Working with Substance-affected Parents and Their Children

Menka Tsantefski, Stefan Gruenert and Lynda Campbell

ALLEN&UNWIN

SYDNEY • MELBOURNE • AUCKLAND • LONDON

Allen & Unwin
83 Alexander Street
Crows Nest NSW 2065
Australia
Phone: (61 2) 8425 0100

Email: info@allenandunwin.com
Web: www.allenandunwin.com

Cataloguing-in-Publication details are available
from the National Library of Australia
www.trove.nla.gov.au

ISBN 978 1 74331 949 9

Internal design by Julia Eim
Index by Puddingburn Publishing Services
Set in 10.5/15 pt Minion Regular by Post Pre-press Group
Printed and bound in Australia by Griffin Press

10 9 8 7 6 5 4 3 2 1

The paper in this book is FSC certified. FSC promotes environmentally responsible, socially beneficial and economically viable management of the world's forests.

FOREWORD

'The challenge of ending child abuse is the challenge of breaking the link between adults' problems and children's pain.' (UNICEF, A League Table of Child Maltreatment Deaths in Rich Nations, 2008)

We have had a longstanding chasm between those services that focus on children's pain and those that focus on adult problems such as alcohol and other drug use, mental illness and family violence. This book builds a strong bridge across that chasm.

It is indeed a very timely bridge. In the past decade in Australia the number of children in the care of the State as a result of child protection proceedings has doubled. Parental use of alcohol and other drugs is a major contributing factor in approximately two-thirds of these families. This group of families is just the tip of the iceberg of a much larger population of children who experience the adverse effects of parental substance use, ranging from foetal alcohol spectrum disorder to children and adolescents carrying a heavy burden of care for their struggling parents.

It is perhaps not surprising that the parents of such children are usually judged very harshly by the community. Yet this can add to the burden for both child and parent. Children can be a powerful source of motivation for a parent to seek treatment for substance use problems but paradoxically, the fear of losing one's children is one of the greatest barriers to seeking treatment. Fear, shame and despair are a corrosive combination.

In the face of this, the book offers great hope. While it acknowledges that some children will need to be raised by members of their extended family or others, it explores the enormous potential for working successfully with parents and their children, both as individuals in their own right and as families. The authors have created a resource which will be of immense value to those working in both child and family services and the alcohol and drug treatment services. It should also enable both of these groups to have a greater understanding of each other and to work together more collaboratively.

The style in which it is written speaks directly to service providers in these two fields in a very clear and engaging way. It is balanced and nuanced, and recognises the great diversity in families in which there is parental substance use. Written from a strengths-based perspective, it invites the reader to reflect on their own assumptions and feelings, and regularly poses the question 'How will I know if I am on track?' A rich array of conceptual frameworks is brought to bear, ranging from an understanding of social networks, child development and family relationships, through to specific techniques such as motivational interviewing and having a purposeful conversation with a child.

Above and beyond the theory and research, this book draws on the values of compassion, respect and hope, and brings a depth of wisdom which is rare in such publications. The rich reservoir of the authors' practice wisdom is abundantly evident, as is their long commitment to this group of fragile families. It is a wise and insightful resource which, if used well, will enable us to deal more effectively with the adult problems such that we might prevent the children's pain.

Emeritus Professor Dorothy Scott
Australian Centre for Child Protection
University of South Australia

ACKNOWLEDGEMENTS

This book has evolved from training resources developed by Odyssey House Victoria, with funding support from the Helen Macpherson Smith Trust and the Commonwealth of Australia, Department of Families, Housing, Community Services and Indigenous Affairs (now the Commonwealth Department of Social Services, with Indigenous Affairs now looked after by the Department of the Prime Minister and Cabinet). That resource development project was informed by a reference panel including Professor Sharon Dawe (Griffith University), Emeritus Professor Dorothy Scott (Australian Centre for Child Protection, University of South Australia) and Professor Leah Bromfield (Australian Centre for Child Protection, University of South Australia), and by consultations with a range of Australian professionals in regular contact with substance-dependent parents and their children. From those consultations came the core practice questions this book seeks to answer.

The authors express their gratitude to the numerous individuals, including Jodi Salinger, Maria Murray and Dr Debra Absler, and organisations who generously contributed their expertise to the development of this book.

We also wish to acknowledge the children, parents and extended family members who have been part of various Odyssey House Victoria programs for over 35 years. Together, we have become more trusting, effective and inclusive. What we have learnt about your recovery journey and the wellbeing of your children, we now aim to share.

CONTENTS

ABOUT THE AUTHORS

Dr Menka Tsantefski is a Senior Lecturer, School of Human Services and Social Work, Griffith University, Queensland. She previously taught Social Work at the University of Melbourne for seven years, specialising in child- and family-related subjects. For many years, Menka worked at Odyssey House Victoria, researching the experiences of children of substance-affected parents and designing, delivering and managing programs for children and families.

Dr Stefan Gruenert is the father of two boys, a registered psychologist and CEO of Odyssey House Victoria. He is Board Director of the Victorian Alcohol and Other Drug Association, and the Alcohol and Drug Council of Australia. He has worked with parents and children, been a strong advocate for family-inclusive practice, and conducted research and taught courses on alcohol and other drug use, men's issues, intimacy, family work and fathers.

Dr Lynda Campbell has over forty years' experience in the child and family welfare sector, including twenty years of teaching and research in Social Work at the University of Melbourne, where she became an Honorary Research Fellow on her retirement. She has written extensively on child and family services, maintaining a long-term interest in the interface between those services and the alcohol and other drug sector.

INTRODUCTION

Working with families where one or more parents has an alcohol or other drug problem can be very complex, stressful and intense. It is particularly challenging because the problematic use of any substance is accompanied typically by a wide range of issues, such as poor mental health, a history of trauma, child abuse and neglect, including in the parent's own childhood, domestic violence and relationship problems, as well as financial difficulties, legal problems, unemployment and housing instability. However, those who choose to do this work will also experience many rewards as they watch families achieve their personal goals, as they see children thrive, and as they journey alongside parents who courageously tackle their problems, grow in confidence and gain greater enjoyment from family life.

This resource has been designed to assist new workers across many different settings to better support parents struggling to overcome substance use problems, their children and their extended family members or other carers. There are many simple things workers can do that will make a big difference. There are also many traps and challenges experienced by those starting out. Based on extensive consultation with professionals from both the alcohol and other drug treatment and the child and family welfare sectors, alongside leading academics in the fields of addiction and child protection, this book has been organised around commonly experienced practice dilemmas. It includes strategies for overcoming these difficulties from workers' experiences, supplemented with content from up-to-date peer-reviewed literature about what works. While this book does not replace a structured program or an academic qualification, it will help workers, whether newly qualified or struggling with this client group, to apply their existing skills and knowledge to working with vulnerable families where problematic alcohol and other drug use is a key feature.

This book is particularly relevant for those working with substance-affected parents who have one or more children under the age of twelve years. These families pose a particular challenge for workers and are frequently brought to the attention of child protection authorities. While much of the book may be relevant to families with older children, the parenting issues and developmental needs of adolescents, who may be beginning their own substance use, would deserve a whole book on its own.

Throughout this book, we will refer to alcohol and other drugs (AOD) as a reminder that alcohol is a drug, too. Sometimes we refer to substances and mean the same thing. We will generally refer to parents whose use of alcohol or other drugs would meet the criteria for a substance use disorder as defined by the Diagnostic and Statistical Manual of Mental Disorders Fifth Edition (DSM-5), although we don't assume that all people will have a diagnosis. Consequently, we may also refer to addiction or to problematic, dependent or harmful substance use or misuse to describe alcohol or other drug use that is clearly having an impact on the user or their families, whether intoxication is irregular or frequent. Lastly, we will also use the term Indigenous peoples to refer to Aboriginal or First Nation peoples, and the acronym **CALD** to refer to people with cultural and linguistically diverse backgrounds. It is assumed that readers will have a basic understanding of many of the concepts and terms referred to in this resource. However, definitions and further explanations for all words in **bold print** can be found in the Glossary towards the end of the book.

In Part 1, we introduce readers to the common issues facing parents and their children (Chapter 1). We then provide several frameworks to help readers understand these problems and highlight common approaches for workers seeking to assist (Chapter 2). In Part 2, we move to more practical assistance and provide readers with foundational skills and knowledge to begin effective practice with families, including how to enhance engagement with parents (Chapter 3) and with children (Chapter 4), and what to look for when conducting an assessment (Chapter 5). In Part 3, we provide more detail about working together with families to facilitate change, with a focus on uncovering the dreams, hopes and goals of the whole family. After outlining the tasks involved in keeping children safe (Chapter 6), we introduce readers to strategies that will help families change the way they function, so that parenting is more effective and family life more rewarding for both adults and children (Chapter 7). Recognising that these changes do not and cannot occur in isolation, we discuss how to activate or build sustainable supports around children and parents, focusing separately on strengthening the informal social network and improving the functioning of formal services surrounding the family (Chapter 8). This is followed by an exploration of how workers can support children and parents during the difficult time when children are placed in care away from home (Chapter 9). In Part 4, we conclude by examining the needs of the worker, and highlight the importance of professional development and supervision to effective practice and a sustainable career (Chapter 10).

HOW CAN THIS BOOK HELP YOU?

If you are a new worker in an adult- or child-focused service, this book is designed to provide you with some helpful information and knowledge. If you have case management responsibilities within either the alcohol and other drug sector, or the child and family services sector, you are likely to benefit most from its content, although many other professionals in contact with vulnerable families may also find it relevant and helpful. We have designed this book to provide general information relevant to a wide range of settings and geographic locations, but we understand that some sections will have more relevance for some readers than for others. While funding and organisational policy may determine your primary role and whom you may support, the content of this book challenges you to consider working in a way that is mindful of all family members, that integrates your work with that of others and that is inclusive of entire families and significant others, wherever possible.

During the consultations that informed this book, workers often asked us to give direct and concrete examples of the sort of actions workers should take when working with families. We have responded to these requests wherever possible. It must be noted, though, that despite our advisory tone, the suggestions contained within this book are not intended to be prescriptive, and may not be suitable for all settings, local areas or with all cultural groups. We aim to develop your awareness of the connection between the problematic use of alcohol or other drugs by parents and child wellbeing, and to promote sensitive responses to the needs of children, parents and other family members, regardless of what type of community service you work in. At a minimum, we hope this book will help you to understand the importance of identifying alcohol and other drug use, parenting or child wellbeing issues, and following up any concerns through more comprehensive assessments and, where appropriate, making referrals to specialist service providers. More optimistically, we hope this book will lead you to engage in more effective and direct work with families and to provide greater integrated care with other community supports or service providers.

Most importantly, this resource should help you to, with confidence:

- create a welcoming and safe environment for your clients;
- identify and enhance family strengths;
- instil a sense of hope and optimism that positive change, the achievement of goals and recovery are all possible; and
- work in partnership with parents, children, other carers and professionals from within and beyond your own discipline to name and address any risks and concerns.

It should be noted that this book was developed in Victoria, Australia. However, as it does not focus on any specific legislation, it is applicable to supporting families elsewhere. As always, strategies must be implemented in accordance with local legislation, protocols and procedures relating to both children and substance misuse.

BEFORE YOU BEGIN

Supporting families affected by problematic alcohol and other drug use requires a multidimensional understanding and approach. You should consider the needs of children, the needs of their parents as individuals, and sometimes as couples, and the life circumstances and functioning of the family as a whole. Equally, the quality of the family's support and its sense of belonging within its wider social network and community are important. This book cannot cover all contingencies across this spectrum of risk and **protective factors**, but it can draw attention to key issues at each of these levels. It is particularly focused on what workers in a variety of service types can do to keep children safe and help them thrive, to support parents in their parenting role, to help strengthen the **attachment** between parents and children, and to ensure responsive, appropriate and effective service provision that leads to recovery for all family members. We have made the assumption that, in most cases, children and their parents will be best served by our efforts to keep families together. This is our starting point. Naturally, clinical and legal judgements may determine otherwise in some circumstances.

This resource is based on the wisdom of those who have been immersed in work with families affected by problematic parental substance use for many years. Nevertheless, all sound practice wisdom is a blending of theory and practice, of ways of thinking and ways of doing, and on the evidence of what works. Before we address the practice dilemmas commonly reported by those working with these families, we will introduce what we understand about parental substance misuse and its implications for children. We will also present some useful theoretical frameworks for thinking about both the development and wellbeing of children and their families, and the process of helping people to achieve change in their lives.

PART 1

FOUNDATIONAL KNOWLEDGE

1

Understanding families with alcohol and other drug problems

Many children throughout the world have parents who use alcohol or other drugs. Use can vary in frequency and intensity, from occasional light social use to heavy dependent use. It is important to remember that there is a significant difference between *use* and *impairment*. As a consequence, the impact on family functioning and the harm to children can vary considerably. In some cases, light and occasional use of alcohol may add to family celebrations and cohesion and place children at no risk. In other families, where regular and heavy drinking occurs, children may be severely impacted by compromised parenting to the detriment of their overall development and wellbeing.

Clearly, not all parents who use alcohol or other drugs are bad parents or incapable of looking after children and meeting their needs. However, parents whose use of alcohol or other drugs is frequent or dependent will often also experience a wide range of other problems, including **family or domestic violence**, poverty, ill-health (e.g. **hepatitis C** and dental issues), mental health issues (e.g. depression, anxiety or **psychosis**), and difficulties with housing and employment (Dawe et al., 2007). While difficult to untangle, each of these issues may impair parenting and children's health and wellbeing, even if parents stop using alcohol or other drugs. Yet parental substance misuse presents distinctive challenges and is worthy of attention in its own right; many workers find the issue daunting. To begin, this chapter will present a summary of current knowledge about parental substance misuse as a social concern, the effects of substance use on users and on their parenting, the consequences for children at different **developmental stages** and some implications for service providers.

PARENTAL SUBSTANCE MISUSE AS A SOCIAL CONCERN

Even though alcohol and other drugs have long been used by adults across societies, public concern about parental substance misuse has accelerated over recent decades. Initially, concern regarding substance use among women drew attention to the impact on their children and, in particular, newborn infants (Deren, 1986). Over time, both the child protection and family services sector and the alcohol and other drug treatment sector have begun to pay more attention to the needs and rights of children of all ages in substance-using families, and boundary issues have emerged between these two separate arenas of discourse and practice. Defining this as a social issue has involved counting, locating and differentiating the populations of concern.

It is difficult to establish clearly *how many* children are adversely affected by their parents' substance use, but estimates are that over eight million children in the United States are living in households where at least one parent is dependent upon or is abusing substances (Hedges, 2012). In Australia, at least one in eight children live in a household where there is problematic parental substance use or dependence on alcohol or other drugs (Dawe & Harnett, 2007). This currently translates to more than 500,000 children under the age of fifteen years. United Kingdom figures suggest almost one million children are living with a drug user and that 3.4 million live with parents who currently binge drink (Manning et al., 2009).

Changes in the types of drugs used, their potency, availability and patterns of use, including polydrug use, have further fuelled community concern. Globally, between 3.5 and 7.0 per cent of the population aged between 15 and 64 years used an illicit drug at least once in 2012. In addition to alcohol, the most widely used drugs were cannabis, opioids, cocaine and amphetamines. The *World Drug Report* (United Nations Office on Drugs and Crime, 2014) notes increases in amphetamine-type stimulants seizures (mostly methamphetamine) in the US, Mexico and the Middle East, with emerging markets in Central and South West Asia and Africa. Globally, cannabis use seems to have decreased, which is especially noticeable in Europe. There has also been a move towards decriminalisation and greater medicinal use of cannabis, especially in the US. While this has contributed to an increase in the rate of illicit drug use, the use of most other substances in the US has remained steady or declined. Consumption of alcohol by those who are underage, binge drinking and heavy use of alcohol have all decreased. Australia and New Zealand have comparatively high rates of cannabis and meth-amphetamine use. The decline in alcohol consumption, evident in New Zealand since 1990, has only recently started to reverse. Australia has seen declining use of some illicit drugs and a reduction in risky alcohol consumption, but an increase in the misuse of pharmaceuticals. Tobacco use is steadily declining. In the past few decades, smoking rates among adults in Australia and the United Kingdom have halved. Smoking is at an all-time low in the US; Canada and New Zealand similarly report reductions in tobacco use.

The number of synthetic and prescription opioid-dependent users continues to rise around the world, overtaking heroin in many cases. While the reported number of people who use amphetamines has remained relatively steady, there has been a significant increase in the purity of methamphetamine, the frequency of its use and greater harms associated with its use, including crime, violence and presenta-tions to hospital emergency departments and drug treatment services

(Australian Institute of Health and Welfare, 2014). In particular, the switch from the powder form to the more potent form of the drug ice (crystal methamphetamine) has drawn considerable media attention and community concern.

Child protection and out-of-home care statistics have fuelled unease about links between problematic use of both legal and illegal substances and child abuse and **neglect**. Neglect is a common form of maltreatment, and as it is often both chronic and pervasive in relation to the child's physical, emotional and intellectual needs, it may have greater impact on children's long-term development than other forms of abuse, which are more likely to be episodic. It is often neglect that is the primary concern when parents are substance-affected (Dawe & Harnett, 2007). However, adolescent and adult children of substance-using parents have reported higher rates of physical and sexual abuse compared with those whose parents have not experienced problematic substance use (Walsh, MacMillan & Jamieson, 2003).

Despite attempts by parents to reduce the impact of their substance use on their children, between 50 and 80 per cent of families engaged with the child welfare system involve parental alcohol or other drug use in Australia (Council of Australian Governments, 2009), in the United Kingdom (Forrester & Harwin, 2008) and in the United States (Blythe, Heffernan & Walters, 2010). The infants of **substance-dependent** women tend to be notified at an earlier age. These children are also more likely to be removed from parental care and to remain longer in **out-of-home care**. Repeat notifications to child protection authorities occur more frequently when parental alcohol or other drug use is identified. Child removal occurs most often when parents are **polydrug** users. Problematic parental substance use tends to cluster with mental health, severe financial difficulties and, unsurprisingly, with higher rates of homelessness (Jeffreys et al., 2009). The type of drug used can influence outcomes for children and parents. Lloyd and Akin (2014) argue that risk for children whose parents use methamphetamine may be overstated, that children and families may experience a different 'system level' response whereby children are removed for fewer reasons with less likelihood of reunification to parental care than children whose parents use other substances (page 78). As socioeconomic factors are the most critical variable in child protection involvement and the greatest barrier to reunification (Lloyd & Akin, 2014), service providers need to examine their own biases and to conduct a thorough assessment of risk and protective factors in order to ensure the best outcome for children, which may, or may not, be placement in out-of-home care.

Who are the parents whose alcohol or drug use is likely to escalate to substance misuse or a substance use disorder? Despite widespread acceptance of the use of alcohol and drugs as recreational and social lubricants, particularly in Western cultures, there is less societal acceptance of excessive or uncontrolled substance use and the personal and social problems it leads to. The result for the substance user, and sometimes for the communities in which they live, is social stigma, and even criminalisation. As a result, few people would choose to be labelled as a substance-misusing parent, yet it seems that few extended family groups or communities are exempt from such problems. When we are tempted to define this as an issue for others, we would do well to examine the impact of alcohol or other drugs on children within our own social networks, and it is likely that we will find evidence of such harm within our ranks. Yet some social groups and communities do seem to be more seriously affected than others.

Rates of drug use tend to be higher among minority groups who have experienced sociopolitical and economic disadvantage. These groups typically have less access to education and employment, face discrimination and live in more stressful neighbourhoods, all of which constrain the ability to achieve feelings of belonging, comfort and pleasure in socially-acceptable ways. After controlling for socioeconomic factors, differences among ethnic groups often become statistically insignificant (Unger, 2012, page 391).

The discussion on prevalence among different groups is complicated. To begin with, it is possible for an individual to identify with more than one ethnic group. Further, the experience of belonging to an ethnic minority in a majority neighbourhood may be different from that of being surrounded by other members of the same minority group. Also, minority groups typically undergo a process of acculturation to the values of the dominant group which has implications for substance use patterns. As the process of acculturation, with its associated shift in attitudes, beliefs and values, is often not shared among family or community members, stigma towards drug users can be greater and increase isolation from valuable support networks. For example, rates of drug use increase among immigrant women as they become distanced from the protective quality of traditional collectivist values (Schwartz et al., 2010, in Unger, 2012), while at the same time, limited understanding of **pharmacotherapy** (medications to treat addiction) by family members can complicate treatment. Greater stigma towards drug-users in the culture of origin can lead to greater social isolation which increases women's reliance on male partners and other drug users, many of whom are also male (Higgs et al., 2008). As most child care in families affected by parental substance use is provided by mothers, regardless of whether the father, the mother or both parents are substance-users (Lawrence et al., 2015), substance-using women from immigrant backgrounds may receive less support from the social network than their counterparts.

Differentiating substance-misusing parents from other groups with special needs can be difficult because of the overlapping problems they experience. Relationship problems and family violence are commonly associated with heavy alcohol or other drug use. As we have mentioned, many substance-dependent people also have mental health problems (often referred to as a **dual diagnosis**), which may impact on their ability to provide adequate care of infants and children. There are overlaps between the experiences and the needs of children whose parents have a mental illness and those whose parents are substance-dependent. Parental behaviour can be erratic; periods of **relapse** can be contrasted by periods of **recovery** or wellness; and children can become '**parentified**' or assume a caring role in the family. Both groups can be subjected to stigma and become socially isolated and impoverished. Similarly, children living with parental mental illness and/or substance use are more likely to be removed from their parents and placed in alternative care than other children. Compared with children of parents with a mental illness, those of parents with **substance abuse** problems are more likely to develop their own substance use problems. Many will have observed illicit substance use; some will have seen or been involved in drug-related crime and other illegal activities—for example, being present while parents buy, sell or use drugs. A small number will have witnessed parental overdose, or even death. Some will have been present during police raids on their home or visited parents incarcerated for drug-related crime (Gruenert, Ratnam & Tsantefski, 2004). Even when they do not experience such distressing events, children are often acutely aware of negative societal attitudes towards users of illicit substances, and are alert to public health warnings of the dangers of use. Unsurprisingly, children can live in heightened states of vigilance and **anxiety**, feeling concern for their parent's or parents' wellbeing and possibly fearing removal from their care (Harbin, 2002). Also, in families where the predominant concern is mental ill-health, members of the extended family may qualify for services as carers, whereas the family members of substance-users may not be afforded such recognition. Clearly, this has implications for the level and type of support available to children, parents and the extended family.

SUBSTANCE USE AND ITS EFFECTS ON THE USER

Evidence suggests that humans have been using substances such as alcohol and other drugs for a very long time. It is thought that Stone Age people from 8000 BC made alcohol, and that this occurred on a large scale in Egypt with breweries from 6000 BC, and wineries from 2000 BC. Many Indigenous peoples around the world made alcoholic drinks from fermented grains or flower nectar and most traditional societies knew of particular plants which had powerful effects on human thinking, mood and behaviour. Such drinks or drugs had a variety of social, religious or medical uses and were generally well controlled by a society's rules and structures. Today, an enormous range of drugs is available, with hundreds of new synthetic drugs being created each year.

Synthetic drugs are generally chemically manufactured psychoactive substances which have been designed to mimic the effects of more common, more established or plant-based substances. Sometimes called 'legal highs', well-known synthetic drugs include 'bath salts', 'mephedrone' ('meow meow'), which mimics drugs such as cocaine and amphetamines, or 'K2' ('Spice'), which mimics the effects of cannabis. Some synthetic drugs may also be marketed as 'herbal highs' or 'party pills' and contain ingredients such as caffeine, geranamine or guarana. Demand for these drugs is largely driven by those who are seeking a legal alternative to well-established but currently illegal drugs, or those seeking a new type of high. As their manufacture is uncontrolled, and the exact composition is changed regularly to keep one step ahead of legislators, there is very little research or knowledge about their harms and side effects. Consequently, synthetic drugs are considered particularly risky and may be more harmful than the drugs they seek to mimic.

The impact that drugs can have on humans is complex. The frequency of drug use, the amount used and the type of drug used are all important factors. A useful way of understanding the effects of different drugs is to classify them into three types (depressants, stimulants or hallucinogens) based on the impact they have on our central nervous system. The central nervous system consists of our brain and spinal cord, and it coordinates and influences the activities across all parts of our bodies.

Depressants slow down the activity of the central nervous system, meaning that communication between the brain and the body will be slower. In small doses this can induce people to feel calm, relaxed or sleepy, but in larger doses it can lead to a loss of physical coordination and consciousness, stop your breathing or heart, and in some cases cause death. Common depressants include alcohol, gamma-hydroxybutyrate (GHB) and opioids such as heroin, morphine, codeine, methadone, buprenorphine, pethidine and oxycodone. Many inhalants are depressants. Cannabis can also act like a depressant in small doses.

Stimulants speed up the activity of the central nervous system, increasing the communication between the brain and other parts of the body. Typically, stimulants increase alertness, physical activity and feelings of pleasure or euphoria, but in high doses they can lead to heart attacks, agitation or aggression and feelings of paranoia. Common stimulants include tea or coffee (caffeine), speed, cocaine, ecstasy, amphetamines (including methamphetamine) and some inhalants like amyl or butyl nitrites.

Hallucinogens interfere with the communication of the central nervous system. This can lead to distortions of perception and reality, as well as feelings of relaxation, creativity or euphoria. Hallucinations may occur, such as experiencing images, sounds and sensations that don't actually exist, in addition to unusual thoughts and behaviours. Common hallucinogens include cannabis in high doses, LSD (lysergic acid diethylamide), magic mushrooms (psilocybin), PCP (phencyclidine), ketamine and mescaline. Effects for an individual can depend on a variety of factors, including: the user's physical, psychological and genetic makeup; their current physical and psychological state; the quality, quantity and strength of the drug taken; and the method of use (e.g. swallowing, injecting or inhaling). In addition to the desired effect of the drug, many unwanted side effects are also common, such as nausea, paranoia or anxiety.

The context within which a drug is used, the amount used, the purity of the drug and the person using a drug, can also have a large impact on how the drug is experienced. All workers should obtain basic familiarity with different drugs and their effects, and understand that the same drug can have different effects on different people, depending on how much is smoked/consumed/injected, depending on someone's tolerance, their body mass, their use of other substances and on the person's mood, mental health and their environment.

SUBSTANCE USE AND DEPENDENCY

Many people who use alcohol or other drugs experience very few, if any, negative effects. However, all drugs have the potential for harm in either the short or the longer term. Harm may result from a drug's actual immediate effect on the body, or from the accumulation of damage over time. Harm may also result from a drug's impact on someone's behaviour, mood or thinking. Generally, the more of the drug used and the more frequently the drug is used, the greater the risk of harm. Nevertheless, harm including death has been noted in isolated and single use of some drugs due to acute intoxication, high-risk behaviours or contaminants.

People who use drugs regularly can become dependent upon or addicted to them. They may build a tolerance for the drug (needing more for the same effect), lack control over the amount they use and experience persistent cravings. The regular user may continue to use drugs despite experiencing legal problems or negative impacts on their health, their employment or their personal relationships. They may begin to prioritise obtaining and using drugs over other activities such as sleeping, eating, catching up with friends, going to work or meeting their parenting responsibilities. Dependent use of a drug can also lead to physical or emotional symptoms of withdrawal when use of that drug is ceased.

Withdrawal symptoms differ between drugs but may include anxiety, restlessness, insomnia, headaches, poor concentration,

depression, sweating, racing heart, muscle tension, tightness in the chest, difficulty breathing, nausea, vomiting or diarrhoea. Sudden withdrawal from some drugs like tranquillisers or alcohol can lead to very severe and dangerous withdrawal symptoms such as grand mal seizures, heart attacks, strokes, hallucinations and delirium tremens (DTs). As a result, withdrawal from dependent drug use should be medically supervised either in a clinical setting or through a home-based **withdrawal service**.

VIEWS ON DRUG ADDICTION

Opinion is divided as to the cause of drug dependence and the available evidence has been interpreted in many different ways. Some believe that drug use is always a matter of personal choice, which generally stems from a habitual or behavioural response to an event or feeling, although it is acknowledged that not all of us have equal choices (the cognitive/behavioural approach). Some view drug dependence as a loss of self-control, a disease or personal pathology (e.g. the philosophy underlying **Alcoholics Anonymous [AA]**). Others regard drug dependence as stemming from a genetic, biological or physiological problem and are more likely to describe addiction as a brain disease for which some individuals are more likely to be predisposed than others. Much of the evidence suggests that some combination or integration of the above is most likely. Most experts in the field would agree that genetic factors and some personality traits such as impulsivity make some people more vulnerable to addiction than others, and that choice plays some part in recovery, if only to influence help-seeking and treatment compliance. Nevertheless, due to the different views on dependency, treatments for substance use disorders vary significantly, and each type of treatment places a different emphasis on either the psychological, physiological or moral aspects of drug use. Each substance-user, too, is likely to have a perspective on his or her use or dependency.

DOES THE DRUG MATTER OR IS ALL ADDICTION THE SAME?

While some differences in a person's experience of addiction and its treatment depend on the type of substance used, there are probably more similarities than differences. Typically, problematic substance use is associated with a range of social and emotional problems regardless of the drug type used. Difficulties in understanding and managing emotions is very common, as are limitations in the social skills and behaviours required to establish and maintain positive relationships. A history of **trauma** or of relationship problems with childhood caregivers is also common, as are problems with someone's sense of identity or belonging. As a result, part of the treatment for addiction will usually focus on addressing some or all of these underlying issues.

However, there are, of course, different legal classifications for various substances which can make a difference. For example, alcohol is a regulated but legal substance whereas heroin is illegal. This distinction may have an impact on how someone's drug use is viewed by an employer, a neighbour or by extended family, and illicit drug use may have more severe consequences for the family as a result of legal issues. Some drugs, like heroin, have very well-established and effective medications or pharmacotherapy treatments such as methadone or buprenorphine, while others currently do not. Many people with drug problems use a range of substances in various combinations, sometimes depending on what is currently available to them. Others will only use or experience difficulties with a single substance.

It is commonly observed that drugs with a depressant effect like alcohol and the opiates are used as a way of coping with the psychological effects of trauma. Likewise, drugs with a stimulant effect, such as methamphetamine, cocaine and ecstasy, are often associated with people suffering from depression, self-esteem issues or sensation seeking. As a general rule, however, it is important to remember that no two individuals will be exactly the same in terms of their pattern of drug use, the issues underlying their problematic substance use, the difficulties they may be having with parenting, the impact their drug use is having on their children, and the treatment and family support that will be of most benefit. Consequently, as discussed further in Chapter 5, it is important to spend a significant amount of time gaining an understanding of each family's unique circumstances, their patterns of drug use and how this may be impacting upon their own functioning and on their parenting and on their children.

HARM MINIMISATION AND HARM REDUCTION

Different countries around the world have adopted different policies and strategies for dealing with the problems caused by alcohol and other drugs, and for ensuring the wellbeing and protection of children. In Australia, the United Kingdom, parts of Europe and the United States, strategies tend to be multifaceted and acknowledge that no single approach on its own will prevent or minimise the harms associated with alcohol or other drugs. Australia's national strategy of **harm minimisation** has three core pillars: supply reduction, demand reduction and harm reduction. Supply reduction receives the greatest funding and focuses on strategies that aim to prevent and limit the availability of drugs through regulations and law enforcement, including customs and policing. Demand reduction focuses on strategies to prevent or reduce people's uptake or use of alcohol and other drugs through education programs and treatment services. **Harm-reduction strategies** assume that some people will be using substances at any point in time, and they consequently focus on education to help people use alcohol and other drugs in the safest way possible. Some well-known harm-reduction programs include roadside breath and saliva testing to ensure people who use alcohol or other drugs are not driving while intoxicated, and needle and syringe exchange programs and education to ensure injecting drug-users minimise their chances of contracting **blood-borne viruses**, and to keep streets free from used syringes.

It is particularly useful to have some understanding of demand reduction and harm-reduction strategies when working with families. While abstinence may be the ultimate goal for many workers and individuals experiencing alcohol or other drug problems, different people are likely to require different strategies, depending on their motivation and goals for change. Some useful frameworks and techniques will be covered in more depth in Chapter 2 to assist workers to incorporate these strategies into their thinking and work with families.

RECOVERY

Recovery generally refers to the *process* of achieving one's own personal goals for health and wellbeing in relation to alcohol or other drug dependence, but it also sometimes refers to an end *state* of freedom from substance dependence. Recovery may involve abstinence from drug use, but this is not always the case, as recovery is typically seen as an individually defined journey. For example, people on methadone programs may consider themselves to be in recovery. Recovery typically involves addressing the harms caused by problematic substance use as well as working on aspirations to be independently and actively engaged in and connected to the community in a meaningful way. Recovery oriented services tend to be more holistic and work on an individual's health, wellness, relationships, hobbies, education and employment. They embrace and integrate harm reduction and various types of treatments, including medical, abstinence-based and peer support approaches, while acknowledging that there are multiple paths to recovery.

Evidence suggests that more than 50 per cent of people with a substance use disorder at some point in their life will see themselves as being in full and sustainable recovery. However, the average time taken to move from first drug use to problematic drug use, and then to seeking help and eventually achieving sustainable recovery, is thought to be in excess of 25 years. While many people 'achieve' recovery without any professional help, instead relying on personal resources and support networks (sometimes referred to as 'spontaneous remission'), most people will require multiple episodes of treatment and experience at least one or more relapses to alcohol or other drug use along the way.

SUBSTANCE USE AND PARENTING

The time span from someone's first use of drugs to their recovery might encompass the full duration of the childhood of their sons or daughters. Given this, it is not surprising that alcohol and other drug use and parenting may exert conflicting demands on the substance-using parent. Parents can reduce or cease their problematic substance use and improve family management practices, but this can take a significant amount of time and may occur under multiple stressful conditions. Common issues for parents who are substance-dependent are:

- a preoccupation with substance use;
- impaired physical health;
- impaired mental health and poor emotional regulation, often related to their own past trauma;
- a fragile capacity to nurture self and others;
- an identity shaped around their substance use culture;
- fractured family of origin and community support;
- limited financial and material resources and financial difficulties, including debt;
- unstable housing;
- disrupted educational and work histories and disengagement from normative leisure options; and
- unsafe or violent family and community relationships.

Drug use itself impacts variously on parenting. The lifestyle associated with illicit drugs generally differs from the use of alcohol or medically prescribed drugs if obtained legally. While individual drugs also affect people differently, as mentioned above, whether they are legally or illegally obtained and used, polydrug use is common among problematic substance-users and it is therefore difficult to single out the effects of one substance in isolation from others; research on individual drugs and parenting capacity is therefore limited. There is some evidence to suggest that heroin use correlates with child neglect and that alcohol is likely to increase the risk of physical abuse of children (Forrester, 2000). Less is known about the effects of amphetamines on parenting than other drugs, but observation suggests that parents experience long periods of alertness (days) while using, which are then followed by long periods of sleep during which time children are not supervised or cared for. Recent research from the United States indicates that the rise in methamphetamine supply and use correlates with children's entry into foster care, attributed, at least in part, to increased rates of neglect and physical abuse (Cunningham & Finlay, 2013). For practitioners, in the absence of a clear general indicator, it is important to establish, on a *case by case basis*, the particular impact on actual parenting behaviours of episodic or chronic states of incapacity or aggression that are often associated with drugs such as alcohol, the hyperactivity and paranoia often associated with stimulants, and the disordered thinking that may accompany hallucinogens. It is also important to note that symptoms of substance use can be particularly acute during episodes of withdrawal and that behaviour can become erratic and unpredictable. In fact, parents may become more irritable and less functional during periods of withdrawal than during substance use or intoxication.

The quality of parenting and the incidence and severity of maltreatment can be influenced by the duration of addiction, types of treatment obtained and history of abstinence (Hogan, 1998). Risk is significantly elevated when both parents have substance use problems. Even if the risks associated with the environment that the child is raised in are not immediately threatening, they are likely to shape the child's behaviour and attitudes through social learning of cultural norms and values (Klee, 2002). Children who witness substance use by parents or older siblings are more likely to develop their own substance use problems and to also experience a range of additional problems. However, the association is not clear-cut, as observing problematic behaviour and the impact this has on the wider family can have a counter effect and discourage use (Rose, 2010).

While the association between parental substance use and child abuse and neglect has been well established, the numerous interrelated factors implicated in this relationship mean that caution is needed in examining whether substance use is actually leading to abuse or neglect. Frequently, parents who are focused on obtaining, using or withdrawing from drug use pay insufficient attention to their children, compromising their social and emotional development through neglect. Basic requirements for shelter, food and clothing may not be met. Inadequate supervision can be deadly for young children. Medical neglect of a child with acute or chronic health problems can have significant implications for long-term health and development.

Many parents acknowledge that their ability to parent adequately is compromised by their substance use, and many employ a variety of measures to protect children from harm. Strategies range from periods of abstinence, through to seeking treatment; reducing or limiting their substance use to periods when their parenting responsibilities are minimal; protecting children from drug-related activity; maintaining a stable, safe and secure home; avoiding incarceration; and finally, placing children with trusted caregivers and maintaining as active a parenting role as possible (Richter & Bammer, 2000). Parents may also substitute one drug for another if they believe it is less detrimental to parenting (Klee, 1998; Tsantefski, 2010).

CONSEQUENCES FOR CHILDREN

The impact of parental substance use on children ranges from effectively little to profound, depending on the pattern, context and duration of use, and on parental mental health, the availability of other support and the age, characteristics and stage of development of the child.

Pregnancy and the perinatal period

Pregnancy is a time when most women reduce or cease their use of substances. For a small number of children, exposure to parental substance use begins in pregnancy, where damage to the foetus or disruptions to development can occur at any stage. Infants born to substance-dependent women are at greater risk of premature birth. They are more likely to have lower birth weight, to be small for gestational age, to have a smaller head circumference and lower length, and to have respiratory conditions. Feeding problems are more common among this group of infants. Neurological changes and congenital abnormalities are possible. Some changes, such as those resulting from the most widely used illicit substance, cannabis, can be subtle and affect neurobehavioural outcomes. Some infants will experience **Neonatal Abstinence Syndrome (NAS)** (Hudak, Tan, The Committee on Drugs & The Committee on Fetus and Newborn, 2012), otherwise referred to as 'withdrawal symptoms', mostly caused by opiates and opiate analgesics. Severity of withdrawal is not determined solely by levels of maternal drug use as it is possible to have low levels of illicit drug use or pharmacotherapy but severe symptoms of infant withdrawal and vice versa (Jones et al., 2014).

Reports of lasting consequences for children of exposure to substances in pregnancy are conflicting due to a number of inter-related factors in maternal lifestyle that make it difficult to attribute causation. First, smoking is almost universal among substance-using women. Second, many women use multiple drugs in pregnancy and it is difficult to disentangle the effects of one particular drug, including tobacco, from other drugs used. Third, as many substance-dependent women live in poverty, poor diet may be a factor in infant outcomes. Fourth, many substance-dependent women present late for obstetric care and do not derive the full benefit of medical attention (Bell & Harvey-Dodds, 2008). Sudden drops in drug levels can increase the risk of miscarriage, and it is, therefore, critical that cessation or changes in drug use during pregnancy are medically supervised.

While much stigma is directed towards pregnant women who use illicit substances, the greatest evidence linking detrimental effects on neonatal outcomes involves two readily available and widely used licit substances: tobacco and alcohol. Smoking in pregnancy is associated with lower birth weight, shorter gestational age and small for gestation age infants (Kalland et al., 2006). Increased risk of small-for-gestational-age births has been found even among passive smokers (Nafstadet al., 1998). Smoking in pregnancy also increases the risk of **Sudden Infant Death Syndrome (SIDS)**.

Maternal binge drinking (more than five standard drinks on a single occasion) during pregnancy also increases the risk of low birth weight (Pascoe, Kokotailo & Broekhuizen, 1995). Critically, alcohol use in pregnancy can have negative life-long consequences and result in **Foetal Alcohol Spectrum Disorders (FASD)** or, worse, **Foetal Alcohol Syndrome (FAS)**. FASD refers to a range of adverse effects which include growth restrictions and distinctive craniofacial abnormalities, as well as central nervous system dysfunction. FAS is considered the most serious end of the spectrum, and is associated with defined facial features, as well as neurobehavioural symptoms. FASD is the leading cause of preventable intellectual disability in children. White and deep grey matter as well as total brain volume can be reduced. Children can have difficulties with memory, executive brain function, attention and behaviour (Riley & McGee, 2005). It is likely that FASD is more common than earlier estimates suggested and that many children (and parents who may also have been affected as unborn babies) remain undiagnosed and misunderstood (Chudley et al., 2007).

Although children exposed to illicit substances are more likely to suffer Neonatal Abstinence Syndrome (NAS), they are more likely to be healthy, to have no growth restrictions and to perform well academically compared with children exposed to alcohol in pregnancy. Nevertheless, children in both groups are more likely to meet the criteria for Attention Deficit Hyperactivity Disorder (ADHD) than children whose mothers did not use alcohol or other drugs while pregnant (Elgen, Bruaroy & Laegreid, 2007). Consequently, with the exception of alcohol, and to some extent tobacco, foetal exposure to substances seems to have less long-term impact on a child's outcomes than parenting and family environmental factors a child is exposed to as they develop.

Many of the problems seen in newborn infants of substance-dependent women are preventable through good diet and provision of pharmacotherapy—for example, methadone or other opiate substitutes—to stabilise drug levels. Public health and child protection policies can also influence outcomes. Studies from the UK, in particular, highlight the critical role of obstetric services for substance-using women and their infants, with some studies reporting outcomes among substance-exposed infants comparable to matched controls (Scully et al., 2004). By contrast, a recent study comparing the effects of prenatal methamphetamine exposure and early child growth in the United States and New Zealand found no difference in birth weight; however, infants born in New Zealand were longer in length at age 36 months (Abar et al., 2013). Differences in neonatal and infant outcomes may result from higher use of obstetric services in countries with free health care. It is also likely that mandatory reporting requirements for medical personnel, particularly in the United States where prosecution of substance-using women is possible in some jurisdictions, may deter women from availing themselves of health care for themselves and their children (Wu et al., 2013).

Good, regular antenatal care can help to ameliorate the effects of exposure during pregnancy but it does not alter the caregiving environment where, with the exception of alcohol, differences in children's long-term outcomes are found (Dawe et al., 2003). Among all mothers, commitment to the infant typically commences in pregnancy. Alcohol and other drugs can affect the mother's emotional and cognitive state and impair bonding with the unborn baby. A number of additional problems, more common among substance-dependent women, can also negatively affect bonding or mother–infant attachment, which is viewed as a critical factor in a range of long-term outcomes for children. For example, some mothers may have been poorly parented themselves and lack understanding of the behaviours that promote a secure attachment. Substance-dependent women are more likely to experience family violence, which can lead to housing instability, which further increases the risk of child protection intervention and loss of infant care. Bonding to a subsequent infant can be reduced among mothers who have lost the custody of older infants or children.

Infancy and the preschool years

As we have noted above, infants exposed to substances in utero can experience NAS shortly after birth. Depending on need, some infants will remain in-patients alongside their mothers while receiving treatment; those requiring more intensive intervention may be placed in specialist paediatric units for treatment for varying lengths of time, which separates them from their mothers (and fathers) at a critical stage in family formation. As the severity of symptoms and the duration of treatment are unpredictable, ranging from days to weeks, parents can be ill-prepared for this separation and experience high levels of anxiety. They may also struggle to conceal maternal substance use from family members or friends who have been unaware of the mother's use before and/or during her pregnancy. Separation while the infant undergoes treatment places mothers, and their partners, at increased risk of relapse if they consider this a 'safe' time to use before the infant is discharged from hospital to their care.

Infants are reported to be difficult to settle, even after treatment for NAS, with disrupted sleep patterns and problems feeding. They can be discharged from hospital to the care of a mother who is less responsive to her infant's cues and unpredictable in her interactions, which can lead to compromised bonding and attachment. Research indicates that bonding problems are likely to be worse for women who continue to use substances in the postnatal period, particularly among those with higher rates of drug use; however, socio-demographic and psycho-social characteristics factors also play a part (Minnes et al., 2005). The mother may also suffer from co-morbidity (multiple conditions)—for example, anxiety and depression or other mental illness may inter-sect with substance use problems and pose further challenges to the mother's ability to parent effectively.

While their infants may have high care needs, there is often less help available for substance-dependent mothers. Recovery from substance use, often attempted in the perinatal period, usually requires severing ties with alcohol or other drug-using networks, which reduces the availability of support when it is most needed. Rates of domestic violence are higher among this group of women. It is not uncommon for perpetrators to use social isolation as a tactic of abuse (Humphreys, 2007). The association between women's substance use and trauma makes it more likely that women will have been maltreated in child-hood, or experienced family violence. Some will have come to the attention of child protection authorities as children and have been removed from parental care. As a result, substance-using women may not be able to draw upon the family to the same extent as other preg-nant and parenting women. In addition to receiving less social support, substance-dependent women experience more depressive symptoms, each of which in isolation has implications for attuned, sensitive parenting. Low socioeconomic status, sole parenting and family size also exacerbate parenting difficulties.

The overwhelming body of evidence suggests that, again with the exception of alcohol, the caregiving environment is the key variable in individual children's developmental and cognitive outcomes, which tend to be worse the longer a child lives with an actively using parent, when both parents are substance-users or when the child continues to live in a high-risk environment. Poor outcomes include higher rates of affective and anxiety disorders and lower levels of social competence (Luthar et al., 1998). As mentioned above, with the exception of in utero exposure to alcohol, the lowest cognitive scores are found in children who suffer severe environmental deprivation rather than those whose parents use substances. Overall, while infants can be reared in an impoverished environment with less reciprocity and poorer interactions with their mothers, the critical variables in infant outcomes are maternal depressive symptoms and socioeconomic differences (Pajulo et al., 2001). **Developmental delay** is sometimes not detected until later in life, when the gap between children of substance-dependent parents and their peers widens.

Cognitive and other developmental outcomes are improved when mothers (and fathers) cease or reduce their alcohol and other drug use and when the caregiving environment is enriched. Weekly home-based interventions, especially those focusing on the parent–child relationship, have been found to increase maternal responsiveness and mother–infant interactions (Schuler et al., 2000) and to improve infant developmental scores (Schuler, Nair & Kettinger, 2003). Home visitor programs focused on parenting education and emotional support to caregivers have also been shown to reduce perceived behavioural problems in young children and to improve family functioning (Dawe et al., 2003). Despite the value of home visitor programs, referrals to services are often not taken up or engagement does not endure (Campbell, 2002; Tsantefski, 2010). Many short-term gains—for example, breast-feeding rates, infant immunisation and parental drug use outcomes—are not sustained (Bartu et al., 2006). This suggests that intensity and duration of service provision and assertive **outreach** are key variables in the effectiveness of home visitor services to families affected by parental substance dependence.

Middle childhood

When children start school they begin a process of learning to understand themselves, their parents and their social world in a wider context. They become vulnerable to many small but compounding experiences of stigma and exclusion, which may be interpreted by them as personal failure: simple things such as being late for school, personal hygiene, not having uniforms or lunch, using inappropriate language that attracts censure, or parental absence from important school events. While parents often try to conceal drug use and to protect children from its consequences, children as young as seven years can be well aware of drug use in the family and concerned about the potential impact on themselves, their siblings and parents. By the age of ten, children can observe and report fluctuations in substance use and accompanying changes in parental behaviour, some of which can be disturbing, if not alarming, such as witnessing a parent lose consciousness or suffer or inflict violence. Parental nurture cannot be taken for granted. The parent's unpredictable cycle of behaviour may mean that primary school children have significant periods of responsibility for caring for themselves and siblings, and perhaps the parent (Gruenert, Ratnam & Tsantefski, 2004).

With unstable and isolated parents, many of these children have limited access to social activities that promote **pro-social development** and social connections. Disrupted schooling, frequent moves and poverty can lead to educational and social disadvantage for this group of children. During the bad times, friendships cannot be sustained. Children and parents are sometimes embarrassed to invite friends home and may not receive invitations from others. Learning is not continuous and the resources and time commitment needed for extra-curricular activities are unavailable. While many children develop great resilience to the environmental problems they are exposed to, others begin to show the signs of not managing or coping. Children's social and emotional problems generally take on one of two forms during this age: behaviour becomes either internalised (withdrawn) or externalised (acting out).

Adolescence

Some experimentation with alcohol and other drugs is a normal part of late adolescence, but the children of substance-dependent parents are at increased risk of developing their own alcohol and other drug use problems. This is not to say that all adolescents who use substances come from homes where parents or other caregivers are problem users or that parental or caregiver use invariably influences children's own uptake. For some, substance use commences by the time they are twelve to fourteen years old. Early onset is associated with longer and more extensive use, the use of more dangerous drugs and increased propensity for criminal activity, including drug dealing. Typically, this follows a trajectory from the use of legally available substances such as tobacco, alcohol and inhalants to the use of illegal substances, often commencing with 'softer' drugs—for example, cannabis—and progressing to harder drugs—such as opiates or stimulants. This group of children is also more likely to leave school early and to experience mental health problems and teenage pregnancy (Robertson, David & Rao, 2003).

Much depends on the relationship between child and parent and the quality of home life. Parents can be emotionally unavailable, model low levels of self-regulation and poor impulse control or they can be responsive to their children's needs for attention and affection and display maturity in their interaction with others. Within the family, the process of transmission of substance use involves the internalisation of beliefs, norms and values that influence identity formation, a normal developmental task of adolescence. Children can observe not only their parents, but also members of the extended family engaging in problematic use. In more extreme cases, use can be 'normalised' to the extent that children may join with adults in rites of passage as a means of bonding with family members (Hedges, 2012). Many children assume caring responsibilities for themselves and younger siblings, becoming what is sometimes referred to as 'parentified' when behaviour exceeds that generally expected of a child at a given age and developmental stage. This role reversal is associated with higher rates of depression, anxiety and conduct problems in children and is a likely precursor to their drug use (Hedges, 2012), yet required helpfulness can also engender a sense of self-efficacy among some older children and adolescents that stands them in good stead for the future by promoting resilience (Werner & Smith, 1992).

Parental substance use influences children's own use less when constructive family routines are maintained, when parental behaviour is predictable, when interactions between parents and children are rewarding and when parenting practices are positive. Importantly, parents can choose either to continue to model problematic substance use or to ensure their children are aware of the efforts they are making to curb use and to deal with problems associated with addiction. The distinction is an important one as attitudes to alcohol and other drug use may be more influential in adolescent use than actual use by parents. The likelihood of adolescent use increases when there is a greater number of problem drug users in the family.

As children mature, the peer group is increasingly an influential route to substance use and other problem behaviour. Individual differences are also critical to outcome: children with positive attitudes towards substance use are more inclined to experiment with alcohol and other drugs, while those with difficult temperaments are more likely to develop substance use problems, particularly if they are poorly bonded to school. Early onset of problem behaviour and a greater number of **risk factors** are predictive of longer-term difficulties across a range of areas in an additive manner. For example, a child with lower cognitive functioning, who has difficulty regulating their emotions, living in a family with high levels of conflict and who has a poor relationship with their parent, may gravitate towards antisocial peers. This in turn increases exposure to substance use at a comparatively young age, which further increases the likelihood of not completing school. Future employment options are then limited, leading to greater risk of engaging in criminal activity, particularly to fund drug use. Parents monitoring where children are and who they are with, children's engagement in pro-social recreational activities and continuation at school can mitigate peer influence and protect against the development of problem behaviours.

IMPLICATIONS FOR SERVICE PROVIDERS

Make use of opportunities to connect

The issues are complex, but opportunities for change are numerous. The diverse problems experienced by substance-using parents, their own conflicted histories with official service providers and the different difficulties thrown up by children's developmental stages all mean that these families might be encountered across a wide range of services— child and family, alcohol and other drug, education, health and mental health, housing, and so on. Each entry offers some potential for prevention and intervention, but it is easy to focus only on adults or children in isolation, rather than on both simultaneously. Parents can be receiving a range of adult-focused services without assessment of parenting capacity or risk to children; the needs of children may therefore not be identified or addressed. Alternatively, children may be receiving appropriate children's services for the moment, yet opportunities to engage and support their parents to deal with their substance misuse may be missed, with detrimental long-term consequences for all family members.

Some parents will come to services voluntarily, others will be coerced. Some parents will be functioning quite well; others will present as disorganised and in crisis. Concern for children can be an incentive for parents to seek support from services and to enter treatment. However, it can also be the reason they avoid treatment if they fear it will lead to professional scrutiny and possibly children being removed from their care. The parenting role can also be insufficient motivation for treatment as many parents believe they can continue to use without this adversely affecting their children. Real change often comes about when parents see the detrimental effects that substance use is having on their own health and their lives more generally, and when they decide to take action to reduce or cease use. Helping a parent come to this understanding in a supportive and non-judgemental way can bring about positive change for children. However, being insensitive or confrontational can often trigger a defensive reaction and jeopardise any chance of establishing a meaningful and cooperative working relationship (Miller & Rollnick, 1991).

At a minimum, to make children visible, adult-focused services working with substance-using individuals should seek to establish if their clients are parents, and if they are, the ages and living arrangements of children (Gruenert & Tsantefski, 2012). They should be asked whether they would like to establish contact with children no longer in their care. Any areas of concern should be further explored. Potential or actual pregnancy should also be inquired about and relevant information provided to both genders about the risks of alcohol and other drug use in pregnancy and the critical importance of good antenatal care for pregnant women. Chapters 3, 4 and 5 will examine these issues of engagement and assessment in greater depth.

Safely pursue the wellbeing of children and their parents

Although parental substance dependence poses significant risks for infants and children (see Chapter 6), it is important that interventions are not driven entirely by rare occurrences of child deaths, or by negative or naïve attitudes towards substance-users. Rather, interventions should be directed towards positive outcomes for children, parents and the wider family (see Part 3) and draw on the family's strengths, dreams and their own goals. Children need provision for their:

- physical health;
- mental and emotional wellbeing;
- belonging/identity and relationships;
- material needs;
- learning and development; and
- safety.

To ensure this, the general goals of the service system are to build the conditions under which the family can provide for these needs, by helping to build strong attachments and connectedness between the child, the family, the wider network and their community; enriching the environment children are raised in; nurturing strengths in families; and helping parents recover from trauma and dependence, while ensuring child and parent safety. Despite their difficulties, some children of substance-dependent parents do well. These children are likely to have a resilient temperament, good social skills and the support of the extended family and a broader social network. The role of the worker is to optimise these resilience factors wherever possible.

SUMMARY

Parental substance misuse has increasingly become defined as a social issue that must be tackled by a range of services across what, historically, has been a fragmented service system. The diversity of substances available, the variability of substance-users' own life stories and needs, and the complexity of the associations between parents' patterns of substance use and the experiences of their children makes this a challenging area of work for professional helpers of various disciplines. It is apparent that there are no simple cause and effect chains on which to build a standard formula for practice. The complexities revealed make it clear that any approach to practice in this area will need to be informed by learning from the alcohol and other drug treatment field, and from child and family services. Chapter 2 will elaborate our perspective on the purpose and nature of this work and provide some foundational knowledge required to undertake it.

2

Conceptualising needs and professional responses

If you work with families anywhere across the spectrum of human services, it is likely you will meet parents whose alcohol or other drug use impacts negatively on their parenting and ultimately on their children. If you work in the child and family services sector or the alcohol and other drug treatment sector, it is likely that you will have some case management responsibilities. Your responses will be shaped by the setting within which you work, the opportunities it offers and the constraints it imposes. Regardless of the setting, however, there will be opportunities to intervene and obstacles to overcome. The underpinning assumptions, core goals and methods of practice within the child and family services sector have evolved quite separately from those in the alcohol and other drug treatment service sector. The former tends to focus on child safety and development and the provision of home-based family support, while the latter has typically focused on an individual's recovery from substance dependence and on **relapse prevention**. There is generally more urgency about change in child and family services, particularly where child protection authorities are involved, while it is acknowledged that alcohol and other drug treatment can take a long time, with several setbacks along the way. The child and family services sector is likely to expect abstinence and see the child as the primary client, while the alcohol and other drug treatment sector may emphasise harm reduction and see the parent with the substance problem as the primary client.

For families to thrive, however, input from both sectors is likely to be needed, provided they work together in an integrated way, rather than impose further strains upon already stressed families. This chapter aims to bring together these perspectives as a foundation for your work. Though not yet mainstream, there are examples of services which challenge this divide: examples include Parents Under Pressure (PUP), devised by Sharon Dawe and Paul Harnett (Australia and the UK), and Odyssey House Victoria's child and family programs (Contole et al., 2008); see Useful websites and resources.

Regardless of your workplace and role, it is helpful to have a multi-dimensional conceptual framework to guide your thinking about the family, your approach to helping and your communication with other helpers. Such a framework will draw upon theories of children's development in context, of parenting and family functioning, and of substance dependence, trauma and recovery. It will be informed by practice theory about the processes of change and helping drawn from both child and family and alcohol and other drug services. In this chapter we suggest components for such a framework to underpin your work and to provide a shared platform for collegial discussion.

UNDERSTANDING THE CHILD AND FAMILY

The developing child in context—an ecosystemic view
In this book we view child wellbeing from an ecological or ecosystemic perspective, owing much to the foundational work of Bronfenbrenner (1979) and Garbarino (1992). There are several elements to this approach:

- The child is an individual, with his or her own innate qualities and vulnerabilities, and his or her own inherent dignity, worth and emergent capacity for agency and citizenship throughout the dynamic process that constitutes childhood. Through this process, the environment helps shape the child, but the child also shapes aspects of the environment.

- The quality of the attachment between a child and his or her parent/s (or primary caregivers) is crucial. The child must feel loved, secure and 'special', and be known or understood by the parent. Parents, too, should derive comfort and inspiration from the relationship with the child if they are to survive and thrive through the challenges of child-rearing.
- The family is seen as a system of mutually contingent carers evolving together in particular times and places (Elder, 1978). Members' needs and behaviour interact, and developmental changes, crises or achievements experienced by one member will flow through to changes for other family members. The eminent sociologist, Glen Elder, has demonstrated over many years that these mutually influential life courses are deeply influenced by social history.
- No one can rear a child alone; a supportive, informed, well-resourced social network is needed. Ideally, within this network are natural helpers who understand and promote the needs of children and their parents, and who do not impose impediments to child-rearing or hazards for the child's and parent's health and wellbeing. As the child develops his or her own social network, the quality of the relationships between that network and those of his or her parents will also become important to the child's wellbeing.
- Social structures and institutions, including health agencies, schools, government departments and various community service organisations, can make or break family life through the resources they offer or withhold, the developmental opportunities they open up, the demands they impose upon parents and children, and the ways in which they do or do not work together for the family's benefit.

Parenting and family functioning

For many people, parenting is a key, even unquestioned, life goal and a great joy, yet it involves onerous responsibilities on behalf of the wider society to nurture and socialise the next generation. Becoming a parent adds a whole new component to our identity and how well this component is integrated into our sense of self, and how successfully we take up the challenges of parenting, will be subject to many influences. These include the parenting and nurture we have experienced as children; how others around us respond to us as people and as parents; the resources at our disposal to assist us to adapt; the sheer volume and nature of our competing developmental and life tasks; and how the child responds to us. Many substance-dependent parents, though not all, face threats to successful parenting from each of these directions, making it difficult to respond to the community's expectations of them. These include the expectations that parents will ensure that children have:

- a safe and stable home;
- access to a loving extended family or substitute;
- sensitive and loving attention from parents or other carers;
- medical treatment and preventative medicine—for example, access to a **Maternal and Child Health Services** nurse;
- full daily access to education;
- friendships and opportunities to develop their own social and recreational interests and talents; and
- moral education and socialisation into citizenship.

The parent is the child's gatekeeper to these experiences. Faced with these expectations and the community's judgement about whether they are met adequately, parents can feel that their own needs, even their core sense of self, has been submerged, and when they seek to have their own needs met, tensions arise. Such tensions can be particularly potent at times of relapse from recovery. Whether or not parents can meet community expectations and resolve these tensions will depend in part on how the family as a whole works together. On the basis of practice with troubled families and research into apparently 'normal' families, Froma Walsh (2006) argues that some families are simply more able to respond successfully to their troubles. She defines family resilience in terms of:

- family belief systems: making meaning of adversity; positive outlook; transcendence and spirituality;
- organisational patterns: flexibility; connectedness; social and economic resources; and
- communication processes: clarity; open emotional expression; collaborative problem solving (pages 49ff).

To enhance such resilience, workers need to focus on helping families define who they are and want to be, manage the daily tasks of living well and regulate the expression of emotions so that communication can be effective.

Summary: Risk, resilience and intervention goals

In short, our practice suggestions throughout this book rest on the premise that to understand the needs of the child and parents and to respond to these needs effectively, you will need to assess and work across the layered environment of the child's life, paying particular attention to the family unit and how parents are supported to meet children's needs.

Risk factors/hazards	(Focus) and desired outcomes	Resilience or coping factors
Infants, young and disabled children cannot fend for themselves; older children are overburdened or socialised into drug use	**(Child development)** Child/ren—safe, loved, nurtured and supported; positive psychosocial and emotional development is promoted	Adequate food, shelter and caring and responsible adults

Risk factors/hazards	(Focus) and desired outcomes	Resilience or coping factors
Alcohol and other drug use (and associated conditions) impedes parental responsiveness	**(Attachment)** Children and parents have a positive and secure attachment	Good pregnancy, birth and early parenting experiences; recovery from trauma; parents keen to learn about child and parenting; parental emotional regulation
Severity and impact of alcohol and other drugs; parental trauma; family violence	**(Adult development and relationships)** Parent/s carers are safe and well and work well together for the children	Parent/s' readiness to change; relapse prevention strategies; pro-social skills and emotional regulation
Complex family with many competing needs; recurrent crises	**(Family functioning)** The family functions well as a unit and works well together for the children	Adequate income, housing, education; children respected as family members
Parents isolated; extended family alienated, problem-ridden or over-demanding; friendship networks focused on substance use	**(Social support networks)** A support network of friends or family helps both children and parents	Parents have regular contact with non-using, child-aware, supportive adults; pro-social skills and attitudes; children have friends in the community
AOD services undervalue parenting role; child and family services naïve or punitive about substance use; services inaccessible, contradictory or poorly coordinated	**(Organisational and service system arrangements)** An accessible and responsive service system addresses both parental substance misuse and children's wellbeing	Accessible, responsive and well-coordinated services; workers not judgemental but knowledgeable
Poverty, stigma and social exclusion; housing in crime- and alcohol and other drug-dense neighbourhoods	**(Community and societal conditions)** Local communities and social structures are inclusive and support healing, resilience and recovery	Community acceptance; preventative health orientation in social policy; safety nets for provision of basic necessities of family life; affordable housing

Working through such a descriptive framework, it is easy to see how a parent may have multiple care burdens—the self, the child/children and perhaps the partner. Those working with Indigenous peoples or with CALD populations report that this is compounded by complex care burdens across generations and laterally across a kinship group. Of course, this is not always so across all dimensions, but the dynamic interaction between the parents' and the children's needs and imperatives must be understood by any worker, and responded to in a multidimensional way, often by a team of workers or a service and social network. A core paradox is that, when a family is particularly disengaged from a supportive network and community, such links are more than usually needed to supplement children's care.

THE PROCESSES OF CHANGE AND HELPING

Approaches underlying child and family services

Child and family services cover a broad range of services from **early intervention** to protection and substitute care. Within this spectrum, the focus and content of the work may vary considerably. For example, child protection, foster care and family services can have very different case management responsibilities and practice priorities, and the search for a single case manager can prove futile (Campbell, 2009), yet the field as a whole does yield some common themes. Often funded from statutory authorities responsible for overseeing the safety and wellbeing of children, child and family services tend to place the child at the centre of attention, and to focus effort on improving the material and social conditions of family life and the interactions or relationships of members within the family, so that children can thrive. If children need additional support, the extended family and friendship group is viewed as the first port of call for help, perhaps through the use of family group/family decision-making conferences (Arney, Chong & McGuinness, 2013; Morris & Connolly, 2012). Special attention is placed on the safety of children, but also on the safety of women, since family violence is commonly encountered. Where children are deemed to be living at an unacceptable level of risk, workers call on statutory **child protection services** to use their authority to impose conditions upon family life, mandate service provision or place children in out-of-home care if necessary.

This book draws in part on the practice traditions within family support and preservation services, where even though much of the work occurs with parents, often with the mother, the needs of the children remain clearly in sight, and particular attention is paid to building parenting competence. The modes of intervention are chiefly in-home practical support combined with in situ family counselling or therapy, individual and couple counselling for parents, parent education and skills development, and child- and family-centred case management. Yet there has also been a strong tradition in family support services of the use of group-work, mentoring programs and community action to foster social skills, networks and social inclusion (Campbell & Mitchell, 2007). While service to troubled families may be episodic and sometimes protracted, there are well-established models of brief intensive intervention (up to a few weeks), such as the *Homebuilders* model of Intensive Family Preservation Service (Kinney, Haapala & Booth, 1991), which originated in the US but has been replicated and modified in Australia and the UK. One variant, *Option 2* in Wales, is designed to respond to child protection concerns arising from parental alcohol and other drug use by incorporating motivational interviewing and solution-focused work into the home-based therapy model. *Option 2* has been evaluated as worthy of wider replication and adaptation, on the basis of reduced need for children to enter care, cost savings to government, reduced parental alcohol and other drug abuse, improved family and parental wellbeing and clear appreciation by parents of workers' accessibility, helpfulness and trustworthiness (Forrester et al., 2012).

Philosophically, family services are designed to be accessible, flexible and empowering (Campbell & Mitchell, 2007) and have come to draw upon counselling approaches that are **strengths-based** rather than deficit-focused, such as **solution-focused** work (Berg & Kelly, 2000), and that make use of **narrative** methods to 're-story' distressing life histories and options (Elliott, Mulroney & O'Neil, 2000). These approaches de-centre the worker, asking clients to explore their own options and build on what they know to work well in their own lives, even within child protection services, wherever possible. *Signs of Safety: A case management approach for child protection practice* was devised in Western Australia by Turnell and Edwards (1999), partly in response to the need for a more strengths-based response to child welfare issues in Indigenous communities. Increasingly, in recognition of client groups weighted towards survivors of family violence, sexual abuse and cultural marginalisation and exclusion, child and family services seek to be trauma-informed.

The family-centred practice tradition is well summarised by Scott, Arney and Vimpani (2013, page 18) who exhort us to 'think child, think family, think community' and to strive for practice that places the family as the central unit of attention, maximises choices, takes a strengths (not deficit) perspective, is culturally sensitive and is delivered via relationship-based practice that is expressed through empathy, respect, genuineness and optimism.

Approaches underlying alcohol and other drug treatment services

Alcohol and other drug services, too, have diverse philosophical and theoretical underpinnings; however, many themes and elements of evidence-based practice are common to their programs. Often funded from public health authorities, alcohol and other drug services tend to place the adult client or young person with the substance use problems at the centre of attention, and to focus effort on reducing harm from substance use to the individual user, and sometimes more broadly to the family and wider community. Typically utilising and building on motivation for change, services utilise a variety of **psycho-educational** methods to strengthen emotional and behavioural self-regulation and positive social networks with a view to longer-term abstinence or managed substance use.

It is generally accepted that the treatment intervention itself is only one factor influencing treatment outcomes. For example, Lambert (1992) found that the percentage of the outcome that could be explained by different factors in individual counselling included: the therapeutic relationship (30 per cent); the actual intervention (15 per cent); the hope for change experienced and the expectancies of the client (15 per cent); and external or client factors that the counselling has no control over (40 per cent). As a result, many alcohol and other drug treatment approaches place great emphasis on the recruitment and selection of staff members who have the ability to develop a strong therapeutic alliance: those who have a lived experience of recovery and are therefore often able to project hope and expectation that change is possible, as well as the knowledge of and skills in treatment interventions.

Best evidence currently exists for pharmacotherapy treatments and psychosocial approaches that draw on **Cognitive Behavioural Therapy (CBT)**, **Motivational Interviewing (MI)**, **Solution-Focused Brief Therapy (SFBT)**, **Family and Systemic Therapy** and **Dialectical Behaviour Therapy (DBT).** Given the importance of developing positive social supports for recovery, approaches that utilise self-help or peer support/mutual aid have also been shown to be effective and these can include community programs such as Alcoholics Anonymous and **Narcotics Anonymous**, as well as therapeutic communities which utilise peer support and professional staff in a residential setting. More recent evidence has also shown great promise for mindfulness-based interventions in assisting individuals to recognise and manage their emotions.

Alcohol and other drug treatment services and supports

Alcohol and other drug treatment services vary in different parts of the world, but a treatment system will generally include many, if not all, of the following treatment and support elements:

- intake and assessment;
- withdrawal or **detoxification** (hospital, residential or non-residential);
- community treatment or support (including counselling, day programs, self-help and peer support groups);
- residential treatment (residential rehabilitation or therapeutic communities);
- supported living or accommodation;
- outreach and case management (including care and recovery coordination and aftercare);
- pharmacotherapy (using a general practitioner prescriber and pharmacies); and
- harm reduction (including needle syringe exchange and peer-administered naloxone).

Intake and assessment

Most alcohol and other drug treatment services begin with an assessment of need. Some may utilise a brief screening or triage process to determine the level of dependency and a risk assessment, together with the extent of associated problems such as homelessness, mental health and domestic violence. This allows services to determine eligibility and to prioritise immediate assistance to those most in need. This may result in a more comprehensive assessment or a referral to a more appropriate service. In some service systems, each organisation or service will have its own assessment process, while in others it may be centralised and provide access to the full suite of available services. Waiting times to access treatment will vary. There will also be great variation in the extent to which an assessment will examine whether a person seeking help is also a parent and what the ages and caregiving arrangements are for their children. Some will carefully consider a client's parenting support needs and complete a more comprehensive assessment of the wellbeing and safety of the children, while others won't (Gruenert, Ratnam & Tsantefski, 2006).

Withdrawal (detoxification)

A withdrawal program may be a necessary first step for parents seeking to reduce or cease their drug or alcohol use. Some parents may be able to simply stop their alcohol and other drug use on their own, sometimes called 'going cold turkey'. However, where use is frequent and significant, withdrawal can be uncomfortable and sometimes quite hazardous if done without medical supervision, especially in the case of alcohol and where there are other medical considerations or health issues. Withdrawal or 'detox' services can assist with this process. A residential withdrawal involves a short stay (usually 7 to 10 days) in either a community service or in a hospital, depending on the expected risks and severity, and will be monitored or managed by a medical practitioner. Home-based or outpatient withdrawal may be done when the withdrawal is of mild/moderate severity and support is available from a family member, another service provider or friend. These will be supervised by a registered nurse, with the support of a medical practitioner as needed. Withdrawal is not considered a treatment in and of itself, as relapse rates are very high when it is not followed up with other therapeutic interventions.

Community treatment or support

Many different types of treatment and support may be available in the community. These include brief interventions, counselling, structured day programs and support groups. Some brief interventions may be provided opportunistically online or by general practitioners, nurses or support workers, while longer-term interventions are typically provided by counsellors, social workers or psychologists. Many of these interventions will focus on emotional regulation and relapse prevention strategies. Given the critical role that positive social supports play in long-term recovery, self-help and peer support groups (including twelve-step programs) should also be considered where available. Many treatment programs will incorporate some group-work where problems and solutions can be shared by those experiencing similar issues. These may be facilitated by trained professionals, peers or a combination of both.

Residential treatment
Although more resource intensive, residential rehabilitation programs may be necessary for those with more acute and complex problems, or where other forms of community-based treatment have failed. Residential programs typically provide a combination of individual and group counselling, meaningful activities that contribute to the operation of the program such as cooking and gardening or maintenance, and opportunities for recreation. Therapeutic communities are specialist residential programs which emphasise peer decision-making and support. Some residential programs will allow parents to attend with their children and include parenting skills development training and parent–child therapeutic sessions.

Supported living or accommodation
For those wishing to sustain positive changes in a less intensive but supportive environment, supported accommodation programs typically involve community-based housing with an element of professional or peer support through weekly visits or a 'lead tenant'. Housing may be publicly funded or privately rented, and may be suitable for individuals, families or groups.

Outreach and case management

Due to the high incidence of relapse and ambivalence around alcohol and other drug treatment, most systems of care will include some element of assertive outreach to attract or re-engage people into treatment. Likewise, due to the high occurrence of multiple associated issues, most systems will also include case management to coordinate and integrate care. A critical, but often under-resourced part of the system are services that focus on supporting people to reintegrate into the community, and help them engage in meaningful social, vocational and recreational activities (recovery coordination). Likewise, aftercare services that provide occasional support or 'check-ups' following more intensive treatment have been shown to be beneficial to sustaining long-term recovery.

Pharmacotherapy

A substantial body of evidence demonstrates the cost-effectiveness of treating people for dependence on some drugs from a physiological or medical approach through the administration of pharmacotherapy medications. In the case of opioids, this refers to the prescription of methadone or buprenorphine as **maintenance therapy**, and acamprosate, disulfiram or naltrexone for alcohol dependence. The evidence for effectiveness is much stronger with the pharmacotherapies for opiates. Some of the medications (such as methadone) are agonists which produce a similar analgesic effect to the dependent drug, but without the high and must be taken daily. Others like naltrexone are antagonists, which block the opioid receptors in the brain from other drugs. Research suggests that naltrexone is effective but compliance tends to be poor. Although sustained-release forms, including subcutaneous naltrexone implants, have been developed, studies to date on these have been equivocal (Ritter et al., 2013). Some pharmacotherapy medications act as both agonist and antagonist. Pharmacotherapies are generally prescribed by a specially trained general practitioner or an addiction medicine specialist, and are dispensed from pharmacies.

Harm reduction

Policies and interventions which aim to reduce the harms associated with substance use, without necessarily reducing their use, are deemed to be harm-reduction strategies. Examples of harm-reduction services include needle and syringe exchange programs to prevent the spread of blood-borne viruses, supervised injecting facilities, pill testing and peer administered naloxone to prevent overdose or death. With alcohol, roadside alcohol (breath) testing, liquor licensing restrictions and taxation are also considered harm-reduction strategies.

Enhancing motivation for change

Motivation influences the likelihood that a person will enter into, continue and comply with any change-directed behaviour. Motivation is transitory, and may fluctuate, depending on a variety of factors, including internal conditions and external events. Engagement in treatment is difficult for many people, and motivation for change is typically low for many problem substance users. For many years, there was a widely accepted assumption that you couldn't assist anyone to change unless they wanted to. This is captured by the saying, 'You can lead a horse to water but you can't make it drink.' Prochaska and DiClemente (1986) and Miller (1989) detailed a shift in the thinking of treatment for addiction, by placing more responsibility on the counsellor or case manager to identify the motivational stage of the client and implement strategies to enhance client motivation and treatment readiness. Strong evidence supports the effectiveness of this approach. Consequently, it is now also accepted that effective treatment need not be voluntary, and that sanctions/enticements (such as pressure from family, child protection, employers or the criminal justice system) can increase treatment entry and retention. Evidence also suggests that treatment outcomes are similar for those who enter treatment under legal pressure/sanctions when compared to those who enter voluntarily (ANCD, 2007).

Stages of change

Recovery from substance use generally involves a series of steps or changes that a person goes through before they make permanent lasting change. People go through the various stages at their own pace, not necessarily in any order, and most people go through the stages more than once, with multiple relapses. A usual framework for assessing someone's readiness to change, and the strategies required to move someone from one stage to the next, is captured by Prochaska and DiClemente's (1986) **Stages of Change model** below.

Pre-contemplation

The person is unconcerned about their drug use. At this stage, the benefit of substance use outweighs any negative consequences for them. People are therefore unlikely to want to change. Strategies to motivate for change include:

- building rapport and engagement; and
- raising doubt and increasing awareness of risks and problems.

Contemplation

The person has mixed feelings about substance use and is aware of some of the negative consequences of use. They are generally open to receiving information or education. Strategies to motivate for change include:

- expanding awareness of the consequences of use and the benefits of change; and
- discussing their dreams and goals for the future.

Determination/preparation

The person has decided to act and do something about their drug use.

Strategies to maintain motivation for change include:
- developing an agreement;
- enhancing commitment; and
- beginning planning.

Action

The person has begun to implement strategies to change their behaviours. Strategies to maintain motivation for change include:
- supporting specific steps to implement the plan; and
- assisting the development of new skills and discussion of barriers/ obstacles.

Maintenance

The person has adopted the change and new behaviour has become the norm. Strategies to maintain the change include:
- dealing with challenges and new opportunities as they arise.

Relapse

At any time there can be a loss of motivation or a relapse into a previous stage, sometimes accompanied by a regression in behaviour or substance use. Strategies for enhancing motivation include:
- quickly identifying the current stage and activating associated strategies; and
- minimising harm and considering which strategies did/did not work.

Motivational interviewing

Motivational interviewing is considered an effective way to enhance motivation for change in individuals who are either ambivalent about, or reluctant to, change. The examination and resolution of ambivalence is its central purpose, and any discrepancies between the person's current behaviour and their goals are highlighted as a way to trigger behaviour change. Motivational interviewing accepts that it is normal to feel torn between wanting to change and not wanting to change, and that ambivalence will usually continue even after a decision to change is made. It also aims to enhance the skills and confidence required for change (Miller & Rollnick, 2002). Motivational interviewing has five key strategies:

1. Express empathy
- gain permission to explore the issue;
- normalise ambivalence;
- use reflective listening and avoid labels; and
- aim for understanding the client's perspective and accept it (this is different to agreement or approval).

2. Avoid arguing
- resistance is a signal to change your questions/strategy;
- arguing is counterproductive and usually results in defensiveness; and
- clients' attitudes are shaped by their words, not yours.

3. Develop discrepancy
- develop an awareness of the consequences to help the client examine their behaviour;
- develop a discrepancy between behaviour and important goals to motivate change; and
- get the client to present any reasons for change in their own words, which are usually more powerful.

4. Roll with resistance
- use momentum to your advantage, follow their lead on what the problem is;
- try paradoxical statements or exaggeration to elicit reactions in their words;
- shift perceptions;
- invite new perspectives, don't impose them; and
- clients are valuable resources in finding solutions to their problems.

5. Support self-efficacy
- enhance the belief that they can achieve new behaviour or accomplish a particular task;
- emphasise client strengths because belief that change is possible is an important motivator; and
- ultimately, the client is responsible for choosing and carrying out actions to change.

Common motivational interviewing tools and techniques include generating a list of the pros and cons (decisional balance) with clients, asking them to describe a typical day, asking them to look back and look forward in their life, and inviting them to describe themselves when not using substances versus when using substances.

THEMATIC LINKS: TRAUMA AND GENDER

In both the child and family services and in alcohol and other drug services, practice is complicated by issues of trauma and gender. You can expect that any work you do with substance-affected parents will be affected by the likelihood and impact of trauma in the background of adults whose alcohol and drug use has become problematic. The gender of your clients will also influence their experiences of substance use and their relationships with the service system.

Substance dependence and trauma

Trauma refers to an event when we experience or are threatened by severe physical and emotional harm to ourselves or others and experience intense feelings of fear, helplessness and horror. For the substance-using population, commonly reported traumatic events include childhood physical and sexual abuse, drug overdoses and violence from partners and others in adulthood. Response to trauma is variable, with all manner of suffering and coping, but Covington

(2007) urges workers to be aware of the possibility of post-traumatic stress disorder among alcohol and other drug users, defined within DSM-5 by symptoms such as flashbacks and nightmares, emotional distancing and numbing, avoidance of stimuli linked to the traumatic event, and hyper-vigilance.

Rosenberg (2011) suggests that there is now sufficient evidence that 75 per cent of people entering substance-abuse treatment programs report histories of trauma, and that 'the greater the number of adverse experiences, the greater the risk for negative outcomes' (page 429). It is easy to see how this risk might compound when we consider a serious but not unusual client life story: a child physically and sexually abused in childhood may be further traumatised by police and court interventions and placement away from home; the child may be further abused by caregivers and peers; multiple disrupted placements ensue and the child may be forced prematurely into supposedly independent living; early adoption of substance use draws the young person into street life, especially if homeless; the young person is then vulnerable to physical and sexual violence in the community and may also witness or experience severe drug reactions and deaths. Vicious circles of crisis and problematic adjustment are not uncommon. There are many humiliations experienced. It is not surprising then that persons with a history of trauma may experience a sense of shame and a deep distrust of strangers, and indeed of officials and professionals. Rosenberg (2011) makes a strong case that while stories of trauma are hard to tell and to hear, to ignore them isolates the sufferer and perpetuates harm, so respectful listening is vital.

Because of the likelihood of trauma history and the variability of its manifestation, both Rosenberg (2011) and Covington (2007), along with many others, advocate for trauma-informed practices and services. For Rosenberg (2011), this means that workers and services will understand symptoms as attempts to cope and survive; recognise both the vulnerabilities and strengths of trauma survivors; work according to the empowerment principles of *safety*, *voice* and *choice*; be culturally competent and gender specific; and be coordinated across multiple service systems (page 429).

Clearly, strategies to manage post-traumatic symptoms and unhelpful coping mechanisms may need repeated attention, with a special focus on replacing troublesome behaviour with effective self-soothing and stress management. Individual counselling is just one arena for trauma-informed practice. Covington (2012) also presents materials to inform group approaches to both therapy and education. When trauma has been trans-generational and has become a significant factor in a culture, as Atkinson (2002) has testified in relation to Indigenous Australians and Stevenson (1999) in relation to Canadian First Nations, healing practices will need to become culturally embedded at a community level.

Both the substance use and trauma histories of men and women may differ. For women, there is more likelihood of a history of both physical and sexual abuse, continuing through to partner violence in adulthood. While women substance-users who are trauma survivors tend to present with symptoms indicating anxiety and depression, men may present with chronic medical complaints (Keyser-Marcus et al., 2014).

Substance use and gender

Substance use by women has steadily grown and the gender gap in incidence and prevalence has significantly narrowed. Globally, illicit substance use tends to be higher among men; however, the gender gap in rates of drug use becomes insignificant when pharmaceutical drugs are included (United Nations Office on Drugs and Crime, 2014). Multiple drug use has become the norm, further increasing the risk of drug-related harm. This is of particular concern among women of childbearing age as there are implications for maternal, infant and child health and wellbeing and for society at large, including, but by no means limited to, high use of scarce medical resources in the neonatal period (Kelly, Davis & Henschke, 2000). For the woman substance-user who has a traumatic past, mothering may be an overwhelming challenge, even while being an exciting and welcome opportunity. For Covington (2007), trauma-informed practice with substance-using mothers requires us to be alert to several possibilities: the mother's feelings of shame and guilt that might interfere with parenting; inter-action with her child may 'trigger' her traumatic past, and sometimes neglecting the child is a way of avoiding such emotions; she may be over-protective; and she may have not been nurtured as a child, and so lack the internal resources and knowledge that informs parenting.

It is very common for substance-using women to live with men who also use substances. Male substance-users, by comparison, are more likely to have the support of a non-using partner. Having been introduced to drugs by their male partners, relapse among women tends to be closely tied to intimate relationships with men (Sun, 2007). Covington (2007) suggests that this is because women are strongly attuned to relationships and connections, and may use substances in order to fit in with available relationships, and that subsequently '. . . they change themselves to maintain the relationship' (page 2). For vulner-able woman with few alternatives, the relationship may offer a sense of protection, yet still embody a power imbalance. Gender patterns have been noted in injecting drug use, with men more likely to use before women, which increases the likelihood of transmission of blood-borne viruses from male to female partners. In a two-parent household, if the mother uses, children are more likely to be living without the protective quality of a non-using parent.

Gender also plays a key role in domestic violence. The association between substance use and violence is complex. Dependent use of illicit drugs is more predictive of family violence than other drug use, including alcohol; however, evidence suggests that **antisocial behaviour**, rather than substance use per se, is at the root of the problem

(Feingold, Kerr & Capaldi, 2008). Put simply, this means it is likely that there is a group of people, more commonly men, who engage in antisocial behaviour, including, but not limited to, drug use, and that these men are at greater risk of perpetrating more severe violence. For some men, a history of trauma leads to antisocial personality and poor impulse regulation. This predisposition towards low empathy and impulsive discharge of emotion can be reinforced by a social context in which conflict is resolved by violence, and by the disinhibiting qualities of alcohol and excessive stimulants.

The prospect of parenting elevates risk, as the biological, material and relational imperatives change within the family. It is common for violence to commence during pregnancy, and for violence to be greater when drugs are used in combination with alcohol, resulting in serious injury or homicide, not only to partners, but also to other family or household members. In work with this population, then, safety plan-ning is an ever-present imperative.

Although the potential for male violence towards mothers, and possibly towards workers, is significant, we should not reduce our understanding of men to this issue. Historically, alcohol and other drug treatment services were initially designed for men, with women's needs poorly addressed. In contrast, many services for parents, including universal parenting support and wellbeing services, have been designed largely for, and are welcoming of, women, who often take on the primary caregiving role in the majority of families. Nevertheless, there are many fathers who have taken on this role with young children in families affected by alcohol or other drug problems. This may be because the mother is currently incarcerated, has become unwell or died from a drug overdose, or has separated after forming a relationship with a new partner.

Mothers who use drugs often invoke more active social stigma and condemnation from society and kin, whereas fathers are often dismissed and feared. Yet when men are in an active parenting role, social expectations of them might be lower than for mothers. Alcohol and other drug treatment services often have a unique and privileged access to these men who may struggle to engage with other services. Few organisations, however, make the most of this opportunity to support these fathers and their children. Workers should familiarise themselves with local programs that have proven effective in working with men, and particularly fathers, and look for ideas about engagement and for referral options. While some men respond well to counselling and support groups, many men will initially engage more readily with parenting services if they are not expected to start talking straight away, and where there are opportunities for fathers to engage in fun family activities that match their own interests. Examples may include family barbecues, sports or games, or family camps. Activity and strengths-based approaches can help to disrupt unhelpful stereotypes.

CHILD AND FAMILY SERVICES AND AOD TREATMENT PRACTICE

Much of what has been learnt from the alcohol and other drug treatment field has been learnt from close attention to the private lives of individual clients, and this learning can enrich practice with families. Yet it will be important to bear in mind that, once children are involved, the highly personal journey of substance use, dependence and recovery is not one that is travelled alone. If you see the family as a system of mutually influential developmental pathways, you will be alert to the parallel experiences of the child, the mother, the father, other partners or parent figures, including grandparents, and siblings all influencing each other for better or worse. While it may be necessary to focus on the needs of one person at any given time, you will need to constantly bear in mind the dynamic interaction between the developmental trajectories of the various family members.

Interventions on behalf of one family member may have important repercussions for others; there are many intervention opportunities, many different pathways to help.

Drawing upon both the child and family and the alcohol and other drug service sectors, and their practice theories, this book is fundamentally humanist in its approach, enriched by cognitive/behavioural and motivational approaches to change within the positive and hopeful orientation offered by solution-focused and narrative approaches to individual and family counselling and support. The major elements of this approach, which will be evident throughout this book, can be described as follows.

Blending practical assistance with counselling and support

- The heavier the burden, the harder it is to achieve change. Multiple problems and disabilities can overwhelm the best of intentions, particularly if the world is experienced as hostile. Giving parents practical help with life's tangible needs may create hope and help clear the way for attitudinal and behavioural change, while ensuring that children receive what they need when they need it.
- Counselling is a very small part of the process of change, most of which occurs as life is lived differently in a changed and supportive world. Effective change requires workers to coordinate their efforts with each other, and with the range of effective informal helpers available in the family's continuing social network, from the outset.

Listening to lived experience

- Over time, people develop stories about their lives which incorporate themes about their efficacy or passivity, about hope and hopelessness, and about shame and their personal worth in society. These themes develop through the person's direct experience in their world, and destructive themes must be countered by new positive experiences and liberating ways of viewing their world. The structure of daily life itself might need to be changed for those new experiences to be available.

Building trust

- When people have been abused, traumatised and stigmatised or socially excluded over a long time they learn to expect these responses from others. Trusting others, particularly officials, or those in authority or power, is difficult and workers must actively earn trust through continuously avoiding abusive or demeaning behaviour. Trust also requires absolute honesty, especially given substance-users may be more prone to practise deception as a means of self-protection.

- Workers who are seen as trustworthy are consistent in word and deed, congruent in their presentation of self, always respectful and are willing to listen to stories of suffering and degradation without judgement, while offering hope for a better outcome.

Regulating emotions, thoughts and behaviour

- Patterns of both thinking and behaviour are learnt, and can be changed, if opportunities to do so are created, recognised and seized, but enduring change must be reinforced many times in different supportive social contexts.

- In the context of a trustworthy, helping relationship, change can be facilitated by identifying and replicating socially acceptable behaviour that already serves the child and parent well (building on strengths), by encouraging and developing more enjoyable and rewarding daily activities, by emphasising the creation of a secure attachment between parents and their children, and by shifting the way the family identifies itself from worthlessness and failure to worthiness and achievement.

- Powerful forces (such as substance dependence, violence or submission to a controlling partner) need powerful alternatives. Envisaging a better future requires strong dreams with real resources to help fulfil those dreams. The dream of a better life for one's child is often an important part of the dream for a better personal life.

Planned management of risk and crises

- Since substance dependence tends to be a chronic and relapsing condition, it is necessary to plan for lapses into substance use and the attendant crises these may create for children and families. Early warning signs and triggers for use should be identified, and strategies to handle lapses should be planned and practised.
- The association between substance misuse and criminal behaviour often poses specific threats from the environment for children. Sources of potential threat should be identified and responses planned. Help-seeking may need to be rehearsed.
- Lapses and failures need to be defined as learning opportunities, if incremental gains are to be made.

Enhancing the quality of daily family life

- Competency and motivation are linked through experiences of success. When opportunities for rewarding family experiences are structured into daily life, they provide a substitute 'virtuous circle' to counteract the tendency to become stuck in 'vicious circles' of self-reinforcing destructive behaviour. Enabling, noticing and furthering children's developmental steps and expressions of talent will bring rewards for both children and parents.
- Children, and their parents, need joy to thrive. Factoring in fun times and celebratory rituals lifts family life from the mundane and encourages imaginative engagement with alternative life scenarios.

Building networks of support for child and family resilience

- Formal and informal sources of support need to work together for the sake of the child, the parent and the whole family. Workers need to remind themselves and the families they work with that they cannot remain forever, and that the child and parents will still need someone to turn to in the future.

SUMMARY

Brought together, an ecosystemic approach to child development and family life, and a humanist, strengths-oriented, socially embedded approach to change in thought and behaviour, offer a way of working with families affected by problematic parental substance use that keeps the wellbeing of children at the centre of attention, but does so in a way that is respectful of the complex challenges facing the parents, and is realistic about the resources and time they will need to effect substantial and sustainable change. A layered response is called for.

Within both the child and family services sector and the alcohol and other drug treatment sector, clients' personal vulnerability and social stigma have been acknowledged, and forms of intervention have been developed that emphasise the facilitative quality of the worker–client relationship, making the most of the windows of opportunity for change, and building support for the durability of change. Professional helpers need to take initiative but to be realistic about the limits to their own influence. While positive change in clients' lives may be achieved as a result of planned professional intervention, it may also occur as a result of intense private personal effort, the actions of family and friends, and happy coincidences of personal and social factors (serendipitous windows of opportunity, such as new housing, a new non-using or recovered partner) at particular stages in the personal and family life course (moments of readiness).

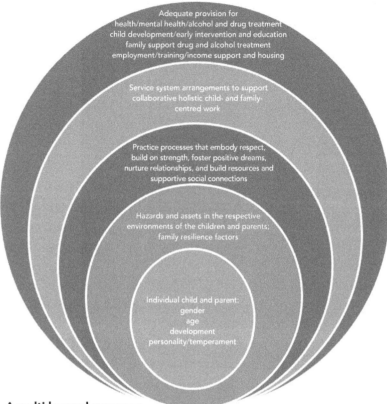

A multi-layered response

Readers will note two key words recurring throughout this book: *respect* and *hope*. This emphasis is deemed necessary because, as a group, parents who use substances in problematic ways have a high incidence of traumatic and demeaning life events underlying their initial and continuing substance use, and as they become identified in the community as substance-users, they experience further stigmatisation, rejection and even abuse. Many have come to expect to be treated as unworthy of help and view workers and services with extreme caution. Both this caution and the stigmatisation that prompts it may place them and their children at further risk of harm if services are not made available in an acceptable and timely way.

PART 2

SOUND BEGINNINGS

3

Connecting with parents

In this chapter, we discuss the importance of engagement with parents and we identify common barriers to a constructive working relationship between the family and the worker. Relationships are built through action, spending time together, listening, providing some early and tangible assistance, and demonstrating understanding and empathy; here we explore how these play out in work with substance-affected parents. (We reserve for Chapter 4 most discussion of direct communication with children.) To illustrate some of the ideas we will present, two case studies that will be followed in subsequent chapters are introduced in this chapter.

The notion of 'engagement' can be understood differently; to some it is an early task in building a working relationship, to others it is a continuing process underpinning all supportive work. We will use the latter interpretation as work with substance-affected parents can be especially prone to interruption for many reasons, including: the physical effects of substance use and withdrawal; parents' own difficulties with emotional regulation; and legal, financial, housing and other crises such as domestic violence, which, as we have noted, frequently accompany problematic alcohol and/or other drug use.

This stigmatised group of parents is usually all too aware of negative assumptions about alcohol and other drug use and parenting capacity, so engaging with them can be a challenge, particularly when they present intoxicated. Parents can be evasive and their behaviour erratic if they are actively using alcohol or other drugs, when experiencing withdrawal symptoms, or when they are preoccupied with multiple difficulties. In Chapter 7 we provide further strategies to help workers stay goal focused and to set priorities, so that competing demands can be managed and real and positive changes can be facilitated.

Many substance-using parents do not differ in important ways from their peers and can provide good enough, if not comparable, care of, and nurturing for, children. Such parents may never come to the attention of service providers. Some parents know when they are struggling to manage alcohol and other drug use, and when their capacity to provide adequate care of children is therefore compromised. They welcome respectful, non-threatening intervention, for their own sake, and for the wellbeing of their children. Others may deny even very significant problems, and may try to convince themselves, and others, that they can manage substance use and parenting responsibilities. The extent to which parents acknowledge their problems can be understood in relation to the Stages of Change model developed by Prochaska, DiClemente and Norcross (1992), as outlined in the previous chapter.

Some clients are mandated to accept services, for example, as conditions on children's court orders, or through family drug courts, which offer comprehensive assessment of parental substance use, and risk and protective factors for infants and children, combined with statutory authority. These are a promising development across international jurisdictions (Harwin et al., 2013), with many in the US but isolated pilot examples in Australia and in the UK. While the court order can create an opportunity for engagement, intervention is frequently perceived as a threat. Compliance with orders can be low or superficial, potentially increasing the risk of infant and child removal from parental care and reducing the possibility of reunification (De Bortoli, Coles & Dolan, 2013). Parents can also be defensive and aggressive as a consequence of trauma, fear of involvement with services, past experience of stigma and low expectations of service outcomes. From their perspective, parents often experience services and workers as unhelpful and hard to communicate with. Some parents will have experienced child protection involvement in their own childhood or have lost the care of other infants or children, either temporarily, or to permanent care. Determining whether they can trust a service or worker is therefore a prime concern. Key strategies for engaging substance-using parents in alcohol and other drug treatment services include providing a safe and welcoming environment, establishing credibility, demonstrating an understanding of their concerns and needs, and using techniques such as motivational interviewing to determine and enhance their motivation for change.

Families will often present as single parents, typically sole-parenting mothers; however, family structures can be complex and variable. When multiple caregivers are involved, you may need to engage with them separately and together if children's needs are to be met effectively, subject to consideration of the gender and relationship issues involved. When there is family violence, it is important to consider whether you can all work safely together. It helps to understand the different functions of substance use for men and women. For example, men are more likely to use alcohol and/or other drugs prior to perpetrating violence whereas women are more likely to use as a means of coping with violence (Humphreys et al., 2005). Considering your own safety can be a good gauge for the safety of family members (see Chapters 5 and 6).

Whether working with mothers, fathers or couples, engagement and work towards change is a mutual and shared process in which both parties, clients and workers, have responsibilities. Therapeutic intervention will require that at least one professional is well-engaged with the family. Some worker attributes reduce tension and conflict and foster good helping relationships with families. These qualities are authenticity and the ability to challenge parents gently and wisely, combined with a style that is understanding and compassionate.

INTENDED OUTCOMES

Positive engagement is purposeful, requiring continuous attention to achieving intended outcomes. First, it aims to build a deep understanding of the needs of all family members in order to match families with appropriate services. Second, it aims to establish a working relationship able to withstand honest feedback to improve parental functioning and outcomes for children by helping parents and children understand the past, cope with the present in a constructive way and create hope for the future.

HELPFUL ATTITUDES AND VALUES

Practice experience suggests that there are some key values and attitudes that help workers achieve a positive working relationship with parents.

Respect for parents as individuals and in their role as providers for, and protectors of, their children is crucial. Many parents have become accustomed to receiving disrespect, dismissal and condemnation. *Acceptance* or a *non-judgemental attitude* is a key tenet of helping relationships generally. In this context, it means not being judgemental about alcohol or other drug use and trying to understand its value from the client's perspective. For example, is this the parent's way of self-medicating anxiety, depression or trauma? It is important to note, though, that acceptance does not imply giving permission for, excusing or condoning any form of abuse or violence.

Conveying positive regard, empathy and compassion for parents despite appearances and challenging behaviour, and *being sincere* in all interactions with parents, children and members of the extended family and network are ways of translating respect and acceptance into action. Similarly, *positive advocacy* demonstrates respect. For example, ensuring substance-using parents are not discriminated against and that they receive the same services as other families will do a lot for the worker–parent relationship and the establishment of trust and respect.

Open-mindedness helps. Workers need to be willing to seek to understand situations from the parent's and child's perspective without prejudgement based on intake, referral or file information. While not disregarding critical referral information, it helps for the worker to see clients as the experts in their own lives, by asking them what they understand to be happening and what they find helpful. Being open-minded also leads to trying to accommodate the family's priorities, including being flexible about meeting times and places, consistent with worker safety.

Hopefulness provides a launching pad for change. This does not preclude honesty about the difficulties to be faced. On the contrary, the cautiously optimistic worker demonstrates that change is possible in the face of learnt patterns of demoralisation and fatalism among clients who have come to accept such things as substance dependence and relapse, relationship turmoil and material crises as givens in their lives.

For these values and attitudes to lead to productive mutual engagement, they need to be accompanied by clear behavioural expectations of both clients and workers, and these expectations need to address questions of safety.

EXPECTATIONS OF YOURSELF

You will need to monitor your personal attitudes and values and their impact on the formation of a working relationship with substance-affected parents. Am I demonstrating reliability, sincerity and mutual respect in all interactions? How have I demonstrated acceptance of the person without necessarily condoning behaviour (e.g. drug dealing, sex work)? Am I making sure that I am not placing anyone in danger through what I ask of them? Have I paid sufficient attention to the child's safety? Having modelled respect and honesty, it is then appropriate to ask that clients reciprocate.

EXPECTATIONS OF CLIENTS

In negotiating the terms of how you will work with parents, it is reasonable to ask them to be reliable, sincere and mutually respectful in all interactions, while knowing that this might not always be sustainable. Parents should be invited to engage in honest, open conversations about the challenges of parenting and substance use; this is more likely to occur if parents do not feel threatened, blamed or punished. Limits to unacceptable behaviour should be negotiated within an expectation that all family members and workers are entitled to be safe while working together.

BARRIERS TO ENGAGING PARENTS AND FACILITATING SUSTAINABLE CHANGE

Barriers to engagement may be encountered in several places: in the family, in the family's network, in the worker and in the service system.

Family barriers to engagement

There are many reasons why parents might be wary of entering an honest working relationship with a service provider. Fear of scrutiny by service providers and the potential for child removal are the major barriers to engagement with parents, especially when parents are aware that their parenting practices are flawed. Those who are subject to family or other violence may feel unable to speak honestly for fear of retribution from the abuse perpetrator. Children, too, can fear being removed from parents or getting parents into trouble if they disclose information about the family and its network. Some parents will avoid services, directed at themselves or their children, in an attempt to shield children from knowledge of substance use within the family. Substance use and a history of trauma can limit parents' and children's ability to understand and remember conversations and induce difficulty in communicating emotions; they may be emotionally reactive or unresponsive.

Network barriers to engagement

Many substance-using parents have social networks that are depleted of natural helpers, but busy with people and activities that draw their attention away from child-rearing. They may experience lack of time due to juggling the demands of the drug-using lifestyle, in which parents spend time and resources buying (and/or dealing) drugs, with trying to meet their own and their children's basic needs for shelter, food and clothing. Under these conditions, meeting with workers can be difficult, and there are many disincentives to being open about their daily lives. In addition, both substance use and the use of social services may have variable meanings and associations across cultures, so that some parents may not know what to expect of services, may fear that their specific cultural obligations will be misunderstood, or may fear disapproval within the social network if they are open about drug use and seeking help with substance-related problems.

Worker barriers to engagement

The worker may erect a number of barriers to engagement through his or her emotions, presentation, knowledge, choice of words and skill. Body language and clothing convey status and degree of comfort in social situations and need to be monitored and adjusted according to the degree that they are off-putting for particular clients. Many parents will easily spot a worker who is not genuine or is anxious. When a worker is fearful of asking questions about substance use or parenting issues and indicates that he or she does not want to get involved, parents may be left feeling they will not be helped to address the most pressing concerns facing them and their children. At the other extreme, the worker who projects an image of unreasonable optimism and pressure for change may leave parents feeling that their doubts and worries have not been understood.

Workers bring to the relationship their own personal, familial and professional experiences with both alcohol and other drug use and with child-rearing. Any experiences of distress and disappointment around these issues may make it more challenging for workers to engage with parents. For example, the worker who has come to believe 'once a user, always a user' will be ill-equipped to generate the required climate of hope. The worker who has come to believe that substance users do not tell the truth may not be able to understand that lying about substance use, or other problems, can be a parent's way of protecting themselves and their children from intrusion into family life and potential consequences.

A consistent message from parents is their distrust of workers who prove unreliable. Whenever a worker (for whatever reason) does not assist parents to access what they need for themselves and their children, or does not follow through on commitments (e.g. to make a referral to another service provider) in a timely manner, the chance of continued positive engagement is reduced.

Service system barriers to engagement

The way services are publicised, their referral pathways, their culture and practice models and their physical attributes can all affect engagement. Parents are sensitive to stigma; labels such as 'junkie', 'addict', getting 'clean' or even 'user' can be offensive, and services need strong systems to monitor organisational culture and detect language and behaviour that might deter parents from approaching and continuing with the service. At the point of entry, intake procedures that discourage discussion of child-rearing, on the one hand, or substance use, on the other, may discourage parents. Office environments that are unwelcoming to children also act as deterrents to parents. As many substance-dependent parents will also have a dual diagnosis, social anxiety or other mental health problems can prevent parents from leaving the house or going beyond known vicinities. Services that are rigidly office-based, have inflexible appointment systems or are unhelpful with transport all pose barriers.

Poor communication and **collaboration** between different service providers can also limit engagement, including different philosophical underpinnings; different priorities or goals (e.g. abstinence versus harm reduction); identification of the primary client; significant differences in tolerance for risk; and different policies and practices. Such tensions undermine engagement by pulling the client in different directions, and diverting worker attention to inter-organisational conflicts and away from the parent and child. These issues are further addressed in Chapter 8, where we consider professional collaboration in more depth, alongside ways of improving collaboration between services and families.

KEY STRATEGIES FOR ENGAGING PARENTS AND FACILITATING SUSTAINABLE CHANGE

Engagement with families in which there is parental substance use involves establishing and demonstrating comfort, respect, honesty, choice, hope and action.

Comfort

Beginning with comfort, it is important to provide a safe environment for all family members to speak openly. This may mean scheduling separate appointments in a neutral and safe location for women if family violence is suspected or known to occur, or offering some sessions without children present if parents do not wish to have substance use discussed in their presence.

Begin with 'where the parent is' and direct attention to the family unit and the presenting concerns rather than to parental alcohol or other drug use alone, and allow family members to define 'the problem'. When you do ask about alcohol and other drug use, do so in an open matter-of-fact manner that invites disclosure but does not suggest judgement. Clearly express why you need certain information. For example, comments such as 'Understanding past alcohol or other drug use, and the treatment or harm-reduction strategies you have already tried, can be helpful when we prepare treatment or case plans' can help to allay parental anxiety.

Reassure parents and children that communications will be confidential, except in cases of likely or actual harm or if files are subpoenaed. Most clients understand and respect limits to **confidentiality**.

Provide assertive outreach to families, particularly those who are isolated and/or have not had positive experiences with service providers. Home visits can reduce anxiety about involvement with services in both parents and children but they can also be frightening, particularly in the first instance, if parents think the home environment is being scrutinised or judged. Given this tension, offer a choice of location if possible. This may pave the way for access to the family home after trust has been established. If sessions occur in office settings, posters or images of culturally and structurally diverse families can create a welcoming ambience.

Since upheavals in lifestyle and alcohol and other drug relapses are common, families are likely to enter the service system repeatedly. It will be important to have an open-door policy which allows parents to return to the service on an 'at-need' basis wherever possible, and ideally to meet with their previous worker or another familiar team member.

Respect

Model respectful behaviour in all interactions with family members. Ask parents how they wish to be addressed. Use everyday language rather than jargon or words that are not understood by parents or children. Allow parents to express their concerns and needs without interrupting or becoming defensive. If the parent is responding with hostility, engage in further conversation when they have calmed down. Consider postponing the discussion or rescheduling the meeting if the parent is unable to regulate their emotions, remains hostile or appears substance-affected.

Many substance-dependent parents will argue they are able to safely use and care for children, which may well be the case in some instances. Such statements, however, cannot be taken at face value. The association between parental substance use and child maltreatment means that many will struggle to manage addiction and meet their children's needs. Rather than confronting parents with the impact of their substance use on children, which is likely to result in denial and resistance, use motivational interviewing techniques to assist them to consider the function and impact of alcohol and other drug use in their own and the family's life. For example, you may change your topic of conversation and inquire about the parent's goals for their children, and examine the benefits and costs of their current lifestyle and choices in attaining those goals.

Originally devised for work with individual problem drinkers, motivational interviewing has been adapted for use in the child and family welfare sector and has been shown to enhance potential engagement with parents without leading to loss of focus on the child (Forrester et al., 2008; Holman, 1998). This discussion should be undertaken in relation to stages of change which render individuals, including parents, more or less receptive to counselling and other interventions. It should be noted that child care responsibility may not be sufficient motivation for the parent to stop using and more intrinsic motivation may need to be explored and built upon. For example, you may also explore the parent's own health or deleterious impact on other aspects of their life, including relationships, employment and housing.

Honesty

At the outset, and periodically as needed, address parents' and children's anxieties by clarifying why you are meeting. Discuss openly the status of the referral and differences in power and authority (between parents and workers and between parents and children), and consider whether an advocate is needed. State the voluntary nature of involvement, if applicable, and indicate what the service is able to offer the family. If engagement is involuntary, clearly explain what the parent needs to do for services to withdraw. This may involve complying with conditions on children's court or family drug court orders. Providing parents with practical assistance to meet expectations placed on them can go a long way to fostering a solid working relationship.

Problems, including alcohol and other drug use, need to be 'named'; to not do so could lose the respect of the family. Parents, adolescents and children are more likely to disclose information if they know how the information may be used, so this needs to be discussed explicitly. Be up-front about the possibility of contacting child protection and the circumstances in which this might occur. Parents can be angry about a report while understanding that action may need to be taken to ensure child safety and wellbeing. Anxiety can be reduced by informing parents that a potential report will be discussed with them beforehand, provided that doing so does not further compromise the safety of the child or another person. It is worth remembering that involvement by statutory child protection services is not always unwelcome by families. In fact, some parents, especially mothers experiencing family violence, can be accepting, and even appreciative, of the need for increased monitoring if it improves safety.

Choice

Maximise decision-making by parents and children by offering as much choice as possible. Let parents know they are in the driver's seat, and that work will be focused on their goals and conducted at a pace that suits them, as long as this is consistent with the safety of children and/or other family members. It is important to understand this may involve some 'regression' as parents cycle through stages of change, and display denial or minimisation of alcohol and other drug use.

Where possible, give parents and children choice in workers but don't make assumptions on their behalf. Many families with substance use issues prefer the anonymity of accessing a mainstream service or a service in another town or city where they are not known. Also for anonymity, some people from culturally and linguistically diverse backgrounds and some Indigenous service users do not want a CALD worker who shares the family's ethnicity or culture. Some fathers may prefer a male counsellor, others may not. Even if you cannot offer a choice, ask about such concerns and seek to address them. Workers in all services need to enhance their cultural understanding and be familiar with translation services and other supports for the communities in which they are likely to work.

Hope

Avoid contributing to self-fulfilling prophecies—for example, by writing or expressing comments such as 'parent is unmotivated to make changes'. Focus instead on strengths that can be built on and blockages that might be overcome. Many substance-dependent parents have had difficult lives and lack hope for change; it is therefore important to demonstrate the professional ability to help people make important changes in their lives by offering both practical and emotional support. Review progress towards goals and reinforce achievements, however small, to sustain engagement and to build the therapeutic alliance by encouraging further progress (see Chapter 7). You can also help parents create a new, more hopeful and positive story about their achievements and their future.

Action

Meet parents and children more than half-way without being discouraged by initial indifference or reluctance. The onus is on the professional worker to keep trying to engage the client, and quick delivery of results on manageable requests can demonstrate good faith. Many substance-using parents struggle to keep appointments; when appointments are missed, have procedures to invite parents to re-establish contact with the service. For example, post a friendly card after a missed appointment inviting a telephone call, or send a gentle text message reminding the parent to reschedule. Be aware though, that when a relapse occurs, parents will often cease contact with services and this may be an unsafe time for children and families.

If you represent a service families are mandated to accept, find out who else is involved with the family and seek the family's consent for collaborative practice. Do a thorough **handover** between team members and when making referrals to avoid parents and children having to repeatedly tell their story. Assist families to access other services through active referrals and handover, ideally in person (see Chapter 8).

Families are more likely to get to, and stay involved with, services that provide transport and child care. Social events with food for children and parents also encourage attendance. Parents with histories of chronic substance use sometimes feel uncomfortable in social settings where they fear rejection or if they believe they have little in common with others. Specifically designed and run programs or groups with their peers can encourage attendance. An example might be a playgroup for substance-using parents from a specific ethnic group. Once engaged, the parent may be more inclined to attend or accept other services on offer.

TIPS FOR NEW WORKERS

- Engagement is often a staged process in which parents test the service by dropping out or missing appointments. Parents will be checking you out to see if you can be trusted, if you know what you are talking about and how you will react. A dismissive or punitive response at this stage can deter the parent from persisting with the relationship. Letters and cards are effective ways of re-engaging parents who may be embarrassed by missed appointments or who do not want to be seen when they are not doing well.

- Develop a thick skin, and do not be easily put off if early attempts at engagement fail.
- Try to reduce defensiveness by using motivational interviewing techniques in conjunction with strengths-based approaches, which acknowledge the parent's struggle and compliment them for it; for example, such statements as: 'It can't be easy doing this on your own. I wonder how you manage to cope as well as you do' can go a long way towards reducing defensiveness and facilitating a productive working relationship.
- Preparing parents for difficult questions can make conversations easier—for example, 'There's a sensitive question I need to ask you'. **Open-ended questions** and empathic responses reduce resistance and increase the amount of information provided by parents.
- Parents are often more receptive to professional involvement when services address children's needs rather than just focus on changing parental behaviour.
- Parents often try to shield children from knowledge of their drug use; respect parents' wishes but inform them that children are often well aware of parental substance use and may welcome the parent receiving help.
- Provide a child-friendly environment with toys or youth-appropriate magazines in clinical settings, or carry play/drawing materials for children when conducting home visits. While this is primarily a tip for engaging children, it also signals to the parent that you take their children, and their parenting, seriously, and it builds common communication tools between the parent, the children and the worker (see Chapter 4).
- Childlessness is not a barrier to engagement when the worker is

able to demonstrate an ability to help with parenting issues such as establishing bedtime routines for children or implementing behaviour management strategies.

- Consider initially meeting on neutral territory; for example, a hospital cafeteria is helpful when parents are highly anxious about involvement with services after the birth of an infant.
- Establish rapport through friendliness and minimal but appropriate use of self-disclosure. Bear in mind that personal revelations can be destructive to parents if they convey the message that the worker is a superior person or parent.
- When parents present aggressively, try to understand if you have contributed to the development of hostility. A useful strategy for managing client reactivity is to let the parent know you need to have a difficult conversation and ask how they will manage their emotions.
- A relaxed manner is likely to reduce resistance or hostilities: be calm and respectful regardless of the parent's presentation; be sensitive to non-verbal cues (e.g. body language in adults such as arms firmly crossed and held tight against the chest or a child hiding, cringing or crying) and change strategies to reduce anxiety or hostility.
- If the parent is significantly intoxicated, especially if they are behaving aggressively, consider if a more meaningful conversation can be held at another time and arrange to come back.
- Be sure to inform authorities—for example, child protection or police, or a helpful, responsive adult family member—if you have serious concerns about a child's imminent safety (see Chapter 6).

TRAPS FOR NEW WORKERS

Some of the key traps for new workers include:
- Mistaking compliance-based actions for a real commitment to change—for example, a parent superficially meeting conditions on children's court or family drug court orders.

- Accepting and giving superficial responses in place of meaningful dialogue or action, particularly if the worker is feeling anxious and struggling to have the necessary difficult conversations. This includes giving unrealistic positive feedback that makes it hard for parents to admit to lapses—for example, 'You were so pleased with how well I was doing I couldn't tell you I was using again'.

- Jumping to solutions and trying to solve a problem before the parent or child has identified it, or pushing your own solutions/ goals onto the family.

- Referring parents to other services before establishing motivation or commitment to attend, and assuming the parent will contact the other service provider or that the other service provider will actively follow up the referral.

- Feeling personally hurt and disappointed when parents are unavailable or fail to return text messages and telephone calls or respond to letters or emails, and then giving up on families too soon.

- Speaking down to, or being patronising towards, parents or other family members.

- Hiding behind a professional mask and using jargon and/or organisational power to create distance from the client, particularly when feeling ill at ease. For example, statements such as 'Unless the department's conditions are met . . .' can be replaced with 'I'm concerned about the care arrangements for your child when you are using'.

- Expecting too little or too much of parents and children.

- Not visiting through fear of your own safety and neglecting to take appropriate action to ensure child safety, which may include visiting in pairs or arranging a visit at a public location.

- Failing to see the child or infant during home visits, and as a consequence remaining unable to satisfy your concerns about their wellbeing.

HOW WILL I KNOW IF I'M ON TRACK?

- Parents' and children's responses will not be defensive or evasive.
- You'll establish a partnership with parents to work towards meeting child and family needs.
- Parents will willingly allow you to see the children.
- Parents will be available for appointments, return calls and follow-through with goals and case plans.
- Parents will disclose alcohol or other drug use, parenting difficulties or other problems and struggles.
- Parents will introduce extended family members or other significant people in their informal network, including close friends or neighbours.
- Parents will call before there is a crisis or shortly after to seek assistance and support.
- Children will be welcoming, relaxed and communicative.

ENGAGING STELLA

Stella used heroin throughout her pregnancy and delivered a premature baby girl, Mia, at 24 weeks gestation. Stella informed her hospital social worker that she and her partner, Daniel, were homeless and having relationship problems. After first considering a report to child protection, the social worker referred Stella to a specialist alcohol and other drug (AOD) family support program for drug treatment, relationship counselling and assistance with housing.

Stella was highly anxious about involvement with a service as she feared it may lead to loss of her infant. The first meeting between Stella, the hospital social worker and the AOD worker was held at the hospital. In response to Stella's obvious anxiety, the AOD worker suggested they meet in the hospital cafeteria for the next visit, which Stella hesitatingly agreed to. The next two meetings were also held at the hospital, during which time the worker built trust and rapport. Towards the end of the third visit, Stella invited the AOD worker to meet her mother, Joan, who was visiting Mia in the neonatal ward. She also disclosed domestic violence, perpetrated by Daniel, which included financial and physical abuse. Stella wanted to leave him but was scared of retaliatory action on his part. A **safety plan** was implemented and an intervention order taken out to help Stella safely separate from Daniel in the days before Mia's discharge from hospital.

ENGAGING KEVIN

Kevin was mandated to receive AOD counselling after committing crime to fund illicit drug use. He resented attending and usually slumped in the chair, remaining largely non-verbal. The AOD worker responded with warmth and friendliness, initially focusing her attention on the issues that were of most concern to him: a housing transfer; assistance with overdue bills; and warm clothing for his ten-year-old son, Zac. Zac had been returned to Kevin's care after three years in out-of-home care after being removed from his mother while Kevin was incarcerated. After receiving assistance with the issues he considered most pressing, Kevin became more vocal, even jovial, and open to other discussions, including questions about his substance use and how it may affect Zac.

SUMMARY

In this chapter we have argued that there is a logical sequence to be followed and some key strategies to use in order to establish good engagement with substance-using parents, just as there is in most other helping relationships, even though we can expect setbacks and stalemates from time to time.

Build engagement by:

- reaching out with respect;
- creating a comfortable setting for parents and children;
- responding to expressed needs; and
- avoiding confrontation when motivation for change is absent.

Build motivation for change by:

- focusing on their hopes and dreams;
- honestly clarifying expectations and limits;
- negotiating priorities;
- demonstrating utility through action; and
- keeping the door open!

4

Connecting with children

Having explored barriers to engagement with parents and how to over-come them, this chapter stresses the importance of direct engagement with children and the need to bring their developmental needs into prominence in work with the family and others. The process of engagement with children echoes that of engagement with parents. They, too, need a comfortable environment, demonstrated respect, honest communication, choice in matters affecting them, a climate of hope and the reassurance of action. This chapter therefore talks not only about communication but also about initial interventions which will be built upon in later chapters. In the discussion below, it will become evident that these elements are always shaped by the child's developmental stage and needs, but of course child development theory, research and practice is a vast arena of learning in its own right beyond the scope of this book. No worker can know it all, so search out your local experts, encourage your agency to invest in relevant key child development texts and familiarise yourself with the many online resources available. The website of the Raising Children Network in Australia has many resources to inform workers and parents alike, structured according to the age of the child. It provides an excellent starting point when you or the parents you work with have queries about what to expect of a child. In the United Kingdom, the Research in Practice organisation has a number of relevant professional resources available for purchase (see Useful websites and resources).

As we have noted, recovery from substance dependence is typically a long process of change and relapse, but there is immediacy in children's physical, emotional, cognitive and moral needs: children cannot simply wait for parental recovery to occur. Consequently, workers often struggle with potentially conflicting needs and competing time-frames. Ideally, each child will live with a loving family in a stable home with low levels of conflict; this in turn requires support to parents to help them create a protective and nurturing environment. Even so, it is important to consider if the child needs services in his or her own right because, despite obvious advantages for children if parents reduce or cease their substance use or have other needs met, this may not, in itself, sufficiently improve the child's situation. Many problems may remain unchanged; for example, parenting stress may not decrease, or the family might still be impoverished.

Bringing children to the foreground in families affected by alcohol and other drug use involves overcoming child, family, network and systemic barriers to child-inclusive practice. Intervention needs to begin with immediate child safety and to prioritise the child's needs for physical and emotional care and nurturing (see Chapter 6), but be wary of making assumptions about how parental substance use has affected the child. This can vary according to whether the child remains in the care of an actively using parent; if there is a protective, non-using adult in the home; and the type and severity not only of parental substance-use, but also of withdrawal (as discussed in Chapter 5).

It is also important to consider differences in children's experiences in relation to the use of licit or illicit substances. Children living with parents who use *illicit* substances are more likely to have been separated from parents following child protection intervention or parental incarceration; they are likely to have been removed from parents at an earlier age and are less likely to be reunified. They may have been exposed to criminal activities and to have experienced poverty exacerbated by the purchase of costly drugs. Changes of address and school are more frequent, resulting in severance of children's own friendships and networks. Children's feelings of shame and stigma are likely to be greater. They are also more likely to be socially isolated. As we mentioned in Chapter 1, some children will have witnessed an overdose; for a small number, overdose will have resulted in the death of a parent (Gruenert, Ratnam & Tsantefski, 2004). But for many children, the raft of problems commonly co-occurring with substance use, such as mental illness, family and other forms of violence and poverty, may have had a greater impact on the child than substance use per se.

At all times, support should be tailored to the child's age and bio-psychosocial development, bearing in mind that environmental deprivation and exposure to in utero alcohol use, in particular, may have resulted in a wider discrepancy between biological age and developmental stage than would typically be expected. Fortunately, with the exception of exposure to alcohol, many of the developmental delays seen in children of substance-dependent parents can be overcome through an enriched and supportive caregiving environment. To help children reach their developmental potential, intervention efforts should target children at greatest risk at the developmental stage when certain problems are most likely to manifest. Appropriate strategies and services for children at different ages and stages are discussed below, but the following general emphases apply. Developmentally tailored interventions tend to:

- begin with support for the pregnant mother to improve the child's in utero experience;
- focus on attachment and direct caregiving in the postnatal period;
- centre on early intervention to overcome physical, cognitive and emotional problems in the preschool years;
- enhance children's educational engagement, social competence, positive sense of self and access to nurture in the middle years, with attention to improving the congruence between the child's experiences at home and in the community; and
- work to avert substance use uptake and build strong educational and community participation in the adolescent years.

INTENDED OUTCOMES

In working with and for the child, several goals guide the worker's efforts, namely, that children are buffered from the direct impact of parental substance use, that their developmental needs are met, that their daily life opportunities are optimised and that they have access to social goods and services.

Buffering children from the direct impact of parental substance use has several components: children will not witness serious parental drug use, excessive alcohol consumption or self-harm; they will not ingest substances used by parents or be harmed by drug-related parapher-nalia (e.g. syringes); and their own uptake of alcohol and other drugs or other problem behaviours will be prevented or reduced.

Children's developmental needs are diverse and numerous, and clearly specific to the child's age and any special needs, but there are core desired outcomes to guide intervention. First, it is crucial that infants and young children get off to a good start with families who provide good quality care and meet their physical, social, emotional, developmental and educational needs. Second, for families to provide that good care requires that children have consistent, available and caring adult figures and that their relationships with non-resident parents and significant others are maintained, as appropriate to the child's safety and wellbeing.

Optimising children's daily life opportunities means ensuring that they simply have a childhood, full of the usual learning, play and chal-lenges of children of their age. For this to occur, they ought not to be what is sometimes called 'parentified', that is, assuming responsibili-ties beyond what would be expected of their peers, whether this be in self-care, care of siblings, household management or emotional and physical care of parents.

That children have access to social goods and services tends to be taken for granted in developed societies, but children of substance-misusing parents sometimes miss out on basic provisions. We suggest you aim to ensure that infants and young children are in regular contact with child health services, and that children receive early childhood education, followed by continuous schooling. In addition, the child's lack of comparative power within the service system should be addressed, so that within the limits of their ability to contribute their perspective, children understand and participate in decisions that affect them.

HELPFUL ATTITUDES AND VALUES

As in work with parents, work with children calls for specific attitudes and values. First is a willingness and confidence to engage directly with children. This entails respect for the child as an active, competent person with their own preferences and ability to make informed decisions, commensurate with age and developmental level, and it is in turn grounded in respect for children as citizens deserving of service provision in their own right.

Even so, it remains important to respect the child's relationship with parents, siblings and significant others, not simply because these people might facilitate or block the worker's access to the child, but also because these are relationships of intrinsic value to the child, even if problematic, and the child might experience disrespect towards family as a personal slight.

EXPECTATIONS OF CLIENTS

The development of trust through careful negotiation with parents and other carers is an important prelude to work with and on behalf of the child, for the worker is asking for their permission to see and speak with the child, and to acquire whatever information is necessary to understand the child's circumstances and needs. Beyond this, the worker also expects parents to prioritise the child's needs, including pro-social development, by not modelling excessive alcohol or other drug use in the presence of children, and asks them to work in partnership with professionals to support healthy child development.

It is more difficult to specify expectations of the child as client, given the developmental spectrum; the worker must recognise that the child is the least powerful person, and the most vulnerable to having their confidences exploited. With this proviso, where a verbal child engages in direct discussion with a worker individually or in groups, it is reasonable for the worker to support the child to be truthful or honest in telling their opinions and experiences, provided the worker in turn undertakes to be honest with the child and to do all that is possible to respect the child's wishes unless the safety of the child or another is compromised. This is always best done with permission from the parent, and where the child hears the parent give this permission.

EXPECTATIONS OF YOURSELF

You will prioritise the child's need for safety and wellbeing across all domains relevant to childhood: health, education, identity formation, family and network connections, social integration and emotional, cognitive and behavioural development. You will be committed to increasing decision-making and participation by children, as appropriate to their age and developmental level. You will promote positive outcomes and improve children's life chances by helping to build protective factors and not just focus on reducing risk. You will be respectful of the child's relationship with their parents and caregivers, and consider the child's attachment needs in all interactions with children, parents and other carers (see Chapter 9).

BARRIERS TO WORKING WITH CHILDREN

Barriers in the child

Children do not like feeling interrogated and can find it difficult to disclose what they know, think or feel to a stranger, especially when they fear the potential consequences—for example, being removed from home or getting their parents into trouble. In addition, children whose early socialisation and education has been compromised may lack the language to put their feelings into words. Parents engaged in illicit substance use, in particular, can demand that children not disclose, or in any way discuss, their substance use, effectively silencing the child who wishes to remain loyal and loved.

Barriers in the family

Parents' own stories of past deprivation or trauma and current difficulties are often compelling and demand time and attention, which can make it easy to neglect the needs of vulnerable infants and children (see Chapter 7). Parents can block access to children, particularly if they feel family secrets will be disclosed or that workers will inform children of their alcohol or other drug use. The most frequently encountered barrier in the family is parental fear that scrutiny will lead to notification to child protection services, or if statutory services are already involved with the family, that monitoring will result in infants and/or children being removed from the home.

Barriers in the network

Extended family and friends may inhibit worker access to the child or discourage the child's trust in the worker. This is sometimes done to protect the child and family from what is regarded as unwanted interference. The child's social network can be depleted, lacking both caring adults and age-appropriate friends, which limits social and developmental opportunities available to the child, and also limits the channels through which workers can assist the child. For example, with few peers, the child misses out on learning to play with others constructively; if the family unit is cut off from positive adult relatives, it is harder for the worker to organise extensions to the child's routine, such as clubs or extracurricular learning.

Barriers in the worker

Many workers lack the skills, knowledge and confidence to work directly with children, both because they have had limited social contact with children in their adult lives, and because much professional education focuses on communication with adult clients. Some workers have had childhood experiences of family problems similar to those of the child. These experiences and the lessons learnt in dealing with them may equip the worker well to work with the child. There is also a risk, however, that the worker might identify strongly with the child and experience **secondary trauma**, or be tempted to feel they have the answers to the child's issues, whether or not these actually suit the specific situation. Alternatively, the worker may overly identify with the parents' struggle and minimise the risk of harm to the child.

Barriers in the service system

Most parenting support programs are not primarily designed to provide direct services to children; support is often delivered to parents with the aim of benefiting the child without necessarily addressing the impact parental substance use may have had on them. For example, housing instability and school disruption may have left gaps in the child's learning; exposure to crime may have corrupted pro-social development. Much work might be required to help parents achieve stable housing and a safer environment, leaving little room to directly counter the child's learning gaps and distorted social development.

Similarly, most alcohol and other drug treatment services are funded to attend to the 'identified client' (the man or woman) rather than the child or family as a whole. This focus on the adult sometimes also results in service providers forgetting to consider the risk of harm to an unborn baby, so that they fail to make referrals to obstetric care for pregnant women or for alcohol and other drug treatment; in planning for detoxification, care arrangements for dependent children might be ignored.

WORKING WITH THE CHILD

See and hear the child

At a minimum, speak with parents and carers about their children's ages and care needs. Since children may be apprehensive about the consequences of speaking to workers, seek the parent's help, where possible, to reassure the child, and make it clear that you seek to help the whole family. Get to know the individual child by finding out what is happening from the child's own perspective. Try to establish a secure and trusting relationship with the child while bearing in mind that this is difficult for some abused and neglected children with disordered attachments, particularly as professional relationships tend to be time-limited, which can leave children feeling abandoned when they end. Allow children to speak about their experiences in a safe environment; this may or may not be the family home. Children may prefer to speak with or without the parent present; where possible, offer children a choice.

Children often do not do 'talk-therapy' very well and child-friendly, age-appropriate alternatives may need to be implemented. For example, drawing can be used to engage the child in a discussion about their family or their lives more generally. Children's perspectives can also be gained by modifying methods used with adults—for example, charts can include the use of colourful stickers or pictures instead of numbers to gauge feelings. (St Luke's Innovative Resources have a range of materials suitable for use with children and parents: see Useful websites and resources.)

Give information and engage children in decisions and processes

Children should be given information appropriate to their age and stage of development and relevant to their daily lived experience, the provision of services and the decisions being made about them and their family. Often, they need help to understand what is going on in their family (for example, why they have to live with grandparents). While they may already know a lot about living with a parent who uses substances, they may need explanations about the effects on parents of alcohol and other drugs and withdrawal. Help them understand that recovery is possible, and if/when it is truthful, that the parent is doing all they can to get better.

Children who have been removed from their families may be especially anxious about a worker being in the home, while those who have been abused may be fearful, distrustful or overly compliant with adults in general. Depending on their age and developmental stage, children should be informed of who is working with their family and why, and they should be helped to understand what is appropriate and inappropriate professional behaviour.

It is in the context of shared information that children may be assisted to express their feelings and preferences, and the more important the decision to the child's immediate living circumstances and long-term prospects, the more important it is for the child to be consulted. Aim to involve children in decisions by seeking their preferences and ideas. Children may be helped to have their voices heard by including them in some appropriate family meetings, provided these are well-planned, sensitively conducted and monitored to ensure children are not subjected to adult conversations that are potentially destructive. For example, a parent with poor emotional and behavioural regulation might be overly critical of the child or the other parent, or discuss graphically violence, crime, suicidal thoughts or substance use.

Help the child communicate

As we mention above, the perspective of younger children can be gained through the use of their drawings. Older children can be encouraged to write a letter to the parent. A conversation, with or without the child present, about the child's experience of substance use in the family can be therapeutic for parents but also very confronting and may trigger a range of painful emotions such as guilt, shame, remorse or embarrassment. In order to manage their emotions, some parents may become withdrawn or outright hostile. Be sure to provide parents with unconditional support and encouragement. If you consider it is too confronting for the parent to hear directly from their child, either in person or through their drawings or a letter, consider providing general information to the parent about the impact of substance use in the family on children.

Help the child receive needed services

If you are qualified to do so, directly assess the child's developmental needs, or refer to appropriate services to ensure that infant and child developmental progress is monitored and that any identified delays are addressed in a timely manner. Even if you do not have a direct relationship with the child, you may play an important part in promoting the child's best interest with the family and within the service system. You can ensure that due consideration has been given to the child's gender, socioeconomic background and ethnicity and that the child's needs in relation to these factors have been addressed—for example, is the child impacted by poverty; is the child linked with their cultural group; are gender expectations resulting in a female child, in particular, assuming a caring role for self, siblings or parents beyond what would normally be expected in the wider community?

Consider the balance of services to the child. Just as with parents, combine social and emotional support with practical assistance either directly or by referral to other service providers—for example, help children to access important people in their lives; link them with therapeutic supports to address the effects of trauma, abuse and/or neglect; refer them to well-regulated mentoring programs (such as Big Brothers Big Sisters) to encourage pro-social development; and assist them to participate in recreational activities with other children to develop social skills and confidence and to build friendships. Prioritise the child's safety and wellbeing with families when attending to other issues and concerns; when parents and children's needs are clearly inconsistent, ensure the obligation to meet the children's need for safety and wellbeing takes precedence over other family matters.

WORKING WITH THE FAMILY TO HELP THE CHILD

Before birth

Support for the infants and children of substance-dependent women should commence in pregnancy and continue in the postnatal period. As a worker, it is therefore critically important that you encourage, and where possible, support regular use of obstetric services as an early intervention strategy to promote good infant outcomes. Attention should be given to maternal diet, the management of any existing medical conditions, and stabilisation of drug use and pharmacotherapy.

Infancy and early childhood

In the days and weeks after birth, you need to be sensitive to the parents' need for privacy, to allay unwarranted concerns and to alert parents to challenges they may face caring for an infant who may be irritable and difficult to settle for days or several weeks after birth. The availability of support is a major consideration in discharge planning from hospital as formal services may need to augment a depleted social network (see Chapters 6 and 8). One of the best means of supporting infants is to help the mother (and her partner) identify current and possible future sources of formal and informal support that promote attentive parenting, especially in the home during the perinatal period when maternal (and paternal) motivation for change is high but when the demands of caring for an infant make it more difficult to attend appointments on a regular basis. This is a time of optimism when families commonly rally around a newborn infant, but such support to substance-dependent parents may not endure as old problems, including substance use, often resurface. For example, a mother who is prepared to leave a violent relationship in pregnancy may resume cohabitation with the father of her infant in the perinatal period. This risks not only alienating family members, but also losing the care of her infant through child protection involvement which often follows a crisis such as a police call-out to the home for intimate partner violence (Hollingsworth, Swick & Choi, 2011; Tsantefski, 2010).

A key intervention strategy with young children is to ensure they receive regular health checks, are screened for health and developmental problems that could benefit from early intervention, and are up-to-date with immunisation schedules. Although parents are often reluctant to engage with services through fear of a report to child protection authorities, a recent Australian study found no difference in notification rates between infants of substance-using mothers who were engaged with child health and those who were not. Infants were less likely to be brought to the attention of child protection if mothers were on methadone, which highlights the value of stabilising drug use (Callaghan, Crimmins & Schweitzer, 2011). Substance-using mothers who overcome anxiety about being monitored, and who allow professionals into their home, are likely to derive a range of short- and long-term benefits for themselves, their infants and children. There can be advantages even for unborn babies. In the US, recovery coaches provide assertive outreach to substance-using women in the postpartum period. The combination of case management and counselling has been shown to reduce maternal substance use and the risk of exposure in a subsequent pregnancy (Ryan et al., 2008), an extremely important strategy in the prevention of alcohol- and drug-related harm. The most effective early intervention programs for infants and young children are home-based, non-judgemental and holistic. The aim is to improve family functioning by combining parenting education and support with concrete assistance such as child care and transport. Some programs explicitly address many of the problems encountered by substance-using women, including domestic violence, poor housing and poverty (Osterling & Austin, 2008). Among the first, and best known, is the Strengthening Families program in the US (Kumpfer & Fowler, 2007). In Australia, Parenting Under Pressure (PUP) has demonstrated improved parental functioning, reduced parenting stress, increased satisfaction with parenting and an improvement in parent–child relationships (Dawe et al., 2003). The program has recently been introduced in the UK for substance-affected carers with a child aged less than 2.5 years (Barlow et al., 2013).

Some alcohol and other drug treatment services have set up play-groups for parents with infants and young children, including some specifically for parents from CALD backgrounds. This is an effective way of engaging parents while assessing and attending to their infants and children's wellbeing. Although there are few published studies to date, the practice of mindfulness, widely utilised within the alcohol and other drug sector, appears to promote secure maternal–child attachment through increased maternal self-regulation and improved responsiveness to infant cues (Snyder, Shapiro & Treleaven, 2012). Similarly, attachment-informed programs are used to address maternal–infant interactions among substance-using women and their infants, either in home- (Suchman et al., 2011) or in agency-based group-work settings.

Middle childhood

While parents often try to conceal drug use and to protect children from the consequences of their use, children as young as seven years can be well aware of drug use in the family. By the age of ten, children can observe and report fluctuations in substance use and accompanying changes in parental behaviour, some of which can be disturbing, if not alarming (Gruenert, Ratnam & Tsantefski, 2004). As we have noted, age and developmental stage can make it difficult for children to contribute their perspective on decisions that affect them. School-aged children need support to develop the ability to function independently as informants on their own lives. However, many children find it difficult to engage in 'talk-therapy' and prefer the medium of **play therapy** (Murray & Tsantefski, 2008). In addition to group-work, which is discussed below, various resources, some of which are specific to alcohol and other drugs, while others are more general in nature, are readily available to help facilitate conversations with children. These resources can be used individually with the child, and with the child's consent, in a mediated conversation with the parent, to enable the child to express his or her experiences, feelings and opinions. This conversation, which, as we note above, can be challenging for all concerned, can be highly cathartic for parents who may come to understand the impact of substance use from the child's perspective for the first time.

To counter the effects on children of unstable and socially isolated family lifestyles, it is important to link children with the wider community through social activities that promote pro-social development and reduce isolation. Find out who is available to the child from among the wider family system and ensure children know who to call when in need. A simple strategy is to trace the child's hand on a piece of paper and write the names of significant people or services who can be called upon in an emergency across each of the fingers, with the name and number of the most significant person across the palm. (See Chapter 8 for more on network interventions.)

One of the most effective ways to promote pro-social development and reduce isolation is through group-work, which can be recreational, therapeutic, educational or a combination of all three. As with playgroups for infants, groups can specifically target children of substance-dependent parents or broaden the membership, with advantages and disadvantages in each approach. Therapeutic groups reserved for children whose parents have problematic substance use offer significant benefits by providing children with what may be a rare opportunity to discuss their experiences with peers, which can help to reduce feelings of stigma and isolation. Such groups can be educative through provision of age-appropriate information on alcohol and other drugs and provide an opportunity for children to learn from each other. These groups can also be confronting: there is a very real risk of children hearing of highly traumatic events experienced by other participants—for example, children witnessing drug overdoses or violent crime—and must, therefore, be handled very sensitively by highly qualified and experienced staff able to facilitate, arbitrate and advocate for individual children within and beyond the group. The sensitive subject matter likely to arise in therapeutic groups specifically for children of substance-dependent parents makes a closed group more appropriate (Harbin, 2002).

Both therapeutic and recreational groups offer children pleasurable activities to offset deprivation and help to build social networks (Murray & Tsantefski, 2008). Animal-assisted therapy is increasingly used in group-work with children. One of the benefits of this modality is that it is likely to address parental concerns about children disclosing intimate details about family life as activities are mediated through access to animals while children still derive therapeutic benefit. For example, children aged between eight and twelve years participating in an equine-assisted group for children whose parents have histories of substance-use have reported a range of positive outcomes, including feelings of safety and security, experiencing happiness, personal development and improved social relations (Dunlop, 2014). Engaging children has the additional benefit of building trust with, and engaging, parents.

Disrupted schooling, frequent moves and poverty can lead to educational and social disadvantage for this group of children. Educational support, including tutoring and goods and services such as books, computers, school uniforms and access to camps and other school-related activities, can increase children's participation in school and help to break intergenerational cycles of low educational attainment and poor job prospects. Children's own talents and interests should also be nurtured and mentored (Gilligan, 1999) as this strengthens their inner resources, develops peer networks and helps to ease transitions between localities and schools. (See Chapter 8 for further discussion on strengthening the child's network.)

Adolescence

As with children in middle childhood, adolescents may require psychosocial and educational support, which could include some or all the following: individual counselling, access to pro-social activities, educational assistance and balanced, non-sensationalised information on alcohol and other drugs. Schools are an important site for early intervention and prevention strategies and can greatly contribute to child and adolescent resilience by building a stronger relationship with parents which, in turn, increases children's own bonds to school and the chances of them remaining engaged in education for longer. They can deliver educational programs that create norms discouraging excessive alcohol or other drug use and they can assist children and adolescents to develop interests in, and gain access to, social, cultural and recreational activities that help to offset the risk of problematic substance use in young people. Alcoholics Anonymous and Narcotics Anonymous run groups for adolescent children to help them understand and cope with their parents' substance use problems (see Useful websites and resources).

MAKING THE SERVICE SYSTEM MORE RESPONSIVE TO CHILDREN

Like adults, children value relationships with professionals who offer emotional support and practical assistance. Like adults, they appreciate an environment in which they can feel comfortable and accepted. To make services more responsive to children, workers first need to review the physical setting, the system of appointments, the time allowed and the customary communication styles and resources to see whether they are indeed child-friendly. An adequate response to children's needs might require quite a different service cluster from the services relevant to the parent's own case plan. Individual counselling, play therapy and group-work can be useful in helping children develop coping and other life skills. Children's perspectives should be sought at the level of the individual child and their preferences. For example, would the child prefer peer-based activities such as group-work or would they rather have a personal mentor through a program such as Big Brothers Big Sisters? Children should also be consulted on the design and delivery of services at the program level. Where possible, children should be given a choice of who they work with and how. They may like to speak alone with a worker or they may prefer to participate in family or group activities. Children have expressed dislike of a procession of workers in their lives who gain their trust and then disappear (Bell, 2002). Continuity of worker gives children time to develop trust and a good working relationship. They can also benefit from knowing more than one worker on a team; in the event of staff turnover, there may still be someone they feel comfortable with.

TIPS FOR NEW WORKERS

- At all times, keep the child at the epicentre of your attention and interaction with the family.
- Provide feedback to parents on your observations of parent–child interactions in a sensitive and encouraging manner and be sure to notice the positives!
- Do not exceed the limits of your professional training, competence and experience when dealing with child trauma or developmental needs; instead make appropriate referrals to other services to support your work with the child and family.

- Have hope for children and do not contribute to a self-fulfilling prophecy; bear in mind that while the children of substance-using parents are at greater risk of developing a number of problems, these figures are based on averages, and that with encouragement and practical support, many individual children do well.
- Remember that alcohol and other drugs have similar but different effects on the family partly due to the illegality of some drugs, which results in increased stigma and changes to lifestyle—for example, greater poverty due to cost—rather than more negatively impacting parenting.
- It is helpful for children to speak with other children who share their experiences as alcohol and other drug use often results in social isolation for all family members.
- Remember that although concern for children often motivates parents to reconsider alcohol and other drug use, the child is not the cause of, or the cure for, parental substance use; help children understand they are not responsible for their parents' problems.
- Many children who live in households with problematic parental substance use regularly witness alcohol and other drug use which can influence the development of their own attitudes through role modelling of socially undesirable behaviour; supporting children to engage in pro-social activities with non-using peers is an important protective factor against the development of future problems.
- Carry, or have in your office, pencils, crayons, books, papers and toys for children and use child-friendly engagement strategies with children and parents.

TRAPS FOR NEW WORKERS

- Depriving the child of support by not wanting to reward a parent—for example, not providing respite which could offer the child social, emotional and recreational opportunities because of the perceived benefit to the parent—or not providing financial assistance to a family because it facilitates the use of alcohol or other drugs by parents.

- Considering that sighting the child will provide sufficient information for forming a belief about the child's wellbeing without speaking to the child or observing the child's behaviour, particularly in interaction with parents and other caregivers or without communicating with relevant health specialists and other key services, such as child protection.
- Patronising children by speaking down to them and not seeing them as intelligent and able to exert some control over their own lives.
- Assuming that the extended family is, or is not, the best option for respite or long-term care without a comprehensive assessment.
- Focusing on risk and forgetting to build protective factors that improve outcomes for children—for example, providing therapeutic respite for parents and children, connecting children to the community through social and recreational activities and providing educational support to children through tutoring programs.
- Questioning children in a way that makes them feel interrogated.

HOW WILL I KNOW IF I'M ON TRACK?

- Children will initiate or contribute to meaningful conversations about themselves and the family, as appropriate to their age and developmental level.
- You will be available, reliable and genuinely concerned not only about the child's welfare and safety but also about how they perceive their world, and you will be respectful of, and responsive to, their wishes.
- You will know about each individual child in the family, including: age; stage of development and whether milestones have been met; temperament and other innate qualities; the quality of attachment

to care givers; typical behavioural patterns; relationships with family members and significant others; attendance at school, kindergarten or day care; friendships; and their participation in social and recreational activities.

- Parents' **treatment plans** or family case plans will reflect consideration of, and attention to, the needs of the child—for example, what goals have been set with the family that directly address the needs of the individual child?
- You will have discussed the risk to the child of parental substance use with the parent and put strategies in place to protect and support the child in the event the parent is unable to do so through intoxication, ill-health or other problems.

WORKING WITH MIA

Each time the AOD worker visited the home, she made a point of seeing Mia and on most occasions held her. Prematurity meant that Mia's growth and development would need to be closely monitored. The support of the local child health nurse was therefore essential. As Stella had a history of not engaging with services, the AOD worker ensured she was linked with a nurse who provided regular home visits. The AOD worker's continuing role with the family helped Stella accept the service of another professional.

WORKING WITH ZAC

The AOD worker encouraged Kevin to bring Zac to some sessions. Toys, art materials and snacks were made available. The worker slowly helped Zac overcome shyness. With time, Zac was able to express some of his own concerns and disclosed being bullied at school. The worker and Kevin discussed strategies to support him, including teaching him coping skills and informing his school principal and his classroom teacher. In addition to providing Zac with individual counselling, the AOD worker referred him to a group for children of substance-dependent parents and enrolled him in a school-holiday program.

SUMMARY

Working with children is not straightforward, especially in services where the adult has been defined as the primary client but the ramifications of parental substance use for children are potentially so significant that there must always be a focus on the child's experience. Even if it is not your role to work directly with a child, you should always endeavour to ensure that there is a responsible adult, skilled in interpreting children's experiences and communicating with children, active in the child's life. Ask: 'Who knows this child, and are they promoting their interests to the professionals involved?' If no one else is doing it, you may have to become that person. Observe and listen attentively. As appropriate, educate the child about substance dependence and the roles of services, and advocate for them to receive developmentally appropriate help.

5

Identifying what you need to know

Workers often begin with the questions 'How do I establish a positive working relationship with the parent?' and 'How do I connect with the child?', but they tend to move rapidly to the assessment question: 'What do I need to know?' This chapter addresses that question, and suggests that what is needed is a holistic family assessment that includes parental capacity and functioning, alcohol and other drug use, and children's needs, within the limits of each worker's particular professional role and mandate. Many assessment frameworks and checklists are available and may vary between services and jurisdictions. Seek out what assessment tools are used within your own broader service network, so that you may speak a common language with your colleagues in other sectors. The hallmarks of a good assessment in work with substance-dependent parents are that it is *continual*, *collaborative*, *holistic* and *relevant* to the worker's role and service offerings, and that it is *conducted with an understanding of the process of recovery*.

Scott, Arney and Vimpani (2013) suggest that parental adaptability is critical to successful child-rearing, and that it comprises perceptiveness, responsiveness and flexibility in the relationship with the child over time. Consistency in these areas is undermined sorely by the volatile substance-use trajectory, with its roller coaster of emotions and practical issues, so that behaviour observed at any one moment, especially in a clinical setting, can be a poor indicator of patterns of behaviour in the home. Inevitably, assessment must be a *continuing process*, not simply an initial task. Parents may have parenting *capacity*, in that they have the knowledge and skills to parent effectively, but their parenting *performance* at any given moment may not match this knowledge. In this case, assessment needs to be focused on the mismatch between capacity and performance to determine what is preventing the parent from competently caring for the child. A one-off snapshot of parental functioning and child wellbeing is unlikely to result in an adequate assessment of either parenting capacity or risk and safety issues for children in the longer term. Assessing the parent's capacity to change behaviour is crucial (Harnett, 2007).

Good assessment is *collaborative*. It gets people involved in a discussion about family strengths and resources, as well as risk factors, laying a foundation for joint commitment to action. In discussing initial engagement we noted how shame, stigma and concealment often characterise parents' and children's interactions with the world. Parental resistance, denial and chaotic lifestyle make assessment and screening more difficult, and the worker needs to take this into account. This can be done by inviting all parties to have their say, both because their distinct contributions matter in their own right, and because multiple perspectives give a more balanced picture of complex family life.

As we have seen in earlier chapters, substance-affected families are likely to have multiple issues. Consequently, the case for *holistic assessment* is clear. Emotional, health, educational, social, financial and housing problems are common. Focus on substance use itself can divert attention from other areas of concern, such as exposure to trauma, mental ill-health and family violence which, as mentioned, frequently co-occur. The vividness with which these problems present sometimes obscures family strengths that may act as countervailing forces, such as a loving relationship between parent and child; a parent's ability to prioritise the child's needs and maintain routines and stability; the presence of a non-using parent or other caregiver; or a supportive network of extended family, friends or neighbours. Outcomes for children are worse when families face multiple risk factors and have fewer protective factors. A holistic assessment will be a balanced assessment. It will consider the parent's capacity for change, willingness to engage with services to improve family functioning and it will measure progress towards agreed upon goals, or lack of (Harnett, 2007).

Although important for children's wellbeing, holistic assessments can be intrusive. The level of intrusiveness needs to be weighed against the worker's capacity to help. Workers therefore need to keep their assessment *relevant* to the service context, conducting as thorough an assessment as possible within the limits of their professional role, skill, knowledge and mandate, and to seek professional assistance for further assessment, as required (see Chapter 8). For example, is it for the purpose of screening and referral processes only, in which case, assessment will be less extensive; or, alternatively, is it to be the cornerstone of ongoing intervention with the family which requires greater depth of understanding of the issues facing them? This chapter is weighted towards the latter purpose.

INTENDED OUTCOMES

For screening purposes, the following goals apply:
- Develop an understanding of the parent/s' patterns of use, noting substances used, frequency of use and the circumstances under/ situations in which substances are used.
- Gauge the impact of substance use on a parent's behaviours and moods.
- Identify risk and safety factors associated with alcohol and other drug use for infants, children and parents.
- Identify indicators of impacts on children.
- Improve short-term outcomes for children, parents and other family by developing safety plans for all family members, but particularly children.

- Minimise the need for parents to be subjected to multiple assessments by different agencies by establishing protocols for sharing information.

If work with the family is to involve more than referral, the following additional goals also apply:
- Help to develop parents' motivation to change destructive patterns of substance use.
- Identify parents' and children's goals, values and difficulties from their perspective.
- Implement harm-reduction strategies while assessing abstinence goals.
- Improve long-term outcomes for children, parents and other family members by developing sustainable treatment plans that address the needs and goals of all family members.

HELPFUL ATTITUDES AND VALUES

First, approach the parent in a spirit of honest inquiry. You need to demonstrate that you are trying to understand the role and meaning of substance use in the life of each individual; what functional value does alcohol and/or other drug use have for the parent, however harmful? For example, is it a form of 'self-medication' for mental health issues such as anxiety or depression in response to past or present trauma? Second, you can avoid a climate of blame by seeking to understand alcohol and other drug use within the social context of use: how has the habit developed and what sustains it? Examples might include family rituals, drug-saturated housing enclaves or exclusion from the workforce. These values can be conveyed by adopting a 'matter of fact' approach to questions about the how and when of substance use without judgemental overtones. It can also be helpful to share assessment with professionals across service sectors (see Chapter 8) in order to gain a broader understanding and open up dialogue with the family about what various professions and services might have to offer.

EXPECTATIONS OF CLIENTS

Assessment is so dependent upon information from within the family that it requires clients to engage in honest and meaningful dialogue regarding substance use issues for parents and their impact on children, and to participate in making decisions and upholding agreements regarding infant and child safety and wellbeing.

EXPECTATIONS OF YOURSELF

You should expect yourself to understand normal childhood development and the signs that a child's wellbeing is impaired but be willing and able to refer infants and children for specialised assessment (e.g. infants and children under the age of six years should be in contact with the local child health service to monitor milestones and health issues). You will commit yourself to inviting and fully considering the child's perspective (see Chapter 4), and will give due weight to the perspectives and needs of other family members, including grandparents and other significant network members (see Chapters 7 and 8). You will also be open to working collaboratively with other service providers to develop a comprehensive assessment of the child and family and minimise the need for duplications (see Chapter 8).

BARRIERS TO ASSESSMENT

Typical barriers to comprehensive assessment include lack of trust between the parent or the child and the worker, leading to concealment of substance use and resulting in inadequate assessment of parenting capacity/performance, or of children's safety and wellbeing. Substance use is often an individual's most stigmatised issue; feelings of shame and fear of judgement can result in the parent justifying, minimising or even denying use to themselves and others. Where family violence is present, pressure may be placed on partners and children to conceal issues. Members of the (extended) family can minimise or exaggerate parental alcohol or other drug use to either protect the parent or child, or to support their own wishes for custody of the child. In addition, mental health problems may complicate presenting concerns, requiring specialist assessment through referral to other service providers.

Worker factors may also limit the feasibility and validity of the assessment. Aggression on the part of parents or other network members can result in workers being reluctant to visit or contact the family, which can increase risk to infants and children. Too much focus on substance use can obscure parenting competence or divert attention from other areas of concern such as mental health issues or family violence, while too little attention to substance use effectively denies 'the elephant in the room' and risks arriving at an unrealistic assessment and over-optimistic intervention plan.

KEY STRATEGIES

Any parenting assessment requires attention to parents as people in their own right: their histories, health status, family relationships, and an understanding of their parenting. It requires attention to the parent–child relationship, and attention to the wellbeing of the child. It places these in the context of the family's basic monetary and material resources, living conditions, their cultural norms and expectations, and their connections to social supports and community institutions. Specifically, it considers current and previous service use, with a particular interest in prior help-seeking efforts and their results, as part of an assessment of the potential for change. This is the starting point, with issues related to substance use effectively threaded through each of these steps to achieve a comprehensive understanding of the *parent's substance use*, of *its relationship to parenting behaviours and performance*, its *impact on the child*, how it is affected by *social context* and its *amenability to change through service provision*.

ASSESSING ALCOHOL AND OTHER DRUG USE BY PARENTS

Assessment is rarely just getting the facts. If we consider our own lives, it is easy to see how all our actions take on particular meanings that will not necessarily be obvious to a naïve observer. It is necessary, then, to seek to understand the meaning alcohol and other drug use has in the life of the parent and the story they tell themselves about substance use: the history of when use started, periods of non-use and attempts to reduce or cease use. This narrative will shed light on the significance of alcohol and other drugs in the parent's life and create opportunities for deeper exploration of current use. Clearly explain the reasons for seeking this information and how you will use it; if inquiries into past use appear to have no bearing on current presenting problems, the parent may disengage.

The following questions are helpful in understanding the pattern of substance abuse: What types of substances are used by parents and other family members, including the amount, frequency and duration of use? Does the user feel that alcohol and other drug use is at continual high-risk levels? Does use feel controlled or erratic and unpredictable? Where and when do parents use and who is with them? What do they identify as the effects on them of these different substances—on their feelings, thoughts and behaviour? How do they come down as the effects of alcohol and other drugs wear off? What costs and benefits do they see as accruing from using? How do parents get their drugs and pay for them?

Find out what harm-reduction strategies have been tried, are being used or could be implemented by the parent, including who is available to ensure they are safe when using. What treatment has the parent tried (e.g. unsupervised withdrawal, supervised home-based withdrawal, residential detoxification and rehabilitation)? Discuss what did and did not work, how any changes were sustained, the circumstances under which relapse into substance use occurred and what might have helped to avoid it. Past attempts at treatment and rehabilitation can shed light on the role of substance use in the parent's life, which may help to inform an intervention or treatment plan. Do they see change as possible and needed and show evidence of past and recent efforts to achieve this? If more than one person in the home is using, it can be important to ask them these questions in relation to themselves and in relation to each other. For example, how might parents work together to increase the likelihood of successful changes to substance use patterns?

ASSESSING THE RELATIONSHIP BETWEEN ALCOHOL AND OTHER DRUG USE AND PARENTING

This sensitive area may be even harder to discuss than substance use itself. Some parents believe that their substance use helps them to cope with their problems, be better parents and assist in the **self-medication** of symptoms of trauma or mental illness. Others might be wracked with shame and guilt and find talking about the impact of alcohol and other drugs on parenting very stressful. Others have learnt that these discussions can lead to child removal, so they may become defensive or close up angrily. Again it helps to take a matter-of-fact approach and also to be open to how parents themselves see these connections. Practicalities of substance use should be observed and discussed: Are alcohol and other drugs kept safely out of reach of children? Where are the children while the parent is using? Are young children adequately supervised? Who has unrestricted access to the children? Are there times of the week when money is short and children go without basic provisions?

Without presuming that parental substance use is harming children, the worker can invite the parent to reflect upon the specific challenges they face in caring for children of specific ages and stages of development. To explore less personally the possible impact of substance use upon these challenges, the worker can call upon issues encountered commonly in this field. Infants and young children are highly vulnerable due to being reliant on a caregiver to meet all their physical and emotional needs. Toddlers and preschool children require high levels of supervision and are at risk of accidents, including drowning, poisoning or choking. Older children may be constantly late or miss school, or may be victimised when clothing and hygiene standards are not maintained. The availability of the parent to the child is a key consideration. Is the child spending long periods of time alone or watching television while the parent recovers, withdraws or is intoxicated? Some substance-dependent parents discourage or do not allow other children to visit the home, sometimes because of the state of living conditions. This can be detrimental to children's formation of friendships with peers and their social development. Adolescents are likely to come to harm through their own risk-taking behaviour which requires stable and emotionally available caregivers who offer responsive guidance and boundary setting. Role modelling substance use or displaying positive attitudes towards alcohol and other drug use make it more likely that children will use substances themselves. Through discussing how each family responds to such challenges in its own way, the worker can invite the parents to consider their own responses and how these affect their children.

Exploring how the parent views their child can provide a useful insight into their parenting. Ask the parent to describe their child. Try to understand their perceptions of the child's personality, development and general wellbeing, in the context of their values about parenting and the relationship between parent and child. Ask parents if there have been any significant changes in the child's behaviour that might indicate a problem for the child, such as: Has the child started refusing to go to school? Is the child bedwetting? Is the child stealing or hoarding food? Parents and other caregivers should be invited to reflect on how different substances affect their patterns of parenting, and whether the child responds differently to changes on the substance use cycle. It is important to establish whether some substances are posing a greater threat to child safety and wellbeing than others (see Chapter 1). It is not uncommon for parents to try to manage substance use and reduce harm to children in several ways, including by substituting one substance for another. However, the attempted solution can bring its own, sometimes unforeseen, problems. For example, the parent may stop using heroin, which may have caused them to be drowsy and unavailable to children, for alcohol, or methamphetamine, which could result in greater propensity for verbal or physical aggression.

ASSESSING THE IMPACT ON THE CHILD AND THE CHILD'S PERSPECTIVE

As with parents, individual children are affected differently by substance use in the family. The combination of individual resilience and the presence of risk and protective factors can lead to quite different outcomes. Children also employ different coping strategies, some of which are more adaptive and constructive than others. To gauge the actual impact of parental substance use on the child, the worker will need to understand normal child development, observe the child and interpret community reports (e.g. from a teacher) about the child, in order to determine if children have not reached expected milestones. It may be necessary to consult with a specialist in children's health and welfare, such as a maternal and child health nurse for children aged 0 to 6 years, a general practitioner, or a paediatrician for more comprehensive assessment. Try to establish if the child is securely attached to a primary caregiver (this does not always have to be a parent). Does he or she have ready access to friends and loving relatives? Is the child receiving age-appropriate support? Does the infant see the maternal and child health nurse? Does the preschooler have access to supplementary care and enrichment activities? Is the school-aged child attending school regularly and able to fully participate in extracurricular activities—for example, camps or excursions? Is the child appropriately dressed and well-equipped with school paraphernalia, such as books or other required resources?

The child's own perspective provides a valuable insight into the impact of parental substance use on the child. While parents may be anxious about allowing workers access to their children, it should be stressed that by getting to know the child, the worker will be better able to understand what the child needs and to help the parent to help the child. To this end, try to establish a trusting relationship with the child (see Chapter 4), as appropriate to your role, or observe the child's behaviour for clues to their emotional and psychological state. Is the child's behaviour internalised or externalised? What might this suggest about their inner state? What do they enjoy? What are their favourite people, times and activities at home? What or who do they worry about? Is there evidence of self-harm?

Establish the child's knowledge of the role of alcohol and other drug use in the family as appropriate to his or her age and stage of development; they often know more, and have more developed opinions and preferences, than parents realise. Include the child's own perspective on the impact of substance use on the child himself or herself and on the family, including siblings. Older children might be reluctant to discuss themselves, but may well have pertinent observations about younger children in whose care they share.

The verbal child will also have a perspective on the impact of substance use on his or her life outside the immediate family. Establish children's school attendance rates and patterns, and explore whether there are particular issues arising at school, such as lunchtimes, excursions, homework, friendship groupings, and so on. Being well connected to school is a vital protective factor against the development of children's own problems. Are there interests (such as hobbies, sports, other talents) the child is prevented from developing because of social and financial problems arising from parental substance use? Explore whether the extended family and social network provides additional emotional and social resources to the child, or whether there are lost relationships causing sadness or anger for the child.

Establishing the child's role in the family can help to determine if the child is assuming responsibility for self and siblings beyond what would normally be expected of a child that age in the wider community. If so, what are the barriers to effective parenting? For example, the overuse of sedatives at night to aid sleep, or a hangover after excessive use of alcohol, may leave a parent unable to function in the morning. **Agoraphobia** may prevent them leaving the home to take children to school. In instances such as these, invite parents to consider how excessive or inappropriate use of alcohol or other drug use or parental mental health issues impact on children's home lives and ask them how you can assist them to provide care that meets the child's physical, emotional, cognitive and social needs. Be prepared for denial. One way to proceed with the conversation is to ask parents to reflect on differences in their parenting between when they are and are not using. Remember to keep discussion strengths-based and solution-focused, using questions such as: 'What kinds of things do you do as a parent when you are not using?' 'How do you manage to do these things when you have been using or are withdrawing?' 'What are some of your favourite activities that you do with your children when everything is going well?'

ASSESSING ALCOHOL AND OTHER DRUG PROBLEMS WITHIN THE FAMILY'S SOCIAL CONTEXT

A well-functioning network of friends, extended family, neighbours and colleagues can provide significant support for child-rearing, but many parents presenting to services have severely depleted social networks, as a result of social dislocation, past family trauma, poverty and escape from violent relationships. Many crises and cries for help may have tried the patience of remaining family and friends, exhausting the goodwill within the network. It is important, therefore, to try to understand the role of trauma in the family's life, to establish if there is current family violence and to understand how this has affected the family's social network. Do the children witness violence, physical injury, verbal abuse and other conflict? Through network mapping identify what support is available to the parent and child. Is there one person that the parent or child really trusts? Who is regarded as helpful and what is the nature and frequency of the help given? Does it feel sufficient? Which relationships feel strong, respectful and mutually beneficial? Where are the gaps? Who and what seem to be missing? What damaged relationships would the family like to heal?

Social networks can also be a mixed blessing, conveying culturally determined demands and problems as well as support. Indigenous women, for example, can be expected to care for many others within the extended family. Some women feel bound to destructive relationships through cultural prescriptions within their family and religious community, while simultaneously being unable to confess to alcohol and other drug misuse, and they are therefore blocked from getting help. In some cultures, saving face is very important and anything that might bring shame on the family is avoided. Consequently, family members may not be able to share their experiences with kith and kin. They may need to assess what responsibilities must be maintained, and what can be relinquished.

Often the parent's network has become weighted with fellow substance-users who exert pressure on the parent to engage in continued social drinking or other drug use, with no real regard for the parent's child-rearing responsibilities. Again, it can be helpful to map with the parent those network elements that impose burdens or draw them away from sound child-rearing and invite them to reflect on what they would like to change, and what relationships will be hard to let go.

Gather information from as many sources as possible, including your own observations, and try to conduct in-home assessment, particularly when children and other family members are present in order to observe how the family functions; if this is not possible, draw on the knowledge of other workers engaged with the family. (See Chapter 8 for network intervention.)

ASSESSING AMENABILITY TO CHANGE THROUGH SERVICE PROVISION

To make a judgement about the feasibility of change, determine if specialist alcohol and other drug and mental health assessments have been conducted and ask for permission to access these as they may help with the current assessment and, if not, consider collaborating with other professionals for more comprehensive assessment. The parent's alcohol and other drug and service use history should illuminate how chronic, entrenched and disabling substance misuse has been in the life of the parent, and should yield an understanding of when and how the parent has lived substance-free. It should also give clues to treatment options to avoid or try again. Consider the parent's values, attitudes towards professional helpers and experiences of attempting change, and explore what they are or are not willing to attempt. In addition to discussing formal service options, invite them to make their own assessment of what lifestyle and social network changes might be necessary to maximise their chances of achieving the desired changes in their substance use. Who needs to be brought on board for the journey, to help make any change sustainable over time?

If your assessment leaves you concerned about the immediacy and severity of risk to the children, consider if a report to, or consultation with, the child protection service is necessary (see Chapter 6).

SUMMARY: ASSESSMENT FRAMEWORK

While we recommend that assessment is undertaken collaboratively with family and other key persons involved, it is important that as a worker you can be clear about the information on which you base your own thinking and decisions in each case. To this end, the chart below provides a way of breaking down the various components of the assessment process. If your assessment is challenged by a client or fellow worker, you should be able to show clearly the evidence on which you have based your decisions (on which there should be little dispute) and have an open discussion about how and why you drew the conclusions you did. These might then be modified in discussion, and new priorities negotiated with clients and others. Since intervention occurs within the professional helping relationship, understanding your own role, strengths and limits in relation to the particular family is an important part of the assessment process.

Domain: core information (at a given time and place)	Assessment: weigh up	Decision: priorities for action
Personal development and wellbeing, emotional, intellectual, physical, spiritual, of all children and adults in home	Strengths, harms accrued, areas of serious vulnerability to further harm, critical interactions between needs of family members, potential for change	Most urgent needs (immediate safety and developmental imperatives) Strategic interventions acceptable to family most likely to lead to sustained gains
Family material wellbeing—assets and liabilities: provision and gaps in core needs such as income, debt, housing, food, clothing, utilities, substance use costs, transport	Adequacy and stability of resourcing, most urgent shortfalls or felt needs, assets to be built on	Resources most likely to stabilise parents' and children's lives

Domain: core information (at a given time and place)	Assessment: weigh up	Decision: priorities for action
Family's network, formal and informal: kin, adults' and children's friends and mentors, service providers	Risks, resources and gaps: Who helps and who impedes child and family wellbeing and development? Where are the gaps?	Most helpful relationships to be activated or supported; most destructive to be curtailed/worked on
Parental substance use: type, amount, patterns and contexts of use, history of use/recovery/ relapses	Chronicity, severity, **impact on all domains above,** readiness to change	Strategic opportunities to minimise harm and facilitate recovery
Worker's own knowledge, resources, mandate and service system links	*Legal, moral and professional resources and limitations; quality of working relationships with family members*	*Own capacity to provide support and when and where to refer*

TIPS FOR NEW WORKERS

- Assessment is a continuous process as parental substance use (and mental health problems) can rapidly and dramatically change.
- Do not assume that cessation of substance use will automatically result in improved parenting; parents may experience prolonged psychological dependence well after detoxification and relapse is common; other problems may still be present and possibly escalate; improved parenting may be a further step in the change process.
- Bear in mind that parenting behaviour can be affected by withdrawal, particularly when not medically supervised, and that some treatments can look like drug use—for example, feeling drowsy due to methadone or other pharmacotherapy rather than illicit drug use; it is therefore important not to make assumptions that could prove false and alienate the parent further.
- Parents may not understand why child protection wants to focus on their substance use while assessing parenting; clear explanations of the reason for, and the importance of, focusing on the impact

of substance use on parenting can be helpful and reduce parental anxiety and/or hostility. Remember that what you all have in common is a desire for the child to be safe and happy and for the parent to be able to respect him- or herself as a parent.

TRAPS FOR NEW WORKERS

- Risk assessment frameworks can result in a false positive by skewing assessment towards risk factors without adequately addressing family strengths or resources.
- Some assessments look like a checklist of failings and shortcomings; such assessments could be experienced as disheartening and are unlikely to motivate parents to change, they are also unlikely to foster engagement between worker and client.
- All-or-nothing assessments fail to account for specific family circumstances: do not make assumptions that alcohol and other drugs are or are not impacting on children, and do not assume all substance-using parents are incapable of providing adequate care of children.

HOW WILL I KNOW IF I'M ON TRACK?

- You will be engaged in an open dialogue with both parent and children; parents will share their struggles and limitations with you.
- You will have a good understanding of the dreams and goals of family members, and know what each member is really good at.
- You will have gathered information from as many sources as possible, to form a comprehensive assessment of how alcohol and other drugs are affecting the children and families who have presented at your service or with whom you are working.
- You will understand assessment as a continuous process in which assumptions are tested and reviewed for changes to parental behaviour, family circumstances and impact on children.

- You will be collaborating with other professionals to form a comprehensive assessment of the safety and wellbeing of children, parents and other family members.
- You will be able to advocate strongly for required services and be able to explain why these services or strategies are needed to both parents and other service providers.

ASSESSMENT OF MIA'S SAFETY AND WELLBEING

Stella was stable on methadone and not using heroin. She provided a high level of care, ensuring Mia's needs were met. In the following weeks, discussions with Stella, and Joan, who was often present on home visits, indicated that Stella's substance use was historically intricately linked to that of various male partners. These relationships were invariably violent, some more dangerously than others, and were the catalyst in the loss of two older children from her care. Loneliness was now beginning to affect her. There was the risk that involvement with men in the neighbourhood, many of whom used illicit substances and drank excessively, could result in a return to previous behavioural patterns that would endanger Mia and place her at risk of removal.

ASSESSMENT OF ZAC'S SAFETY AND WELLBEING

The worker conducted a thorough assessment of Kevin's past and present substance use. While it was evident that Kevin's current use of cannabis was manageable, his history revealed extensive use of heroin. The worker was concerned not only with the risk of relapse but also recidivism to crime, which could jeopardise Zac's safety. The worker asked Kevin to consider his social network and who among those close to him was supportive, or not, of his parenting role. By exploring Kevin's history, along with his present circumstances, the worker was able to sensitively raise the subject of a safety plan for Zac in the event of an escalation in drug use or a return to crime.

SUMMARY

In this chapter we have argued for a form of family assessment that is continual, collaborative, holistic and relevant, infused with close attention to the nature of parents' substance use and drug-using histories, and to the impact of these on them as parents and on their children. It is particularly important in work with these families that the worker seeks to learn how the parent and the child each ascribes meaning to the use of substances, how substance use interacts with the family's social context, and about the forces operating for and against change, including those within the service system itself. With this understanding, it becomes clearer how much the children are currently at risk of harm, what it might take to keep them safe and what plans are needed to enhance the wellbeing needs of all family members. This is the focus of Chapter 6. The assessment also provides the building blocks for a plan of action to help the family develop a more rewarding and socially enriched life, which will be the focus of Chapters 7 and 8.

PART 3

FACILITATING CHANGE AND GROWTH

6

Keeping children and families safe

Much of your work with families will involve identifying their strengths and helping them move positively towards their goals. However, even if workers form good working relationships with parents and children, and commit their service to helping parents improve children's lives over time, you will come across families in which an assessment reveals that children, and perhaps their parent(s), are not currently safe at home. This is an anxious time for all concerned, and immediate risks must be addressed, whatever the longer term treatment plan. Protecting infants and children and promoting their wellbeing is not risk-free; it involves careful management of calculated risks, which is more easily done when the parent is motivated to make changes to their substance use and willing to address other family problems. Without such co-operation from the family, the worker bears substantial responsibility.

Responding to many workers' questions about safety, this chapter outlines risk and protective factors when parental substance use has become problematic. It provides guidance on managing risk to infants and children, including risks that arise from family violence or exposure to crime, which may also compromise the safety of adults in the home. Making a report to child protection authorities is also discussed, together with some strategies to consider prior to, during and after making a report.

Although some risks are counteracted by protective factors in the home, workers need to be alert to the specific risks that may arise when a parent is substance-affected. When a parent is intoxicated, or when they are distracted by drug seeking and other pressing issues, their lack of supervision may give rise to accidental or experimental substance ingestion or injury. Psychological absence in the parent hinders the child forming a sound emotional attachment. Poverty and instability may result in: unsuitable and/or unstable housing; insufficient and poor quality food; inadequate medical attention; and disrupted schooling and child care. Alcohol, and a variety of stimulants or hallucinogens, may lead to an increase in family and other violence, together with an increase in the severity of the violence, with children harmed as both witnesses and victims. Because some parents who misuse substances will engage in antisocial behaviour and have criminal associates, physical and sexual harm is sometimes inflicted by strangers visiting the home or having easy access to children. The child may also lose external support when helpful extended family or network members are cut off, leading to social isolation. At the same time, children are likely to experience the normalisation of alcohol and other drug use and crime. Remember, though, that the most common risk to children is neglect, which often goes unnoticed and can result in accumulated harm over a long period of time.

When professionals encounter such situations, they face difficult decisions about whether to make a report to child protection services or not. While there are no easy answers to the question of if and when to report, resolution generally involves four key considerations:

1. assessment of the type, level and immediacy of risk of harm to the infant or child;
2. parental willingness and capacity to address any risk;
3. the worker's and service's capacity to manage and monitor the risks; and
4. the availability of resources and support to ensure that infant and child safety and wellbeing is likely to be maintained.

Develop familiarity with legislative requirements and child protection risk assessment frameworks currently in operation in your jurisdiction, and refer to them in your practice. **Mandatory reporting** requirements need to be met but a report should not be made solely for the purpose of professionals covering their back. While a range of services can be easier to access with child protection involvement (e.g. **respite care**), there is no guarantee on the outcome of a report. Handing the risk over to an authority like child protection is only likely to increase safety if there are adequate resources to respond appropriately to the identified risks. Due to limited resources, child protection services prioritise infants and children at highest risk. Even when a report is made to child protection, community service workers may still need to take an active role in sharing and managing the risks through regular monitoring and assistance to children and parents, and by modelling a cooperative working relationship with the tertiary child protection service.

INTENDED OUTCOMES

The overall goal of risk management is that children will be safe and thriving, through the timely and appropriate action taken by parents, extended family and network members, and service providers, all of whom are likely to share some responsibility. Each party will bring their own special perspective and knowledge to the task: parents and family members know the child and living conditions; child protection and family support services are skilled at identifying risks to children; alcohol and other drug treatment providers are skilled in identifying risks to adults and in motivating change, but are less experienced regarding children. This expertise will be recognisable in case plans that include shared monitoring of risk and protective factors and conveying of information within the limits of professional role and boundary (see Chapter 8).

HELPFUL ATTITUDES AND VALUES

Workers need to affirm the right of the child to a safe home and competent parent, in both the short and the long term. This must be balanced with respecting a family's right to be together. Achieving this balance entails listening to the opinions of all family members, including children and members of the extended family. We have found that it helps if workers adopt a position of neither expecting the worst of parents, nor wearing rose-coloured glasses and therefore minimising the real risk of harm to infants and children. Workers should seek to convey a belief that parents rarely intend to harm their children and have a crucial role in ensuring their safety and wellbeing. In a social context in which substance dependence is stigmatised, workers can acknowledge that parental concealment of alcohol and other drug use or deceit is most usually an attempt to protect themselves, the child and the family unit, rather than a sign of moral deficiency, while suggesting that this might have unintended consequences.

EXPECTATIONS OF CLIENTS AND YOURSELF

Parents and workers alike need to face issues, rather than avoid difficult topics such as the amount and frequency of alcohol or other drug use; what children may have witnessed; and how children are or are not kept safe when parents are intoxicated, buying or using drugs. Mutual honesty is crucial, and is built on the explicit commitment to making professional decisions and taking actions based on the best interests of the child in the first instance.

All workers need to be aware of their level of experience in managing risk safely, and seek support when the potential for harm to a child, family member or the worker themselves exceeds the capacity to safely monitor and reduce risk. It is important to strike a balance between personal responsibility and collaborative practice; respect the opinions of other professionals presently or previously involved with the family, but be willing to accept professional responsibility for your own assessments and actions. You will need to be clear with clients that information relevant to child safety and wellbeing will be shared with your supervisors and other service providers, including, but not limited to, child protection. As a general rule, you will let them know when information will be shared, unless doing so will further increase risks.

BARRIERS TO KEEPING CHILDREN SAFE

There are many potential barriers to effectively promoting children's safety. These barriers include a lack of knowledge, fear and avoidance, and poor setting of the ground rules. When workers have *limited understanding* of child development, of the effects of alcohol and other drugs on parental functioning and on children, and of the particular parent's own drug use history, they may lack the confidence to ask about substance use or parenting issues, fail to recognise symptoms and make mistakes in interpreting what they see.

This lack of confidence may be exacerbated by *fear and avoidance* by both workers and parents. Evasive behaviour on the part of the parent can make it easier to provide a service without asking difficult questions. When clients present as substance-affected, it is common for policy or practice guidelines to suggest deferring contact until they are sober. This, however, removes an important risk assessment opportunity, for these are the circumstances under which children are living. Intimidating behaviour by family or network members can deter workers from visiting homes where so many cues to the child's daily life are to be found, such as drug paraphernalia, a dearth of children's belongings or evidence of excessive isolation of the child; this leaves infants and children potentially at greater risk of abuse and neglect. Faced with intimidation, it is also hard for workers to question or challenge suspicious or contradictory parental behaviour, to discuss openly the dangers of alcohol and other drug use by parents and adolescents, or to name and address aggression towards children and others. Motivational interviewing (Miller & Rollnick, 1991) and solution-focused practice (Berg & Kelly, 2000) can provide some useful tools to enable challenging conversations to be had, in a way that reduces the likelihood of escalating any avoidance or intimidating behaviour.

Confusion about the ground rules of contact is also of concern. While it might seem to the worker that telling the client information will be shared with other professionals, including potentially child protection, will erect a barrier to cooperation, this is not necessarily so. Many parents assume knowledge will be shared, and appreciate honesty about just how, why, when and with whom this will be done. Failing to address the limits to confidentiality, and to seek consent for information sharing, will itself constitute a barrier to safety planning, so it is usually best to have open discussions about the possibility of a report to child protection authorities from the outset.

KEY STRATEGIES IN MANAGING AND REDUCING RISK

Many risks can be managed by supporting a family to promote infant and child safety and wellbeing, if you remain alert to fluctuations in the parent's stage of change, and plan for the possibility, if not probability, of relapse. Take active steps to reduce risk, but if you find the parent is unable or unwilling to protect the child, you will need to notify child protection authorities to ensure the child receives adequate care and protection, consistent with legislative requirements and formal practice protocols. The following section outlines strategies to consider prior to, during the process of and after making a report.

Prior to making a report

Alternative responses to a report to child protection will be considered if parents, family and network members, together with service providers, can ensure the child's safety and wellbeing. Unless and until it becomes evident that a report to child protection is necessary, the worker's main strategies for keeping children safe comprise continually assessing risk and harm (as part of the comprehensive assessment we have recommended in Chapter 5), developing and implementing a safety plan (which may include temporary alternative care and living arrangements during any lapses) and monitoring the child's wellbeing in the light of the safety plan.

Clarifying the nature of the risk and likelihood of harm

When a child's safety is in question, this needs to be discussed openly, in order to gain a more detailed picture than that yielded by the initial assessment. Keep the language simple and clearly explain concerns to the parents, allowing them, and their children, ample opportunity to ask questions and to explain what is happening from their perspectives.

The critical risk clarification questions are:

- What is the child's direct exposure to substances and drug use paraphernalia in the home?
- How severely, and how frequently, does the parent's substance use impair his or her responsible parenting? This will require a detailed discussion about behavioural, thinking and mood changes in the parent, and the ways in which these can influence parenting decisions and behaviours. At such times, does someone else routinely substitute as carer?
- Does the parent, or do other associates, directly abuse the child in some way, both when intoxicated and when sober? Does the child exhibit fear of the parent or someone else in the immediate home environment? Is there current family violence placing both the child and the primary carer, usually the mother, at risk of harm?
- Is there evidence that the child has already experienced physical, emotional or sexual harm or significant developmental delay? What does the child say or demonstrate about this experience? (Examples of serious risk might include: acute fear of, or for, the parent, self

or someone else; chronic anxiety; hunger, hoarding and foraging; untreated disease or injury; self-harm.)

- Does the child undertake an unacceptably onerous burden of care in the family?

In making an assessment based on multiple sources of reliable information, do not ignore your own senses. If something feels badly wrong, think through the clues that have stimulated that response and explore that hunch in supervision or with an appropriate colleague. Are there visible signs of excessive consumption of alcohol? Is there an odour in the house or on the parent's breath that would suggest alcohol or other drug use? How does the conversation flow? Is the parent's own health visibly declining? Be aware of signs of elevated risk, such as parents failing to keep appointments or return calls, or withdrawing or disengaging from services; parents not allowing access to children; children not attending school or day care.

Consult normal developmental checklists and be alert to behavioural indicators of distress in children, such as sullen or withdrawn mood, anger and aggression. In relation to infants and toddlers in the family, who cannot speak up, be alert to signs of failure to thrive and make careful observations: Is the infant pallid, floppy, unresponsive to faces? Sometimes picking up an infant (with parental permission), may be the only way to tell if a child has been injured, as they may wince when held or moved. Is the toddler passive, unresponsive to the parent? Be alert to the return of a previously violent partner, or the entry to the home of a new partner or housemate who is not committed to the safety of the children. In weighing up these patterns, consider the age and specific vulnerability of each child: how are these issues likely to impact upon caring for an infant compared to parenting an older child or adolescent?

Some parents might provide adequate care to infants and children by reducing or controlling their alcohol or other drugs use, and adopting harm-reduction strategies; others might require abstinence. In either case, support from the family and wider network will be vital to successful outcomes, as it is unlikely that a parent will abstain or maintain safe use practices if their partner or other household members continue with unregulated use.

Developing and implementing a safety plan

Developing and implementing a safety plan requires attention to everyday lifestyle as well as anticipating crises. Discuss with the parent the child's developmental needs and daily routine, and work with them to identify everyday risks amenable to basic safety practices. Is there a locked cupboard for drug paraphernalia or does the family need help in obtaining one? If the parent has trouble with sleeping and waking, what help is needed to cater for the children's routine needs for food, attention or transport to school, and so on? When are the peak child care demands and how do they relate to predictable parental mood swings? How well-equipped is the family to meet these challenges and what reinforcements do they need? Pay particular attention to safety planning if the parent lives alone with the child/children, and if the main carer is depressed or is experiencing other mental health issues.

The threat of violence must be taken very seriously. Are there people in the family's network who pose a danger to the children and the primary carer, and how might their access be blocked? Help parents to take out intervention orders, where required, to deter unwanted people from approaching the family or the home. These might include past or present partners, or other acquaintances, including criminal associates. Where the risk of violence is severe, engage specialist family violence, police or child protection services to enhance safety and assist with relocating the family unit and broadening its support base. With your client, evaluate the safety of the social network: are there links to the abuser that might put the family at risk of harm, or sources of increased protection that can be tapped?

In addition to these fundamental safety measures, contingency plans need to be made for when parents are unwell, substance-affected or otherwise in crisis. This is doubly important if the parent lives alone or if parents typically use or relapse together. Clues to lack of progress include the parent being evasive, unavailable or uncommunicative; distracted by other matters and/or in constant crisis; superficial in response to questions; threatening or passive-aggressive; and incongruent (that is, they may deny use when there is clear evidence of it, or say one thing but do another). Help parents, their partners and significant other family members identify and act upon warning signs of dangerous mood changes and unavailability or lack of attentiveness to infants' and children's needs. It has long been a practice in intensive family services to ask parents to identify the kinds of events that tend to precipitate crises in their lives (whether these be emotional, relational, medical or material), and develop a clear written plan of simple steps to take if these events arise (Kinney, Haapala & Booth, 1991). Similar tools have been developed in relation to family violence. Include older children in this plan, and make sure it is easily accessible in the home so that they, as well as their parents, know what to do and whom to call in an emergency. Needless to say, the crisis plan must cover access to out-of-hours professional help.

Build a safety net around the infant or child by enlisting people to monitor and support parenting, including members of the extended family, friends, teachers and neighbours. Ask the parent for contact details of significant and trusted people, ideally well-known to the child, who could voluntarily commit to daily responsibility for the child during periods of lapse or relapse until the parent is able to resume care. Ensure everyone is aware of their responsibility, knows their role and what to expect from the process. Contact details need to be known to children. Older children, especially adolescents, may need a similar crisis plan of their own, relating to their own vulnerability and volatility. They should be encouraged to call upon supporters without fear of recrimination.

Safety plans are crucial if the children are under school age. Infants and preschoolers cannot act independently to seek help, and do not have the regular safeguard of school attendance checks to monitor their safety. For these young children it may also be necessary to ensure that the parent checks in with the backstop carer on a daily basis. During pregnancy and in early infancy special attention may be needed. To reduce the risk of miscarriage or harm to an unborn baby, make sure that pregnant women receive regular antenatal care as early in their pregnancy as possible, and that they are aware of the risks associated with drug use during their pregnancy, especially from alcohol and tobacco use. Ensure that parents and other carers are aware of the heightened risk of SIDS among the infants of substance-dependent parents and that they are informed about safe sleeping guidelines. Pamphlets and other written material are helpful in keeping this issue at the forefront of parents' and carers' minds.

Have an alternative case plan prepared should the parent be unwilling or unable to address risk on a voluntary basis (or in the case of a report that does not lead to child protection involvement) and continually review the effectiveness of their safety measures.

Monitoring the child's wellbeing

A well-developed safety plan provides a solid and explicit basis for monitoring family functioning and the child's wellbeing. The worker can regularly ensure that parents are following through with safety precautions for alcohol and other drugs and with drug-using parapher-nalia (such as safe syringe disposal), or that they are leaving the child with a trusted family or network member when actively using drugs or drinking excessively. This is facilitated by developing and main-taining the family's openness to active observation with both planned and unannounced visits by trusted family and network members and workers. In families where neglect and financial problems are of concern, monitor food supplies and meal preparation, rent and utility payments and school attendance. Where necessary, help the parent with financial assistance, financial counselling and budgeting strategies, bearing in mind that parents are often more willing to accept intrusion into family life when they receive practical assistance and when issues they raise are respectfully addressed.

Help parents address concerns; do not simply refer them to services in the hope that this will reduce harm, as engagement may not occur. Vigilance is important in the period between making a referral and its uptake; do not assume that somebody else will be keeping infants and children safe. Actively follow up referrals to ensure a service will be provided in a timely manner. Safety plans can be strengthened by trying to ensure that parents receive priority access to services such as detoxification or residential rehabilitation, as access to respite care or other child care arrangements may be extremely time-limited.

During the process of and after making a report to child protection

Monitoring may reveal that children are not receiving the care and protection they need, meaning that a referral to child protection becomes necessary. Any professional working with this vulnerable population of children will need to be aware of when and how such referrals should be made in their area, and if child welfare is not their primary area of work, it can be helpful to consult with local child protection workers for advice and ideas on how to proceed.

If you are making a report to child protection in the context of collaborative service provision to the family, it will be important to ensure that your fellow service providers are clear about the reason for and intended outcomes of a report, particularly if there is disagreement among professionals on the need for protective intervention. We are not suggesting that there is no room for disagreement, or that consensus is required, or that it is necessary to present a united front, but families do need clarity about the process.

In making a report, provide information about your own role and what you have seen and done, to allow others to understand the context of your report in order to make an informed decision on children's safety and wellbeing. For example, child protection workers and the children's court often receive assessments and reports by alcohol and other drug treatment providers who have not visited the home or seen their clients' children; such reports can be misleading and do not necessarily support decisions that are in children's best interests. Similarly, a family worker who does not understand the parent's treatment regimen may not draw valid conclusions about progress towards recovery.

Making a report, and investigating it, can be protracted processes, introducing new stressors into an already volatile situation. Where possible, try to stay connected with your client family and keep them informed of progress while continuing to offer help, but inform child protection if there is a serious deterioration in a situation of risk to children, or if, for whatever reason, you cease visiting the family or working with the parents and children. Maintaining a connection with the family is more likely to occur if you have already established good engagement with the family, if you have adequately explained to them your concerns and the reason for your report, and if you have discussed some of the potential benefits and resources that may result from child protection involvement. The best outcome may be that parents themselves make the report to child protection, and explain the difficulties they are facing. While it might be difficult to achieve, this approach is more likely to be viewed positively by child protection and result in a more supportive approach to the process.

TIPS FOR NEW WORKERS

- Substance use and cycles of withdrawal can cause rapid deterioration in parental functioning. Risk levels to infants and children can fluctuate, which requires monitoring on a continuous basis; it is important to keep your eye firmly focused on the child and ask yourself, 'How is the child faring?' Consider whether the child has already been harmed, and how, and whether further or different harm is imminent.

- Find out what you don't know and don't make assumptions about the effects of using or giving up alcohol or other drugs. For example, do not assume that if parents give up alcohol or illicit drugs 'good enough' care of children will follow. It is not uncommon for people to substitute prescription medication and/or alcohol for illicit drug use, with similar behavioural outcomes, so infants and children may not benefit from the change. Similarly, substance use can mask or mediate mental health issues that may become more apparent after drug use has ceased.

- Discuss your concerns and planned actions with your colleagues and supervisors. Better decisions are usually made when multiple perspectives are considered.

- Parental reluctance to engage with services when there are outstanding child safety matters should be followed up assertively and may require a report to child protection; where possible, make the report to child protection with the parent present. Ideally parents could make the report themselves and clarify the type of support they require.

- **Mandated intervention** is experienced by many parents as a threat, particularly if they have previously lost the care of children; parents who feel threatened are more likely to respond positively when fears are openly acknowledged, and you spend sufficient time discussing your safety concerns with parents before reporting.

- Expect that parents and other family members may minimise or exaggerate alcohol or other drug use in child protection and family court proceedings for their own purposes or because they believe this to be in the child's interests.

TRAPS FOR NEW WORKERS

Many traps for new workers stem from understandable anxiety. For example:

- A worker who is not clear on the type and level of risk may make anxiety-driven, reactive reports that lead to negative experiences for all involved.
- Using jargon with families clouds workers' intentions, and leaves parents confused about what is happening and what is required of them.
- Failing to make a report when required due to fear of losing engagement with the parent exposes the child to continued risk.
- Not openly discussing risk management options with parents deprives them of change opportunities and weakens the worker's capacity to target help.
- Sometimes workers fail to take sufficient action to protect an infant or child through concerns for their own safety, particularly when parents have responded with hostility or are known to be aggressive.
- Professionals can raise one another's anxieties (groupthink) to the point of making an inappropriate report instead of considering alternative action—for example, speaking with a parent and suggesting the child be placed with a trusted family member until presenting concerns are resolved.

Others traps for workers may occur due to a limited understanding of the service system and the worker's own contribution to the case. For example:

- Not understanding or working within the legislative framework may result in under- or over-reporting.
- A preoccupation with management of risk can result in welfare issues receiving episodic child protection responses which do not necessarily result in long-term support to families. This may in fact increase the risk to children, due to the erosion of positive

engagement by support services from multiple reports that are not substantiated.

- Reports may describe parental behaviour but lack clarity about the particular vulnerabilities of infants and other children with special needs. This is particularly problematic if the report is driven primarily by the worker's own values and judgements and lacks sufficient evidence of the impact of the parental behaviour on the children.

There are also traps for workers in simply trying to be responsive to the parent as client, but losing sight of the child, such as:

- Not persisting with efforts to contact parents who are making themselves unavailable, which leaves infants and children at greater risk of harm.
- Not perceiving manipulation or deceit and simply believing parental reports of their parenting, family circumstances or their alcohol or other drug use, despite other indicators to the contrary, and without seeing the child, or witnessing parental functioning at different times and places.
- Colluding with families by being the 'good professional' and leaving responsibility for the safety and wellbeing of clients' children to other workers, regardless of worker mandate or role.
- Offering parents false assurances of confidentiality which can lead to parents feeling betrayed if a report to child protection is made.

HOW WILL I KNOW IF I'M ON TRACK?

- You will be working in partnership with parents and other family and network members to ensure children are kept safe and well.
- You will share responsibility for risk and wellbeing and have established complementary roles with other professionals across sectors.

- Your assessment and management of risk to infants and children will be based on multiple sources of information and include knowledge of the past, understanding of the present and evidence of the parent's commitment to change in the future, as mentioned in Chapter 5.
- You will be clear on why and when a report needs to be made, if at all, and what you want child protection to do as a result; that is, what action do you want taken as a result of the report?
- You will have alternative strategies devised with the family, network members and other professionals as back-up if the first strategy does not go to plan.
- The parent will know, understand and ideally support any protective actions proposed or taken.
- You will be prepared to share some level of appropriate and considered risk to give parents the opportunity to change and so that unnecessary reports are not being made.
- Children will not be harmed. They will meet **developmental milestones**, attend school or day care as appropriate, and their care will meet society's expectations.
- Children, parents and others will enact safety plans if the parent is unable to safely provide care.

KEEPING MIA AND SOPHIE SAFE

Stella gave consent for the worker and her mother, Joan, to have each other's phone numbers and for Joan to contact the worker with any concerns. Within a few weeks, Joan called to say Stella had embarked on a relationship with a man with serious mental health problems who was volatile and aggressive. The worker arranged to see Stella the following day when she informed her of the discussion with Joan. Although initially upset by the information, Stella agreed the

relationship was not a positive one and decided to termi-
nate it. Soon after, she met Jim. Within a year she had given
birth to Sophie. Jim readily engaged with the worker and
described himself as a regular drinker. While Jim's drinking
was well-managed, Stella's became problematic. An agreement was reached that Jim would assume responsibility for
the children when their mother was drinking, and that if he
was also drinking, they would be in Joan's care.

KEEPING ZAC SAFE

In time, Kevin's use of multiple substances escalated. During
visits to the home, he fluctuated between being withdrawn,
agitated and hyper-vigilant. After the worker encouraged
Kevin to discuss his fears for his own and Zac's safety, he
agreed he was experiencing difficulties and that it was
time to take protective action. He and the worker invited a
trusted friend, Melanie, to share the home and to help with
Zac's care. With Kevin's permission, the worker spoke with
Melanie, and with Zac's teacher, both of whom agreed to
inform her if they were concerned with Zac's wellbeing. Zac
was encouraged to speak with trusted adults and to let them
know if he felt unsafe.

SUMMARY

In this chapter we have focused on the safety of the child, arguing that
managing and reducing risk is a core task for any worker involved with
substance-using parents and their children. The task is continuous: it
precedes, accompanies and follows any report that might or might not
be made to child protection authorities. At the heart of safety planning
are steps to protect the child's wellbeing through everyday routines,

harm reduction information and advice to parents and extended family members, as well as explicit plans for handling crises when they arise. At times, safety planning for children is directly linked with safety planning for mothers and others who are subject to family or community violence. Responsibility for plans and their implementation is shared with the family, their significant network members and other involved professionals. Clear and honest communication about exactly what children need underpins each step in the process, including making a report to child protection authorities.

7

Improving family life from the inside

Workers have many opportunities to help families change, grow and thrive. Having engaged well with parents and children, workers will have begun the necessary conversations about parents' emotional challenges, relationship issues and parenting. These conversations can lead to explicit strategies to improve parents' emotional self-regulation, to strengthen relationships between parents and between parents and children, to help the family work well and enjoy daily life together, and to manage threats (such as drug use relapse or problematic use of alcohol) to maintaining positive change. The conversations will not be complete, however, until workers also understand the dreams and goals of family members, including children, and begin to make plans that support families to work towards these.

In this chapter we focus on strategies to strengthen families. There are many approaches to personal, couple and family counselling, and many specialist professionals and organisations to do this work. Clearly, not all human service workers have all the relevant knowledge, skills and a mandate for such counselling. In fact, some of the work will go well beyond professional help and may involve community organisations including sporting and other recreational groups and activities. Even so, whenever workers in alcohol and other drug services, family services or other community sector organisations find themselves involved with substance-affected families, they will need to be able to define and address family goals for change, at least at some level.

Past and present trauma and violence make it more difficult for parents to be emotionally and physically available to their infant or child. Substance-dependent parents often have difficulty managing their emotions, and will instead resort to the use of alcohol and other drugs or other feel-good addictions such as gambling, shopping or excessive eating. Some are so overwhelmed with negative emotions that they have not learnt to self-regulate and find it difficult to remain calm and stay focused when they feel anxious, sad, angry, threatened or disappointed. As families become overwhelmed by personal safety, material and social problems, the focus on children and parenting can diminish, but successful change in any of these problem domains has the potential to improve parents' confidence and allow more room for them to focus on the wellbeing of their children. There may be many routes to change, but the maintenance of motivation and morale is crucial. To avoid work with families becoming focused on problems to the point of demoralisation, a strengths-based approach should be adopted to build on what parents do well, their aspirations and the resources available to them.

Strengths-based practice is not, however, naïve practice, and the many problems that beset the family cannot be ignored. Strengths-based practice may flounder when workers are confronted by parents relapsing into substance use. At such times, they need to ensure they are working safely within their knowledge-base and skill set and to seek the support of other professionals when required. For example, it can be dangerous to encourage a pregnant woman to suddenly stop using heroin as withdrawal needs to be medically supervised to avoid harm to the embryo or foetus. Strength-based practice may also suffer when multiple problems obscure family goals. The parent might arrive at the service in crisis, and the worker is deflected from the longer-term change plans, including the management of substance misuse.

Sustainable resolution of family problems requires *clear*, *measurable* and *achievable* goals. As families sometimes enter the child and family welfare or alcohol and other drug treatment sectors after involvement with child protection services, goals may have been set as conditions on children's court or family drug court orders. Such imposed goals may be resented and resisted. It is still possible and necessary, however, to help parents identify and set their own realistic and important goals for themselves and their family, without compromising child safety.

Many alcohol and other drug-dependent parents do not have much faith in their ability to achieve goals and it is difficult for parents to make changes in the face of multiple difficulties. The difference between this client group and some others is that the process of change can be more unsteady, with numerous setbacks, and progress slower. Parents are likely to make initial progress when support is at its highest but progress stalls when support is reduced. This can be discouraging for professionals, who can easily give up on families and reinforce feelings of hopelessness. Much of what needs to be done is good, solid casework. Goal setting and measuring of progress are important to prevent 'case-drift' (aimless contact with services with no real change), to bolster parental morale and motivation, to prevent and manage substance use and to aid recovery from relapse. In this way workers try to replace a downward spiral into substance dependence with an upward spiral into recovery and autonomy.

INTENDED OUTCOMES

Whether families have indeed changed and grown can be identified by several outcomes. To begin with, parents are better able to manage their own emotional life and relationships. This may be evident in a new family narrative in which there is hope and clear plans for the future. Parents also demonstrate effective use of parenting knowledge and skills. They reduce, and ideally cease, use of illicit and other problematic drugs, and use alcohol and prescription medication responsibly, so that their substance use does not negatively affect the parent–child relationship or caregiving. When threatened with a lapse into substance misuse, they use help effectively to manage this threat and keep their children safe. Doing so involves identifying common triggers and implementing relapse-prevention strategies to avoid resumption of regular or long-term use.

HELPFUL ATTITUDES AND VALUES

When focusing on improving the life of the family as a whole, it is helpful for the worker to view every family member as equally important and deserving of support. This requires a commitment to keeping families together, and, when this is not feasible, a commitment to helping families remain in contact. It helps to see problems seen as opportunities for growth, and to convey belief that new patterns of living can be learnt.

To manage the threat of relapse and maintain progress towards goals, workers need tenacity to hang in there when families present as chaotic and/or unmotivated and when progress towards goals is slow or stalls. They must show that they are willing to maintain a strong therapeutic alliance during relapse to help parents get back on track, and need to resist being judgemental when money is spent on cigarettes, alcohol or other drugs. The therapeutic alliance is supported by belief in the client's willingness and capacity to set and achieve realistic goals for themselves and their family, a commitment to understanding what families value and want in their lives, and optimism about change.

EXPECTATIONS OF CLIENTS

In working towards family change, parents are expected to attend to the needs of all family members, including unborn babies, infants and children. They are explicitly asked to address problems and work towards goals, rather than undertake superficial, compliance-based interactions. This will entail keeping appointments or making alternative arrangements and following through with agreed tasks more often than not.

EXPECTATIONS OF YOURSELF

You will work in partnership with parents and other carers to ensure that children and families are more than just safe, but are working towards long-term wellbeing. You will be considering regularly whether you are making a difference (e.g. is the child living safely at home; is the child attending school; has there been a noticeable difference in parenting?). You will continue to accept clients as people (without necessarily condoning all behaviours) and assist them to find or maintain hopefulness for change, particularly when they feel despair or have 'failed' to make the 'big' changes. By modelling control over your own emotional state, you will assist parents, children and other family members to become more aware of and develop regulation over their emotional responses to problems. You will be aware of the limitations of your own knowledge and skills and be willing to supplement your professional limitations through collaborative practice with other service providers (see Chapter 8).

BARRIERS TO CHANGE

Personal and family change can be threatening, even when desired. Faced with the challenge of change, or when overwhelmed by their many problems, parents can be unavailable for home visits, fail to keep appointments, and may not return telephone calls or respond to letters, text messages and emails inviting contact. Aggressive family members can deter workers and render the most vulnerable infants and children invisible and unsupported. New partners can take centre stage for parents, and suddenly change a parent's motivation. Parental isolation or loneliness can lead some parents to make poor partner choices because they believe that 'any company is better than no company'.

Denial about the role and impact of alcohol and other drugs in their lives, along with unresolved trauma, can result in parents self-medicating and avoiding facing such concerns as substance use, family conflict or child neglect. Some recognise their substance dependence but are focused on having their own individual needs met; for example, a parent's own history of trauma and deprivation can dominate discussion and obscure attention from the needs of children or other adults. Workers and organisations may also set up barriers to change. Lack of confidence in working with children can result in services not adequately considering or addressing children's own needs or including them in family sessions or in decisions that affect them. Unmanageable caseloads, insufficient resources and poor inter-organisational relationships can all make it difficult to attend to the needs of whole families. In addition, services may be offered too late when policies and practices pay insufficient attention to the role of early intervention, so crucial for new parents, infants and young children. A particular barrier to goal-focused practice is parents' chaotic and crisis-ridden lifestyle, which interferes with appointment keeping and hooks the worker into solving the new immediate problem, which rarely results in lasting change.

KEY STRATEGIES

Family-centred practice in families affected by parental substance use requires strategies to support parents as individuals, with a particular focus on strategies for emotional self-regulation and management of the need for substances. While many clients present as single parents, couple households are also common, so there is also a need to work on improving adult-to-adult relationships, both for live-in partners and between resident and non-resident co-parents or co-carers. Strengthening the parent–child relationship is a key focus. Since family life is structured on a daily basis by all sorts of routines and shared activities, many of them stressful, there is also a need for strategies to help the family work together well and enjoy their shared lives. It is important to bear in mind that parents do not do this work in isolation, but we will defer until Chapter 8 discussion of strategies to strengthen the family's support and interactions with the extended family and wider network, and strategies to make the service system more sensitive and responsive to the whole family.

STRATEGIES TO STRENGTHEN PARENTS' SELF-REGULATION

There is much still to be learnt about effective interventions for parents who misuse substances, but there are some tentative points of agreement in the relevant literature. Dawe and Harnett (2013) give a central place to the parents' state of mind, their ability to be calm and in control emotionally, and the empowerment inherent in the process of joint goal setting. Forrester and Harwin (2011) also highlight the nature of the worker–client relationship, and in particular what the practice of motivational interviewing in the alcohol and other drug service sector has to teach us about the centrality of assisting parents to reflect upon and resolve their ambivalence about substance dependence and the desirability of change. They also note the relative importance of strengthening clients' decision-making in the here and now compared with seeking to understand history and causation. It is important to remember that if a person defines his or her personal effectiveness as dependent on substance use, confidence in personal autonomy and power can ebb away. Crucially, workers must avoid reinforcing this sense of powerlessness by over-controlled and controlling intervention processes. People are more likely to change their behaviour when their motivation is from within themselves and aligns to their own dreams and goals, rather than imposed by others; motivational interviewing is a key strategy in helping parents give up substance use or change alcohol and other drug use patterns and is a good way of initiating other life changes as well. In the light of these themes, we suggest several modest, minimally intrusive, but potentially powerful strategies to support parents' self-regulation.

First, comes respect, as stressed in Chapter 3 on engaging parents. Without neglecting children's safety, aim to give parents as much choice as possible about the process of how you work together. Support parents emotionally with unconditional positive regard for the person without condoning aggression or dangerous behaviour. Show interest in them as people beyond their parenting roles by inviting them to identify their personal goals for their own wellbeing and growth, and to explore what is working well for them in their pursuit of those goals (Harnett & Day, 2008). Help parents develop confidence and extend themselves by setting new goals according to a **hierarchy of needs** and personal priorities. For example, once housing and finances have been sorted out, and sufficient nutritious food is available, move to joining activities at the local 'community house' or investigate training and employment options. Make good use of opportunities to work together on the skills of problem-solving, priority-setting and interpersonal communication, all of which will be crucial to their path through family life and the service system.

Second, help parents *identify their own strategies* for recognising when they enter high emotional states, and for returning to more stable emotions, without the use of alcohol and/or other drugs or other self-defeating behaviours like overeating, buying things they can't afford, gambling or seeking negative sexual relations. For example, learning mindfulness or meditation, or doing physical activities such as yoga or going for a quiet walk may be more productive alternatives. Help parents to understand that some parenting behaviours or tasks will need doing regardless of how they feel, like feeding children. It is not uncommon for parents to deny workers' concerns until a crisis occurs which draws the attention of police and/or child protection services to the family unit.

This can be a catalyst for change but it can also cause anxiety and a desire to withdraw from the possibility of scrutiny by service providers. Bearing this in mind, encourage parents to articulate their internal narratives about their use of substances and the process of recovery as it applies to them, and to hold on to those aspects of the narrative from which they derive hope and comfort. Work with them to identify the triggers to them losing a sense of emotional control and to put in place strategies they find useful in helping them manage negative feelings and their impact. Pay special attention to their ambivalence about substance use as a response to feelings of loss of emotional control, and their own decision-making in relation to exploring the positive and negative aspects of their substance use. Pay attention to how they might structure their daily lives to maximise positive experiences and minimise failure events. Seek their cooperation in allowing you to monitor and support treatment plans by speaking with alcohol and other drug treatment providers and other professionals engaged with parents—for example, methadone-prescribing doctors and child welfare workers.

Third, combat disabling self-judgements. Many substance users (especially mothers and Indigenous clients) report a long history of social stigma and a deeply felt disabling sense of shame. To set and pursue goals requires them to banish this barrier to change; for this, it is crucial that, as a worker, you help them build and maintain a sense of hope for the future. Writing for the Dulwich Centre about overcoming cravings for drugs in the context of service provision in Hong Kong, Har Man-kwong (2004) reports the value of narrative therapy techniques, such as externalising conversations and therapeutic letters, for combating shame in order to avert problems such as clients pretending all is well when it is not, or 'saving face' by simply disappearing from the service.

Fourth, help parents reconcile their sense of self and their parenthood. Include in the discussion of personal identity and wellbeing the experience of being a parent, with all its ambivalence. Substance dependence mostly occurs in the childbearing years (15 to 40) and many pregnancies among substance-dependent mothers are unplanned; birth control is therefore an important issue to address with male and female clients when they present to various services, including alcohol and other drug treatment agencies. Bear in mind, though, that for many clients, their children and their role as parents may be a major source of hope and comfort in their lives, and a powerful motivator.

Fifth, offer increased support during child protection crises. The therapeutic alliance and the parents' own personal stability can be thrown into crisis if a child is removed from their care. Your work to improve self-regulation can be overwhelmed by the power of external regulation. Not only can this be a disincentive to stop using, it can escalate use by vulnerable parents: it is important to convey this message to parents and to offer additional support to help them maintain their goals and progress. Inform parents of legislative time-frames for reunification of children from foster or kinship care. While bearing in mind that conditions on children's and family drug court orders typically require parents to demonstrate changes to substance use patterns within a specified time-frame, which may not equate with the parents' readiness to change, inform parents that the best way to have children returned to their care as quickly as possible is to meet conditions; ask what assistance they require and offer hope for a successful reunification plan, if this is realistic, to motivate parents to take positive steps (see Chapter 9).

STRATEGIES TO STRENGTHEN OR RESOLVE ADULT–ADULT RELATIONSHIPS

Meaningful, stable and supportive adult relationships matter to all of us. Because many clients present to services as single mothers, it can be easy to ignore the men in their lives. With permission, and when safe to do so, make sure you include the father, partner or co-carer in your work together, not only for the sake of the children, but also for the sake of the primary parent. Men often feel excluded by service providers or are reluctant to engage with services, particularly if they believe the service is more interested in mothers and children. Some relationships may be less than ideal, even abusive, and workers should not be afraid to invite parents to weigh up their positive and negative impacts. Safe new relationships should be encouraged and parents should be supported to put some new insights and relationship skills into action.

If your client is engaged in a process of change, there may be repercussions in intimate relationships, sometimes generating serious counter-forces. Discuss how to involve partners and significant others in the process of setting and pursuing new goals, and supporting the change effort. This might involve a level of respectful conversation that is not customary, requiring some modelling of mutual listening. Group-work can be a useful tool here, with specialist mediation some-times needed. For some couples, substance misuse is deeply embedded in their joint lives, and personal change is unlikely without a mutual commitment to change. Here, there may be room for parallel discus-sion with the partner about his or her personal goals, and there will certainly be a need for some joint work on how daily life might be restructured as change proceeds. Some couples have identified the need for new rituals, challenges or thrills to replace the part that alcohol or other drug-taking play in their relationship. Invite them to imagine new scenarios, and discuss how these might be enabled, and what the implications might be for their children. Mutual change might not be possible. If there are serious risks involved, develop a safety plan for the management and, ultimately, resolution of the relationship.

STRATEGIES TO STRENGTHEN PARENT–CHILD RELATIONSHIPS

Support the attachment process

Emotional regulation and availability allow scope for the secure attach-ment between the child and the parent; Dawe and Harnett (2013) place this attachment at the centre of improving care by parents who misuse substances. This is what makes early intervention such an important service system goal. When workers encounter young parents, especially first-time mothers, it is important to ensure they receive early intervention to prevent harm to their infants and to reduce the escalation of problems for all family members. Pregnant women should receive information on alcohol and other drug use, and be linked with obstetric care as early as possible.

The parent–child relationship is in part shaped by parents' values and expectations, and these are in turn affected by knowledge. Work out which areas of parenting require further development. Does the parent have knowledge of child development and appropriate strategies for promoting children's safety and wellbeing? Do they need help in learning to recognise and understand the child's signals and communications? We have noted earlier that parents are often unaware of how much their child sees and understands parental substance use and they may need help in learning to read the child. A first step might be to encourage them to reflect upon what the child says and does in particular circumstances, followed by supported conversations between parent and child, or modelling modes of comforting distressed young children. After establishing a trusting relationship with children and parents, it can be therapeutically beneficial to sit with the child and parent and allow the child to express his or her experience of living with parental substance use. If this is too confronting, younger children can be assisted to express themselves through drawing or play; older children can write letters to the parent. Such interventions can be important ways of validating the child's rights to be understood and respected as a person of value in the home and community.

Temporary child care may afford the parent respite and the child some enriching life experiences. If this can be treated positively as a normal part of parenting, and if the contacts between all parties are well managed, this can be an aid to the parent–child relationship, rather than a threat. There are times when children are not able to remain within the home either because it is unsafe for them to do so or because parents are unable to provide continuous care. Even so, try to ensure that the child's positive relationships with parents and also with significant others are maintained. This is discussed below and further addressed in Chapter 9.

Interpret the child's perspective for the parent

Children are often aware of parental substance use at a very young age while parents think they have successfully concealed their use. Help parents to understand the experience of living with a substance-dependent parent from the perspective of the child. Encourage parents to ensure the child has enough information to make sense of their lives. For example, parents who are prescribed methadone or other pharmacotherapy often tell children that they are sick and require daily medicine, which can cause children to fear for their parent's health and wellbeing. It is helpful if the parent can explain what is happening and reassure the child that they are making efforts to overcome problems. It can be very powerful for parents to hear how their alcohol or other drug use has impacted their children, particularly as many will have been in denial or have minimised harm. Ask parents for permission to speak with their children, where possible, and ask parents to convey this permission to their children to reduce the child's anxieties about speaking with a worker. While potentially highly therapeutic for the family, this conversation needs to be handled very sensitively and should only be conducted when the family is well-engaged with the worker and after a thorough assessment of risk and safety, for both child and parent, has been undertaken. The aim is to bring parents and children to a position of shared understanding. If you are not confident in brokering the conversation but nevertheless feel that parent and child would benefit from the parent being more aware of the child's experience, consider speaking with the child first and then gently relaying the child's comments to the parent. Referral to specialist counsellors should be considered.

Help parents become more responsive to children

Excessive or problematic substance use interferes with the capacity to be responsive to others. A downward spiral can develop if children develop emotional problems and disturbing behaviour and parents respond by disengaging further, using harsher disciplinary practices or a combination of both. Unpredictability in parenting can also occur when families are caught up in a boom and bust cycle where periods of deprivation through depleted financial resources, sometimes due to the purchase of alcohol or other drugs, are followed by excessive spending if parents feel guilty and overcompensate. Unsurprisingly, children have been known to hide and hoard food. In addition to improved self-regulation, some parents might need information about the impact of alcohol and other drug use on children, as well as the impact of trauma and violence on their own and their children's lives; a **genogram** may be a way of tactfully bringing intergenerational transmission of alcohol and other drugs, and other problems, to parental awareness. (See the *Parenting Support Toolkit* for Alcohol and Other Drug Workers listed in Useful websites and resources.) Move on to helping parents recognise the unhelpful patterns in their interactions with their children, and help them practise more consistent responses to children's behaviour, including non-punitive discipline and reliable nurturing.

In cases in which parents have been excessively preoccupied with their own needs and emotionally and physically unavailable to their children, recovery can be a time of crisis or challenge. Just as between partners, there needs to be re-evaluation of daily rituals and communications to build stronger and more rewarding parent–child connections. Again, reflection on what works is useful. What do they enjoy doing together? Can that be increased or improved? Has the child been assuming too much responsibility? Plan ways that the parent can respectfully take up the reins and allow the child more freedom for age-appropriate activities. Does the parent find particular children's behaviour challenging? Give information about normative parenting responses if needed, while encouraging the parent to evaluate the utility and appropriateness of these responses for their child. If they have sufficient confidence and social skills they might make use of community-based parenting services; for some, more specialist supported playgroups or parenting groups hosted by the agency might be needed. For sustainable change, encourage parents to undertake their own parenting research (for example, via useful websites and local service networks) and help-seeking.

Set few rules but base these on safety for children and others, including professionals engaged with the family, and have clear consequences if rules are not kept—for example, a notification will not be made as long as the parent attends to children's care needs.

STRATEGIES TO HELP THE FAMILY UNIT WORK TOGETHER WELL AND ENJOY FAMILY LIFE

For families to work well as a unit, members need the mutually respectful and clear communication referred to above, and they also need the family unit to be well organised. Parents are usually responsible for this organisation. Substance-misusing parents are often characterised as chaotic, and some do indeed lack basic life skills, but others do have skills in managing very fluid, complex and challenging circumstances. Explore what they have learnt to do well, and how those skills can be deployed to build a stronger family life. Where necessary, teach parenting and life skills, such as child behaviour management, household routines, budgeting, using a diary to keep appointments, and so on, but keep the process centred on collaboration and mutual exploration, rather than instruction; the emphasis remains on doing *with*, rather than doing *for*.

Since this group of families typically experiences diverse problems, workers do need to be flexible and willing to assist families to address problems in as many areas of family life as possible, including parenting; mental health issues; children's own needs; housing; finances; family relationships; and social isolation. If the number and range of problems overwhelm family members and workers alike, work together to break them down into manageable tasks, ensuring that issues related to child safety and wellbeing are prioritised. To avoid defining the family in terms of its problems, try to balance problem-solving with developmental, morale-enhancing activities, such as exploring new forms of shared leisure activities or new ways of recognising family members' achievements.

Engage with as many family members as possible, perhaps through family meetings, to help them to identify their actual and potential contribution to family routines, and allocate tasks accordingly. Children can have many suggestions to make about such activities. The worker might need to advocate for children if they are over-burdened or under-valued as players in the family's daily life. The worker can contribute to the building of family morale by holding everyone in mind, taking the time to listen to all family members and providing additional support during transitions in the family life-cycle—for example, when parents re-partner, when additional children are born or when a grandparent is no longer available to help the family.

Policy permitting, let parents and children know that they remain in your thoughts during lapses in contact or after formal service ceases (since this can be a trying time), through telephone contact (some may be unable to retrieve voicemail but able to access text messages) and emails, letters or cards; consider inviting parents and children to social and recreational events at the service as a means of re-engagement with the service.

KEY STRATEGIES TO STAY GOAL-FOCUSED AND MAINTAIN CHANGE

For the worker to stay goal-focused, and to help parents maintain the gains they make, requires explicit, measurable and realistic practice. In relation to alcohol and other drug use, establish their readiness to change substance use patterns. Invite parents to measure alcohol and other drug consumption to bring use to conscious awareness, which can begin the process of motivation for change. With them, set realistic goals with time-frames and pitch the goals to match parental efforts and achievement, allowing the parent to set the pace unless infant or child safety is compromised. Break up long-term aims into a set of small achievable goals to begin with. Ensure that recovery and parenting goals are meaningfully related to any underlying problem (Harnett, 2007). For example, getting the child to school on time is unlikely if the parent is unable to establish and maintain routines due to being substance-affected or suffering from agoraphobia. Clarify tasks (who will do what when) and write up the plan with family members. Give copies of this plan to parents and other professionals working with the family to help everyone stay focused and motivated.

Specify indicators for measuring progress and have the parents review these with you. Use the monitoring process to assist parents to identify and overcome barriers preventing them from achieving individual and family goals. Measure progress towards goals with goal-scaling exercises: these can be based on simple five to ten point scales—for example, Life Tweaking cards and other resources available from St Luke's Innovative Resources (see Useful websites and resources). Repeat measures of the Strengths and Difficulties Questionnaire can be helpful (Goodman, 1997). Encourage parents to maintain motivation by providing regular constructive feedback; highlight what parents and children do well and provide encouragement for further achievements. To avoid distraction from the purpose of service, spend a short time at the beginning of each session discussing immediate concerns

(15 minutes may be sufficient) and then get back to working on previously set goals (see Chapter 7).

Assist parents to achieve their goals by coaching them and providing practical support; for example, help parents prepare for the birth of an infant by referring to obstetric services, teach or model parenting skills, take parents to a financial counselling service, assist with housing applications or other practical matters.

WHEN A PARENT RELAPSES INTO ALCOHOL OR OTHER DRUG USE

While relapses to problematic substance use are common, and to be expected, good planning can prevent a lapse from turning back into a relapse. It is critical, therefore, for families to have a realistic and easy to implement relapse plan. This should be agreed with parents, the worker, children (if appropriate) and the extended family members, so take the time to develop the relationships necessary to put the plan in place. In many cases this plan will involve temporary care of the children by extended family members or significant other people in the children's lives. Such a plan will allow for ongoing work with parents around their long-term goals, without compromising the safety of children. Without such a plan, a relapse has the potential to completely undermine the efforts and progress that may have been made, and will generally result in child protection involvement or in high-risk situations.

TIPS FOR NEW WORKERS—HELPING FAMILIES CHANGE

- Sourcing and reading or viewing parenting materials with parents and reviewing progress together is a way of engaging parents in parenting issues when the worker is relatively inexperienced and not a parent themselves.

- Some parents lack basic life skills and struggle to keep appointments; buying a calendar and teaching parents to diarise appointments is a helpful strategy.
- Some fathers may prefer activity- (e.g. family excursions) rather than counselling-based support.
- The parenting role should never be undermined by the worker's competence. Workers need to ensure they do not assume responsibility for tasks that belong to the parent—for example, repeatedly providing food for children, disciplining children on excursions, speaking with school teachers on parents' behalf—but rather that they skill up and support the parent.
- Parents respect workers who can openly express concerns without beating around the bush or being judgemental. Therefore, be direct, honest and respectful in your communication.
- Parents value workers who use their own discretion when working with families; they do not like being stereotyped or subjected to predetermined interventions without comprehensive assessment that includes parents' own perspectives on the problems that they, their children and family face.
- Help families to have some small, early wins! Many of the goals you have created together may take some time to achieve, so make sure there are some goals (especially child-focused ones) that can be easily and immediately achieved. This helps build your engagement with the family, and will help build the family's confidence.
- It is more inviting for parents and children when offices and agencies look child-friendly—for example, some alcohol and other drug treatment agencies have a play-room for children, posters with families on the wall, toys and books in the waiting room and fresh fruit available for clients. Make sure that family images reflect the cultural diversity and gender of the clients you are hoping to engage with.

TIPS FOR NEW WORKERS—STAYING GOAL FOCUSED

- Children's wellbeing can be a powerful motivating factor in parental recovery, but it is not uncommon for parents to think they can manage substance use while caring for children; build on intrinsic motivation for change—for example, is the parent concerned about their health or their finances?

- Some behaviour will take a long time to learn or re-learn; acknowledge and celebrate achievements, however small (without being patronising), to maintain parental motivation and progress towards goals.

- Some workers and families agree on a structure for each session or visit, whereby parents can spend 15 minutes at the start to discuss any current crisis or issues that they have, before returning to work on their long-term goals. This helps ensure progress is being made, without ignoring current or immediate issues that need to be addressed.

- Goals framed positively and focused on the desired outcome are more likely to be worked towards and achieved than negatively framed goals—for example, 'living free of cannabis' rather than 'giving up cannabis'.

- Remember it is possible for a parent to be motivated to make changes without necessarily wanting to enter treatment for alcohol or other drug use.

- Removing the child from parental care can undermine the progress of rehabilitation as parents lose incentive to stop using alcohol or other drugs, or lose the hope for re-unification of the child to their care: provide additional support and encouragement to parents in this situation, particularly as not only may recovery stall, but also substance use may increase in response to emotional distress.

- Peer support is helpful for many people in recovery; invite parents to consider joining Alcoholics Anonymous or Narcotics Anonymous or other peer support groups.

- For some parents, alcohol and other drug use feels like an emotional life raft; asking them to give up evokes fear and therefore resistance; acknowledge the anxiety parents may be experiencing.
- Interventions with families with complex needs tend to be more successful when delivered in the home.
- Good work can be achieved with mandated clients with solution-focused and strengths-based approaches.

TRAPS FOR NEW WORKERS—HELPING FAMILIES CHANGE

- Not taking the time to de-escalate aggression or trying to understand parental frustration or anger.
- Allowing intimidating behaviour to continue without being acknowledged.
- Getting caught up in adult issues and unwittingly neglecting vulnerable infants and children, or directing all attention to children without supporting parents to fulfil their responsibilities to infants and children.
- Colluding with parents by minimising problematic parenting or risk to children.
- Minimising children's feelings and wishes by forgetting that their experiences may not be as we imagine them to be.
- Confusing parental compliance with mandated conditions on court orders or during active child protective assessment or intervention with commitment to lasting change.

TRAPS FOR NEW WORKERS—STAYING GOAL FOCUSED

- Providing crisis-driven, reactive service delivery rather than planned, purposeful interventions with parents, children and other family members.

- Setting goals for families instead of encouraging or allowing family members to set their own goals.
- Expecting that change will happen quickly or that it will be a straightforward process.
- Forgetting to give positive reinforcement for goals that have been achieved.
- Blaming the family when progress towards goals is slow or insufficient and not considering whether the intervention has been appropriately designed and implemented.
- Failing to consider the caring role, usually performed by women, and not providing child care or respite which would enable parents to attend programs or achieve other goals.

HOW WILL I KNOW IF I'M ON TRACK?

- Parents will present less in crisis and will demonstrate, individually and together, more self-regulation in emotion and behaviour.
- Parents will be planning for, and accepting responsibility for, their family's wellbeing.
- You and family members will be clear about what change needs to happen in the family and how progress will be measured.
- Most, if not all, family members will be simultaneously engaged, coming to meetings as arranged and undertaking agreed tasks.
- Parents will be aware of the progress (or lack of) they are making and will understand the rewards or consequences of their actions.
- Children's needs will be known and addressed.
- The family will report a happier and more stable family life.

STELLA AND JIM: IMPROVING FAMILY LIFE FROM THE INSIDE

Stella and Jim became preoccupied with problems: unpaid

bills and hostilities with members of the extended family, neighbours and Jim's former partner initially dominated conversations with the worker. Both parents had a tendency to forget important appointments, such as those with the local housing service. The worker set an agenda for home visits. She discussed the children's developmental needs and encouraged both parents to create a calmer home environment. A calendar was purchased and used as a diary of appointments. Automatic debit was arranged for all utilities. Parenting and individual goals were set and progress, including alcohol use, was measured on a regular basis.

KEVIN: IMPROVING FAMILY LIFE FROM THE INSIDE

Kevin admitted to an escalation in the use of alcohol and growing misuse of prescription medication. The worker provided him with unconditionally positive regard. She helped him understand the legacy of his own traumatic past. When conversations became emotionally painful for him, Kevin was flippant and talked 'off-topic'. The worker gently, but firmly, steered his focus back to Zac to help him see his substance use from a child's perspective. Kevin came to understand that his erratic behaviour was frightening Zac, who coped by spending long periods of time alone in his room, and he became more tolerant of Zac's behavioural problems.

SUMMARY

Each family has its own set of imperatives, relationship dynamics and family lifestyle and aspirations. Even if changes to these are desired, they may not come easily. In this chapter, we have suggested that workers encourage families to reflect upon what is and is not working in their daily family lives, and to set goals for change in several key areas: parental self-regulation (both emotional and behavioural), adult–adult relationships, parent–child relationships, and family routines and activities. The balance between these strands may vary between families and within families over time, but it is likely that sustainable change will require attention to each of these themes if family life is to become more mutually rewarding and stable, and less crisis-ridden. When crises do occur, as is likely, they will need to be dealt with, but it will be important to reflect upon the implications of the crisis for internal family functioning and to re-engage the family in the pursuit of these goals and in monitoring progress.

8

Enhancing informal and formal family support

All families need external support, and each family has its particular social economy in which goods, services, regard and obligations are exchanged via networks of formal and informal relationships (Mitchell & Campbell, 2011). Families in which parents have a history of substance misuse often labour under conditions of isolation from kith and kin, social networks skewed towards substance use and away from good parenting, and intermittent and challenging contact with formal social institutions. This chapter presents two major sets of responses to these problems: repairing and expanding the network of kith and kin to protect and nurture children and support parents; and helping families make good use of the formal social organisations that are necessary for family wellbeing, such as educational, health, housing and employment services. Improving families' interactions with formal services requires the worker to establish and maintain good interdisciplinary communication and collaboration, including the need for assertive outreach and information sharing.

The social life of children of substance-dependent parents can be quite fractured. The volatile path taken by substance-users often arises from and/or results in damaged relationships with the extended family, depriving children from infancy of positive interactions with grandparents, aunts, uncles, cousins and kin-like family friends. In addition, re-partnering by parents may lead to complex family structures, with siblings having different extended family constellations.

Complex extended families may provide diverse sources of help, but they also bring with them potentially competing values and demands for communication, tasks and social activities. We all experience tensions within our kinship groups, and perhaps say and do things we should not that we later regret. Substance misuse, with its problems of emotional and behavioural regulation, can exacerbate these normal ups and downs in family relationships, setting off a vicious spiral of mutual disappointments and recriminations. The path to recovery calls for re-evaluation of these relationships.

Family cultures tend to reflect the dominant culture of the social and ethnic groupings from which the family derives, so that there can be considerable variation in how parents and children are expected to behave towards each other and towards kin, in how news of alcohol and/or other drug abuse is received in the wider family, and in inter-generational caregiving expectations and obligations. For example, Indigenous mothers have reported significant care burdens within the extended family group, even while they struggle with improving their parenting and with their own trauma-related needs and recovery path. Sometimes kin, such as grandparents, try to improve children's lives but volatile relationships with the parents makes this support precarious and fraught with difficulty. Those who would help feel they lack the knowledge or legitimacy to do so, and often their efforts to reinvolve themselves with the client family are ignored by workers who worry about confidentiality issues and loyalty to parents. Yet these are the people who tend to become the first port of call for statutory authorities when children need temporary or permanent care away from home; kinship care is preferred for both philosophical and pragmatic reasons. For many children this allows them continuity of caring relationships with significant family members who can help them understand their parents' troubles. For other children, the estrangement has been such that renewed contact is more like contact with strangers. For a small number of children, entrusting their care to relatives is to condemn them to experiencing the kind of rejection, abuse or neglect their parents had experienced as children.

Beyond the extended family, problems such as stigma, parental withdrawal from community activities, poverty and housing instability may also make it harder for growing children to develop their own friendships at school or in leisure activities, a common way in which families in a community build supportive linkages. Substance-using peers in the parents' network can reinforce substance use rather than abstinence or harm reduction, simply impose distractions from the demands of parenting or sometimes pose an active risk to children through their own unregulated behaviour. Even so, they might be crucial to a parent's sense of identity, and to give up these friendships with no viable alternatives may leave the parent lonely and isolated.

Parents might, however, have peers or older family friends who do or could give considerable support in their child-rearing and in their recovery. While the early constructive engagement of kin and helpful friends in children's lives is generally more desirable than waiting until alternative care is needed, it is important to bear in mind that interventions into the social network are sensitive, and deserve the kind of care and attention given to other therapeutic interventions. While workers may be understandably reluctant to intrude into clients' extended family and peer relationships, collaboration with the family's natural helpers is often vital. Loneliness experienced on the path to recovery can engulf a parent and lead them back to substance-using networks or destructive relationships. As a worker, it is always necessary to ask yourself: 'When I have left, who will support the children and parents and help them confront new challenges?' Typically, the closer the perceived relationship between the user and the network member, the greater the likelihood of continuing support (De Civita, Dobkin & Robertson, 2000). It is also important to consider what help has been provided to significant others to enable them to keep providing support, both for parents' treatment plans and their parenting role, and to children directly. Parents may need encouragement and support to forge new relationships to integrate more fully with community life.

In addition, families often have complex needs and require a range of adult-focused services, such as alcohol and other drug treatment and mental health services, as well as child-focused services, such as maternal and child health or family support services. While each of these may intend to offer support, already stressed parents may experience this 'support' as surveillance and demands. Mothers, in particular, can feel monitored and scrutinised and resent this 'intrusion' into family life if their partners are not similarly under the professional gaze (Tsantefski, Humphreys & Jackson, 2014).

The number and complexity of problems makes it unlikely that any one service will have the skill, knowledge or resources to adequately meet the needs of all family members. Rather than receiving appropriate support, families can be shunted between services, particularly when there is substance use and mental illness, and fall through gaps in service provision. A holistic approach addressing alcohol and other drug treatment, mental health, family violence and children's needs, can be delivered by well-coordinated multidisciplinary and multi-agency services. Professional communication and collaboration spans a spectrum from loose coalitions, to cooperative efforts, to coordination, collaboration and finally service integration (Scott, 2013); however, partnership approaches between various services and sectors involved with children at risk of harm have been minimal. We are yet to see child protection, family support services, teachers and school welfare staff, medical personnel and alcohol and other drug treatment providers routinely form teams to support infants, children and young people. Instead, collaboration often functions on a personal level, based on relationships between individual workers in various agencies rather than on partnership between services; this precarious arrangement can leave families without support when staff changes occur.

Some workers will have specialty training and experience.

Maternal and child health nurses, for example, have considerable knowledge of infant health, child development and post-partum issues, and the skills and knowledge of these workers are needed to inform the practice of colleagues from other disciplines. Other workers bring significant understanding of substance dependence or mental illness and recovery. Statutory intervention has its place and creates an opportunity for collaborative practice between adult-focused and child-focused professionals.

However, even in cases in which a service provider believes child protection involvement is needed, risk to infants and children may not have crossed a threshold for mandated intervention and a report or notification may not be followed up or allocated a protective worker (see Chapter 6). In such instances, the role of case management is less clearly defined but potentially more critical to outcomes for the infant, child or family. Indeed, poor communication and collaboration between professionals is regularly identified as a major concern among the deaths of infants and children known to child protection authorities. Lack of role clarity and inadequate follow-up of referrals are often contributing factors (Frederico, Jackson & Dwyer, 2014). Assertive outreach and information sharing help to ensure children's safety and wellbeing.

INTENDED OUTCOMES

All family members have the benefit of meaningful and supportive relationships with family and friends. They participate in community activities that engage their talents and interests and open up new social relationships and lifestyle opportunities. Helpful members of the extended family and social network feel supported in their roles and relationships with children and parents, who in turn welcome their efforts. Service providers work in partnership with parents, with shared goals and, where possible and necessary, in collaboration with informal helpers, ensuring that parents and especially children receive timely and appropriate help with practical problems and developmental tasks. The family has stable access to housing, education, health services and income. Through planned communication and shared expertise, professionals ensure that complementary roles of different service providers are well delineated and coordinated in order to prevent families being caught in the middle or receiving mixed messages. As a result, families do not experience duplication, delays or gaps in service provision.

HELPFUL ATTITUDES AND VALUES

Collaborative work requires respect for the role and mandate of other professionals and services working with families. You need to dispense with the feeling that you have to do everything yourself and instead see yourself as part of a 'care-team'. This mindset extends to members of the family's social network, especially when they play an important role in keeping children safe and enriching their lives. Be open-minded about roles and relationships in kinship and social networks, and be cautious about imposing your own culturally determined expectations on clients' friends and families. When in doubt about the typical behaviour in a culturally diverse population or in the families of Indigenous peoples, it is always wise to ask rather than to make assumptions. Remember, principles of love and care tend to be common across all cultures, but the way in which they are expressed may look quite different to an outsider. Commitment to working collaboratively with other helpers, professions, agencies and sectors entails seeing collaboration as part of your core role rather than as a time-consuming peripheral component.

EXPECTATIONS OF OTHER PROFESSIONALS/ EXPECTATIONS OF YOURSELF

You will be prepared to listen, learn and liaise with informal helpers and professionals in other sectors and services, and willing to change your ways of working to achieve more efficient and effective coordinated responses. You will seek to understand and reconcile philosophical difference between professional groups—for example, the harm minimisation approach underpinning alcohol and other drug treatment and the focus on the child's best interests in the child welfare sector. You will also regard informal helpers as part of the care team and respectfully include them in decisions and actions.

EXPECTATIONS OF CLIENTS

If families are to experience well-articulated formal and informal care as constructive, they should be encouraged to be open and honest about what is and is not working for them. They need to tell workers if they are finding care too complicated, intrusive or onerous in terms of time demands. They should give direct advice about the practicality and prioritisation of multiple activities with multiple helpers. In relation to the informal network, they may need the courage and determination to let go of destructive ties and review and heal old relationships.

BARRIERS TO COLLABORATION

Collaboration with informal helpers may be impeded by parents' shame or embarrassment about asking for help, and their fears that workers might make extended family relationships worse if they stir up old hurts or use relatives as 'spies' on their parenting. These fears can be reduced if workers are honest about their goals, and work with parents to negotiate the roles and activities of wider family members.

Workers can be passionate advocates for the identified client and fail to see the whole family as the unit of attention or the way children's and parents' needs are intertwined; this is frequently the source of conflict between professionals with different perspectives. Indeed, those different perspectives have some validity, for the parent might present quite differently in different settings, such as the counselling room, the men's group or the playgroup, showing different skills and vulnerabilities. Differences in organisational functions and cultures can result in different attitudes and practices with the same client group; these differences need to be reconciled for good, collaborative practice.

Poor communication and the failure to clarify roles and responsibilities creates a potentially deadly situation for infants and children. Different reporting requirements and anxiety about the release of information and privacy can leave individual workers with snippets of information rather than a whole picture, again a source of risk for vulnerable infants and children. This situation can be exacerbated by hierarchies related to professional status in which some workers do not share information or decision-making with other professionals, by limited understanding of the roles and legal responsibilities of others, and by the lack of information sharing and referral protocols between services. Good practice may be hindered by differences in perception between professionals, and between professionals and families, on who is best placed to support parents and children.

STRATEGIES TO IMPROVE THE FAMILY'S INFORMAL SOCIAL ECONOMY

Map and evaluate the network

Network assessment was discussed in Chapter 5. It can be helpful for parents and children to draw a network map, showing who is in the network, the strength and direction of the flow of care, affection and onerous demands in those relationships, and where there are significant cut-offs. Explore the culture of families of origin and the impact of these cultures on parents and children and on potential helpers. Who is important to the child and family and available to see, nurture and protect the child while supporting the parent? Do they know about the substance use and how have they responded? Are there people in the network who are trusted to monitor the wellbeing of children and parents and to take action in times of crisis? In some cultures, extended family members will play very significant roles in caring for children, and parenting may be shared among a large group of adults, including aunts, uncles and grandparents.

Ask about what obligations the parents carry in relation to kin, and how these obligations impact on their personal functioning, their substance use and their parenting. Potentially more sensitive are questions about who is *not* helpful. Which people and relationships in the network draw the parents' time and attention away from the children and parenting responsibilities?

Repair network breaches

Many substance-using parents have burnt their bridges in their social network through unreliable or criminal behaviour, or excessive expectations of support with no reciprocity. Even so, many family members and significant others are able to distinguish such behaviour from the needs of children and are prepared to rally around an infant or child and to rebuild fractured relationships with support from professionals. Use family decision-making processes (family group conferences) wherever possible to maximise participation by children, parents, members of the extended family and the broader social network, including significant others in the family's life (e.g. friends and neighbours) (Arney, Chong & McGuinness, 2013; Morris & Connolly, 2012).

With parents and children, develop priorities about which linkages should be strengthened, paying attention not only to those that are most desired, but also to those that are most likely to be re-engaged in a timely manner. Work with the family to identify who will reach out to these relatives, and what kind of contact ought to be tried first. Although you do need to consider the children's needs even if parents are hesitant about turning to others, you can still do this cautiously, taking your cues from the parents, by asking questions like: 'Who helped you feel safe as you were growing up?' 'Where are they now, and what might they be willing to do?' 'How would you like to open up contact? Can we help?'

Ask parents for details and permission to contact family, friends and neighbours in an emergency. Extended family and network members may need to be gently reminded that denigrating the parent to the child can be detrimental to children's emotional wellbeing. This is not to say that the parent should be whitewashed but rather that the child needs a realistic understanding of their parent, information commensurate with their age and developmental level, and an empathic response from those close to them.

Reduce threats from the network

Identify sources of danger to parents or children, past and present, both within the extended family and within the peer network. How do children and parents manage that danger and what would they like to do about their future contact with those people? Are legal measures, such as intervention or restraining orders, required to lessen the risk from abusers and, if they are already in place, are they working? With the parents, consider changes in routine or lifestyle that can reduce contact with those whose harmful influence needs to be reduced, or build safety mechanisms around such contact when it cannot be stopped. For example, where a parent has been abused as a child by a relative, and finds contact reactivates trauma reactions, are there advocates and protective people in the network with legitimacy to intervene and block contact with the perpetrator? Family group conferences can be helpful in such instances, because the extended family may have knowledge and informal power that you as a worker may never possess, and they have the capacity to be present at the kind of family events that workers will never attend. Similarly, if parents are trying to move out of a substance-using peer network, encourage them to identify alternative actions when contact with those peers is likely and rehearse ways of handling friends' expectations.

Strengthen the child's own network

In addition to working with the extended family, find out how the child is going at school and establish whether the parent has any involvement with teachers or the wider school community, including other parents and children. Has the child made friends? How can this be facilitated? Real or perceived stigma often prevents parents from engaging with school. Relations can be strengthened by supporting parents to communicate directly with the child's teacher and by encouraging the parent to attend school events.

Find out if the child participates in any sport or recreational groups and support involvement wherever possible as a way of linking the child with the wider community. Nurturing the child's own talents and interests within relevant social groups is a key method for optimising his or her normal life opportunities and reducing the likelihood of the child developing their own substance use and other problems—for example, dropping out of school, teenage pregnancy and antisocial behaviour. Consider what financial or other resources (transport, for example) the child might need to be able to develop a more enriched life, independent of what is happening at home.

Help to build new connections

Overcoming dependence on alcohol or other drugs often requires that parents move away from existing networks, which increases loneliness among people who are already isolated. Provide additional support to parents and children at such critical times, where possible using kin to help. Engagement in meaningful work, education or other socially valued community activity is critical to parental recovery and relapse prevention, and it also has the advantage of widening the family's exposure to new friendships and activities. Encourage parents to take up such opportunities wherever possible, but remember that for some parents, long-seated isolation and social rejection has damaged their social confidence and competence, which need to be relearned and nurtured. It may be necessary to use the resources of your own and other services to provide stepping stones to social engagement through such activities as specialist playgroups, educational preparation programs or volunteer activities. Some families may need suggestions, behavioural coaching or practical resources to help them make use of the social opportunities available to their children through school or extracurricular activities. A variety of models exist for the use of mentors and volunteers to supplement the network, including peers from twelve-step programs, recovery mentors, Big Brothers Big Sisters, older volunteers as grandparent alternatives, and respite carers.

Provide support to significant others

Bearing in mind that extended family members may feel confused and despairing to the point that they feel useless and out of their depth in relation to substance use and the change cycle, establish who might need information and support, and plan how that will be offered and given. Unless they have experienced their own substance use problems, many can lack understanding of addiction or the process of recovery, which undermines confidence and limits the ability to provide effective support. Providing information can therefore be a simple, yet essential, intervention in empowerment (De Civita, Dobkin & Robertson, 2000). It is not uncommon for grandparents to feel responsible for their adult child's problems or for parents to harbour resentments, particularly if children are in the care of grandparents. This makes for an emotionally charged family environment and troubled communication. Family members should be encouraged to speak to one another openly and directly, without attack or blame. If this is too difficult, mediation should be offered. Secrecy, minimisation and distortions of the truth should be discouraged. Instead, the substance-using parent could be encouraged, where appropriate, to invite significant others to participate in their treatment plan. This inclusiveness should be extended to non-using partners, siblings and significant others. Additionally, network members often appreciate help for themselves to enable them to keep caring for parents and children. This often requires outreach to a greater number of people, and greater flexibility in working hours and environments, which may need to include grandparents' homes. Making yourself available by phone can be enough in some instances. Video-conferencing via electronic media offers other possibilities. Whatever form contact with the wider network takes, remember to seek consent for exchange of information first, outline limits to confidentiality and provide reassurance to parents who express reluctance to involve significant others in treatment plans that their needs, and those of their children, will remain central to your practice. This is particularly important as fractured families often try to 'triangulate' the worker in a coalition against others.

Observing the loss of control in addiction and fearing consequences of use, for both the individual and their child or children, can cause great anxiety for significant others who may feel like they are walking on eggshells around the parent (De Civita, Dobkin & Robertson, 2000, page 141). Linking network members with people in the same situation can be a source of comfort, particularly as embarrassment and stigma often drives network members to conceal excessive alcohol consumption or use of illicit drugs in the family. Connecting with others is also important for developing strategies to cope with the erratic behaviour often seen in addiction and in managing the negative feelings it can engender such as fear, resentment and self-recrimination. While there are many benefits for parents and children, involving significant others in treatment is not without risk. Relations can become more conflicted if significant others judge that insufficient progress towards recovery is being made. From their perspective, parents may feel that support is dependent upon meeting unrealistic or unmatchable expectations and withdraw from those who are potentially most helpful (De Civita, Dobkin & Robertson, 2000).

Significant others may benefit from referral to other services for counselling for themselves. If they have children in their care, they may need material resources to ease the financial burden (see Chapter 9).

STRATEGIES TO HELP FAMILIES MAKE GOOD USE OF FORMAL SOCIAL ORGANISATIONS

Secure basic resources

Financial strain and poor, inappropriate or unstable housing are common among families with parental substance dependence, creating a vicious circle of crises and dislocations that sabotage attempts at recovery and make it all the more difficult to build a stable family lifestyle within a supportive network. It is important that families be linked with community resources, ideally before problems escalate. Financial counselling and debt management are often important, and stable housing is crucial. For well-motivated families with infants and young children, residential alcohol and other drug treatment and supported housing models should be considered if available. Families in private rental housing are particularly vulnerable, and may need a lot of your support and advocacy time, and some monetary assistance, if they are to remain housed and become embedded in a community. For infants and young children, some form of supplementary high-quality child care can be an important aid to their development. Explore what your own service and others in its network can offer to help gain access and defray costs.

Strengthen families' interactions with service providers

It is not uncommon for substance-dependent parents to feel stigmatised and isolated, but fearful of professionals. They may need encouragement and coaching to connect with the child's school and other community agencies such as neighbourhood houses, preschool and early childhood development programs. Fast-track referrals when child safety is an issue or when infants and children are developmentally delayed, and ensure other workers involved with the family are aware of any potential delays in service delivery. As noted in Chapter 6, simply making a referral is not enough. Do not assume that referrals will result in services being provided or accepted, but actively follow up referrals and ensure that engagement with other service providers has been established before closing cases. For example, it may be necessary to accompany parents to appointments with the maternal and child health service for advice on child health and development or to parenting support programs such as playgroup until they feel confident to attend alone. For school-aged children, maintaining school attendance and good information flow between parent and teacher will be crucial for their educational experience, their social development and sometimes their safety. Some parents, especially those who have had poor educational experiences themselves, or whose reputation precedes them, may need coaching about how to sustain reliable school attendance and manage communication with the school, supplemented on occasion by mediation and advocacy with the school. If you cannot do this work yourself, seek out the intermediaries within the school support system.

As multiple agencies are engaged, clarify roles and responsibilities for tasks, not only between professionals, but also between workers and family members and ensure parents remain responsible for family life, including children's safety and wellbeing.

Improve service system responsiveness to the whole family

Many social and health services have specialised functions and are not automatically attuned to the needs of family members other than the identified client. To widen the focus takes conscious effort on the part of workers, and inclusive policies and procedures on the part of managers. Advocate for your agency to be represented in relevant inter-organisational network activities, such as joint training and policy development.

Alcohol and other drug treatment agencies need to ensure the agency is inclusive of children and has a safe, child-friendly space with toys, furniture and other resources, so that parents can feel free to seek treatment and bring their children with them. Small innovations can have wider benefits. For example, one agency (ReGen in Melbourne) found that simply starting a playgroup on the premises for parents and preschool children brought children and their needs into view, and helped drug treatment workers to relate to their clients not just as substance-users, but as parents (Gruenert & Tsantefski, 2012). Sharing such innovations with your peer organisations is helpful, through newsletters and conferences. In the UK, ADFAM (see Useful websites and resources) seeks to keep professionals abreast of issues and innovations in the area of families and alcohol and other drug use.

Specialisation also means that workers in any one setting must develop awareness of the types and availability of other programs for families affected by substance use. For example, if you are not in an alcohol or other drug service, you will need to know what drug and alcohol treatment options are available in your area in order to make appropriate and timely referrals. Because many clients will have tried treatment options previously, they may have strong views on what is available and how appropriate it is, but real conversation on these matters requires you to be up-to-date and well-acquainted with exactly what is on offer, how it can be accessed and what efforts it will require of the family. Where clients have had difficulties with particular services, explore how such difficulties might be overcome in a new referral, with both the client and the agency to which you want to refer. You will be better able to work collaboratively and resolve problems between families and services if you maintain links with other service providers, and earn respect as a reliable and reasonable professional. Some parents will require that you, or if this is not feasible, another worker or an informal helper, accompany them to assessment and intake for alcohol and other drug treatment.

Pay special attention to whether services are responsive to infants, since these children cannot speak for themselves and sometimes remain almost invisible. Screening and referral for early intervention with pregnant women in particular, and parents in general, should be undertaken at the earliest opportunity. All services should attend to the particular difficulties of parenting infants. Programs and interventions designed for other populations may not be effective with substance-using parents and their children who may require longer-term and more intensive support. For example, vulnerable parents are less likely to respond positively to general health warnings such as safe sleeping practices to reduce SIDS.

For intensive, change-oriented work with vulnerable families with complex needs, keep caseloads small; four to eight families per week per full-time worker may be manageable.

Build professional communication and collaboration

Identify providers and clarify roles

Establish if another service is engaged with or already known to the family (e.g. a medical practitioner or the maternal and child health nurse), and conduct practice within inter-agency frameworks. For instance, many jurisdictions will have explicit protocols between alcohol and other drug treatment providers and child protection services about their respective responsibilities. Most importantly, establish who will take responsibility for leading the coordination of services; this is a critical strategy in ensuring families do not fall through the cracks. Determine who is best placed to assess child and family well-being, including parenting capacity and alcohol and other drug use. Determine (together with parents) how the wellbeing of children will be monitored: who will see and speak to the child? Clarify roles and responsibilities and set time-frames for action, including review.

Work within communication and information protocols

Use common frameworks and develop shared language—for example, what do 'the child's best interests' and 'cumulative harm' mean in the context of child and family support, and what does 'harm reduction' mean in the context of alcohol and other drug treatment? Enter into a respectful dialogue with other service sectors to reconcile potentially opposing philosophies. For instance, harm minimisation, as practised by alcohol and other drug treatment providers, sometimes clashes with the abstinence requirements made by child protection services. Establish memoranda of understanding (MOUs) or protocols between services providers to promote collaborative practice; these documents should include client consent and release of information forms, referral criteria and information, assessment methods and record keeping or other data collection.

Whatever the differences of orientation, it will be necessary to comply with statutory requirements regarding information sharing, mandatory reporting of child abuse or neglect, and other protective measures. These will vary between jurisdictions. For example, workers need to know the legislative time-frames for reunification of children to parental care before court orders for alternative permanent care are initiated and to convey these to parents.

Information sharing can be experienced by family members as an invasion of privacy and as disempowering unless it has the support and involvement of the parent or family (and even then it can be challenging). Where possible, seek parental consent for release of information and explain why services need to keep each other informed about parental and family progress. Sharing of information needs to include information for service providers and for the family about respective approaches to this particular family: what is the aim of counselling, what approach is used, how will a successful outcome be measured?

Coordinate efforts through a care team

Coordinate efforts with other services to ensure family members receive appropriate and timely help. Consider improving multidisciplinary prevention and intervention efforts through delivery of joint services—for example, you might include an alcohol or other drug treatment worker in a family-focused program or invite a family service to introduce a playgroup or children's group into an adult-focused service.

Even with quite different roles and methods, child protection, mental health and drug treatment workers, and other providers, together with families, can set goals that address both parental substance use and requirements for child safety and development. Avoid setting goals and objectives in silos; instead, develop joint case plans with other service providers focused on the needs of parents and children for an integrated approach to working with families. Use case conferences and other information-sharing forums to arrive at a consensus with parents and other professionals regarding what action needs to take place and how progress will be monitored and measured.

Coordination can simplify the work, streamlining who does what and when, avoiding duplication of effort and reducing competing demands on the family. As problems increase in severity and complexity, simple coordination may develop into serious service integration through a care team that communicates regularly. This will mean substantial knowledge sharing to enable a shared commitment to each other's ways of working. Depending on your professional background and experience, you may need to develop knowledge of the risk and resilience frameworks used by child protection and family support services, or to develop understanding of the pharmacology of substances and issues in use and treatment. At times, you may need to work together in each other's work settings, or in the family home.

TIPS FOR NEW WORKERS

Informal networks

- All parents need support and encouragement in child-rearing; parents with a history of substance use are likely to need much more.
- Even when they are presented as currently alienated from the family, grandparents and other relatives have often had an active role in children's lives and will again. With support and care they may be re-engaged.
- Children's services and schools provide many opportunities for developing alternative social networks, when parents and children are equipped to make use of these; when they are not, families should be assisted to fully engage with their community.

Formal networks

- Basic financial and housing stability provides a platform from which many other positive changes can be launched.
- Other professionals stop providing information or collaborating unless they receive timely feedback; therefore, keep people in the loop.
- Early intervention and timely responses can prevent problems developing or reduce their severity—for example, pregnancy outcomes can be improved, relapse might not last as long, homelessness could be averted, children may not be harmed or removed from parental care.
- Collaboration between adult- and child-focused services can improve the effectiveness of children's court and family drug court orders by encouraging and supporting parents to genuinely comply with conditions.
- Many substance-using parents have had prior involvement with child protection services either as child clients in their own right, or as parents; these experiences are likely to influence their relationship with service providers, positively or negatively.

- Good collaborative inter-sectoral practice can reduce the likelihood of child protection workers being maligned by families fearful of child removal and increase parental acceptance of, and engagement with, the service.
- Written consent for release of information, which includes the limits to information sharing, can ease parental and worker anxieties about privacy issues.
- Side-taking can be avoided by focusing on positive outcomes for both children and parents.

TRAPS FOR NEW WORKERS

- Expecting parents to give up their substance-using friends and lifestyle with no real alternatives on offer.
- Ignoring the information and support needs of extended family members yet asking a great deal of them in a crisis.
- Excluding parents from a team approach—for example, not inviting them to attend meetings due to worker anxiety.
- Not working transparently with other service providers, or changing plans and not informing other workers.
- Attempting to cope with the demands of case work with vulnerable infants, children and parents alone rather than bringing other services and members of the extended family and network on board.
- Not understanding the role and mandate of other professions and consequently having unrealistic expectations—for example, that alcohol and other drug workers will be able to attend meetings or home visits, or that child protection workers will immediately remove a child from a home because of parental substance use.
- Supporting a culture of blame or playing good cop/bad cop and colluding with parents or other service providers.

HOW WILL I KNOW IF I'M ON TRACK?

- Children are kept safe while parental substance use is managed.
- Children and parents have someone other than you to whom they turn in times of need.
- Family members and professionals work in partnership to address child safety and wellbeing.
- Parents understand how each service works and are not confused by contradictory messages.
- The family's needs are met as effectively and efficiently as possible within service availability.
- You know who is working with the family and whom you can call upon to monitor child safety and wellbeing and provide practical and other support to parents and extended family members.
- You know the policies and procedures, court processes and inter-agency agreements that govern child protection practice and meet legal and policy requirements.
- You have a shared perspective and approach with workers across sectors.
- Families understand the need for professional communication and collaboration and feel supported, not threatened, by it.

ENHANCING INFORMAL AND FORMAL FAMILY SUPPORT: STELLA AND JIM

Stella, Jim and their worker talked about what constituted positive and negative social support. The couple decided to see less of some network members and gradually increased contact with Jim's brother, his wife and their children. They maintained a close relationship with Joan. Both parents continued to warmly welcome the worker to their home but did not engage with services other than the child health nurse, and even then only reluctantly. The worker gradually introduced them to new members of her own team who conducted home visits while she was on leave or unavailable. Stella joined in recreational activities held by the agency but Jim chose not to.

ENHANCING INFORMAL AND FORMAL FAMILY SUPPORT: KEVIN

Kevin agreed that the escalation in his substance use was detrimental to Zac's wellbeing and expressed ambivalence about continuing to care for him. The worker strongly encouraged him to enter a detoxification facility. She accompanied him to medical and psychosocial assessments and contacted a family support service for respite care for Zac. After discharge, Kevin resumed care of Zac and continued to use respite care on a regular basis. With time, he decided Zac's needs would best be met in a more stable home and voluntarily relinquished his care.

SUMMARY

Strengthening the family from the outside, by repairing and building strong informal and formal support around the children and parents, is a substantial area of practice, but we can identify several key messages. First, the network of family and friends should not be discounted as an important source of help to parents and especially to children, since they provide a potential source of continuing support and safeguarding when workers have moved on. Involving them in your work with the family may be contentious and require sensitivity to those relationships that are inherently harmful, as well as to those who offer potential for help. Second, parents who are being asked to give up a social network and a lifestyle that reduces their sense of loneliness, however dysfunctional, need to be able to see a viable alternative network and way of living. Third, stability in the basic necessities of family life, especially money and housing, underpins change. Fourth, workers are rarely able to act alone, and collaboration across agencies and sectors on behalf of children and families requires its own learning, practice development and infrastructure.

9

Supporting families when children are in care

This chapter outlines issues for parents, children and carers, many of whom are grandparents, when children are placed in out-of-home care, either temporarily or permanently. As noted previously, parental substance misuse is present in many, if not most, child protection cases. These cases take longer to resolve from notification to closure, including the making of court orders, than cases where parents do not misuse substances. This can leave children and families in a state of uncertainty and heightened anxiety. The children of substance-dependent parents are overrepresented in out-of-home care. Children in families affected by parental substance misuse tend to enter care earlier and to remain in care longer. Removal from parental care is more likely when parents use illicit substances or illicit substances in combination with alcohol than when parents use alcohol only (De Bortoli, Coles & Dolan, 2013). Whether temporarily or permanently placed, many children are there because problems associated with parental substance use left them unsafe. The most important predictor of removal from the home is parental non-compliance with court orders and directions from child protection services (De Bortoli, Coles & Dolan, 2013).

This not only exacts a high personal toll for individual children, their parents and carers, all of whom need support in their own right, it also represents a significant financial burden for tax-payers. Many substance-using parents have been child clients of child protection services or in out-of-home care themselves as children or adolescents;

problems in the family of origin, sometimes across generations, make it harder for parents to access support for themselves and their children, and they may therefore require more support than other families. Placement prevention is an important first measure; when this fails, reunification plans should be supported in most circumstances.

Child removal reduces parental motivation to address alcohol and other drug issues. There tends to be a reduction in contact with parents after children are placed in out-of-home care, particularly if they are in non-kinship placements. The grief, loss and anger parents experience when children are placed may escalate substance use, while emotional responses to contact visits with the child can stimulate relapse even for parents who are working towards resuming care of the child. Many substance-dependent parents have little faith that their actions will result in reunification with children. They often lack an advocate or support. Workers need to know if the jurisdiction under which they are operating has timelines for reunification of children to parental care prior to the making of permanent care or adoption orders, and to inform parents of this possibility. The longer reunification is delayed, the less likely it is to happen. If not well-planned or implemented, reunification often fails and children re-enter the out-of-home care system, having experienced greater instability in care.

Parents often do not qualify for family support programs if children are not in their care, although some family services may accept a referral for a family after a reunification plan has been implemented. All workers involved with parents and children therefore need to know if there is a reunification plan and to support it by working collaboratively on shared goals. If out-of-home care remains an appropriate response to the seriousness of parenting difficulties, and children's best interests are served by remaining in a good placement, it does not inevitably mean that they should lose contact with their families; nor does it mean their parents should lose access to support for themselves as people and as parents. Children need to have a relationship with their parents or, at the very least, a realistic perception of their parents and family for identity formation.

Children are frequently placed in the care of grandparents, usually grandmothers, and members of the extended family. Others are cared for by non-kinship carers in foster care or other formal placements. Children in kinship placements often live impoverished lives without the resources available to children in other out-of-home care settings. Children of substance-dependent parents can be more difficult to care for than their peers. Some have been severely abused, emotionally or physically neglected, or exposed to such traumatic events as witnessing a parent's overdose or domestic or other violence. When the mother has been alcohol dependent, there is a possibility of FASD, possibly undiagnosed. Substance use can be part of significant intergenerational problems in a family's history and functioning. Some of these issues may remain unresolved and be a source of conflict among family members. Grandparents can feel guilty if they believe they have contributed to the alcohol and other drug problems of their adult child. They may also feel resentful if they think that caring for grandchildren enables the adult child to continue with substance use without having to assume parenting responsibilities. Carers therefore often need support to manage children's behaviour, financial assistance, respite care and support in managing their own emotional responses.

INTENDED OUTCOMES

A successful out-of-home placement should achieve several ends. The child is well-nurtured by carers who understand and care about the child and his or her family. The child's attachment relationships are maintained and the child enjoys meaningful contact with parents, siblings, grandparents and extended family and network members based on the child's needs. The child should have stable care and continuity with school and friendships, wherever possible. Contact between the child and parent is safe and valuable to the child, whether or not the parent is still using alcohol and/or other drugs, and the child has a realistic understanding of their family as well as achieves or maintains a continuous and positive sense of identity. If the child returns home, it is to a better functioning family and safer environment in which their needs will be prioritised. In the best of worlds, the child returns home and their parents maintain supportive contact with the former carers so that, again, the child has a sense of continuity of identity and relationships.

HELPFUL ATTITUDES AND VALUES

Once again, respect is needed: respect for all people without dichoto-mising the 'good' carer and the 'bad' substance-using parent, and respect for the child's wishes regarding contact with parents and other family and network members.

EXPECTATIONS OF CLIENTS

When children are being placed in alternative care, emotions often run high, and it can be difficult to set behavioural expectations for parents and kin. Any worker involved with the family at such a time needs to encourage a calm focus on the children, by asking that the needs of the child remain paramount from the perspective of all concerned: parents, family members and other carers. When the children are in placement, parents and other significant family members are asked to work steadily towards achieving goals set for either contact with the child or reunifica-tion to parental care.

EXPECTATIONS OF YOURSELF

Whatever your formal role with the family, your attitudes to the placement can make a difference to the quality of the experience

for the child, parent and carers. Encourage hopefulness as an anti-
dote to despair, even when children have been placed in permanent
care, by helping the parent and child understand they can still have
meaningful contact and play an important part in each other's lives.
Work to remain empathetic and non-judgemental when parents
fail to meet expectations—for example, not maintaining all contact
arrangements—and if your role permits, offer debriefing and assistance. Treat parents with dignity at all times and be respectful of their
parenting role.

If you are in a position of power as a child protection or placement
worker, try not to change the goal-posts, such as adding new goals for
the parent to achieve before reunification can occur, but work towards
helping them steadily achieve goals that have already been set. Consider
the needs of all family members, including kinship and other carers,
and respond in a supportive manner to identified needs or problems
either directly or by referral to other service providers.

BARRIERS TO SUPPORTING CHILDREN AND PARENTS WHEN CHILDREN ARE NO LONGER IN PARENTAL CARE

We have referred previously to shame as an emotion commonly
reported by mothers who abuse substances. Deep shame and fear
of judgement often prevents parents from maintaining contact with
infants and children in care. The more stigmatised they feel, and the
more invidious the comparisons between the child's impoverished or
chaotic life at home and his or her well-resourced life in care, the
sharper the self-judgement and the less parents are likely to visit.
Parents will sometimes use alcohol or other drugs prior to a scheduled visit to numb feelings of emotional pain; service providers will
sometimes refuse to allow a child to see a parent if they consider the
parent substance-affected. A downward spiral leading to estrangement between parent and child can become established.

Understandably, carers of children who have experienced severe neglect and abuse may have powerful protective feelings towards the child which inhibit the process of family contact and reunification. Often, while funding and service agreements support carers, there are fewer services with a mandate to work with parents after children have been removed from their care. This can leave parents feeling alienated, depressed and seemingly unmotivated; the latter can be misconstrued as the parent being disinterested in the child. Despite the resources dedicated to the out-of-home care system, many carers, especially kinship carers, feel inadequately supported in their care of children who may be traumatised and developmentally and educationally delayed. Maintaining good contact between children and their parents is then experienced as a further burden for which they may feel ill-equipped, especially if they have a history of conflict with the parents. Supporting these carers can be inhibited by lack of knowledge of substance use and recovery issues in the placement agency and carers themselves may erect barriers to support if they fear the support will be intrusive and will undermine their surrogate parenting role.

KEY STRATEGIES FOR WORKING WITH CHILDREN AND PARENTS WHEN CHILDREN ARE NO LONGER IN PARENTAL CARE

As we have noted previously, not all workers will perform all the tasks we identify, but regardless of your role, if you are working with any party to a child placement where the parents have substance misuse issues, you should be aware of the range of activities needed, and be alert to whether these are being undertaken in a systematic way by some member of the care team. Whether you are an alcohol and other drug, child welfare, family services or other worker, you can play a part in assisting all family members and carers to reduce negative talk about other family members and carers, particularly in the presence of children. Along with colleagues across the service network (see Chapter 8), you can help ensure that there are clearly designated workers responsible for monitoring and supporting the child, the parents and the carers during any placement. You can also be an advocate for using care preventatively as respite and support for parents, children and families and, where possible, build respite into secondary intervention services as an integral part of a program, rather than something to be used in moments of crisis. Depending on your role as negotiated with the family and colleagues, you may also need to work in any of the ways outlined below. Most of these suggestions relate to common family scenarios of parental substance abuse where child neglect and disrupted lifestyle have been the major issues. In more severe cases, where there is evidence that the child has been severely abused or traumatised, you may need more explicit guidance from specialist child protection or child and adolescent mental health workers to deal with the special needs of children, parents and carers.

Work with children

If you are in contact with the child during placement, assess the child's needs on a regular basis and be responsive to the child's wishes for more or less contact with parents, family members and significant others. Make sure you observe the child's behaviour during access, particularly that of non-verbal infants, for vital clues on the child's feelings and wishes. Support the child's contact with siblings who may be in different placements and try to ensure that sibling relationships are also developed and maintained if they are safe. Offer realistic reassurance that the child is loved by their parent even if they are unable to live together due to problems the parent faces, such as substance dependence, mental health, incarceration or other reasons, bolstering this sense of positive connection by any means possible, such as letters, photographs or transitional objects.

Facilitate positive family contact

Help to build bridges between family members when children are in the care of grandparents or other relatives, or between parents and foster carers, wherever possible. Assist the parent and child to stay in regular contact through cards and telephone calls when visits are not possible; discourage contact only if it is detrimental to the child's long-term wellbeing. Help to minimise the child's disappointment when parents either do not turn up for scheduled visits or are denied access to the child if they present as substance-affected. For instance, the parent can be required to call before the scheduled visit to confirm their attendance and to provide assurance they will not 'use' before arriving. Assist children and parents before, during and after contact visits to enhance the quality of the experience. Prepare the parent for meaningful interaction with the child by encouraging the parent to play with their child and express affection during supervised access when the parent may be feeling scrutinised and self-conscious.

Support parents during legal processes

Inform parents that there are legislative time-frames for reunification of children to parental care before **permanent care orders** are enacted (in some jurisdictions, timelines are dependent on the age of the infant or child and the amount of time out of parental care within a given time-frame, according to the infant or child's age). Be clear about what parents need to achieve before contact with the child or reunification can occur. Provide direct assistance to parents to access services and supports as soon as possible to reduce the likelihood of an escalation in alcohol and other drug use in response to grief and loss, which will make reunifications harder and take longer to achieve, if at all.

Wherever possible, assist the parent to attend to conditions on children's court orders or requirements of family drug courts (e.g. attend alcohol and other drug counselling, obtain more appropriate housing). Work in partnership with parents and legal officers to determine the right degree of access with children; recommending more contact can be counterproductive if the parent is unable to keep up the number of visits due to limited funding for public transport, lengthy travel times or other constraints such as appointments with health or alcohol and other drug treatment providers.

Support parents while children are in long-term care

Parents whose children have been removed still need assistance as parents, albeit those who have lost the care of their children. Consider running groups for parents who have lost the care of children for mutual support; such groups can assist with grief and loss, dignified contact with children and carers, building a new lifestyle and parenting of subsequent children.

In situations where reunification is not feasible, relinquishing counselling, given by an appropriately experienced counsellor, can help the parent accept it is in the child's best interests to receive stable care by an alternative caregiver; in such circumstances, parents are likely to feel guilt and remorse and to require assistance to maintain meaningful contact with the child and to remain motivated to continue with rehabilitation.

Support caregivers

Make sure that carers' voices are heard and responded to in any case planning, review and inter-agency case coordination meetings. Provide flexible financial and other support such as information and counselling to foster or kith and kin carers, within the constraints of funding, role and agency mandate. Ensure grandparents and other carers are receiving social security payments and any other entitlements. Try to link kinship carers with others in the same situation for mutual support, as they typically receive little education on alcohol and other drug issues or practical or emotional support from service providers. Locate, adapt and make accessible to carers any relevant publications, websites, training and mentoring programs from the alcohol and other drug services sector that will assist them to understand and meet the special needs of children in their care, and help them in their relationships with parents. Pay special attention to the help carers may need to understand (and to help children understand) substance use and recovery, and to any assistance kinship carers may need to overcome long-standing tensions and rifts in the family. If you have a formal arrangement for cross-sectoral program coordination and development at the interface of alcohol and other drug, child and family welfare, and mental health services, seek carer representation in that forum.

TIPS FOR NEW WORKERS

- The child's wishes regarding placement is an important predictor of stability of placement.
- Grandparents may not want the substance-use history of their adult children known to grandchildren or others, therefore ask before discussing it with others or in the presence of children.
- Children can be confused by secrecy and denial, and torn by conflicting loyalties to carers and parents; it is important to not only gain an understanding of the child's awareness of the role of alcohol and other drug use in the family, but also their emotional reactions to the impact on themselves and the family.
- Children value honesty; they may feel sad but not abandoned if they are told the truth—for example, that their mother is in jail and for how long, not that she has gone on a holiday and will be back in a few weeks—and ensure that information is conveyed in language children understand.

TRAPS FOR NEW WORKERS

- Services can advocate strongly for the respite/foster carer or the parent and overlook the wishes of the child or the family as a whole.

- Carers and services can perceive the child's distress after contact with the parent as negative, however, it creates an opportunity to explore the child's feelings and the meaning the parent has for the child.
- Forgetting that other children have similar but less stigmatised experiences when they spend time with grandparents and members of the extended family or network, particularly at family transition points—for example, after the birth of a new infant or when there are difficulties in the family such as illness.

HOW WILL I KNOW IF I'M ON TRACK?

- You will recognise that child removal has a profound impact on families and constitutes an emotional crisis for both children and their families.
- You will know if there is a reunification plan and how you may be able to support it by working with parents, family, network members and other service providers.
- You will acknowledge the chronic relapsing nature of recovery from substance dependence rather than assigning moral judgement or blame when parents do not meet expectations for resumed contact or reunification with the child.
- Children's long-term connection to parents and significant others will be maintained unless it is against the child's best interests to do so.

SUPPORTING STELLA AND JIM WHEN MIA AND SOPHIE WERE NOT IN THEIR CARE

Police were called to Stella and Jim's home after an altercation between members of the extended family. Later in the day, child protection removed the children from the home as authorities deemed both parents intoxicated and unable to safely care for them (both parents disputed this in relation to Jim). Mia and Sophie were placed in foster care and a contested hearing was scheduled in the children's court. The AOD worker suggested the conditions on the order be determined with input from Stella and Jim. Child protection agreed to meet with both parents and the worker. Agreement was reached and the contested hearing was cancelled. Six weeks later the children were returned to their parents after they each provided urine screens indicating no illicit substance use or excessive use of alcohol. The worker continued to visit the home and modelled a collaborative working relationship with child protection.

SUPPORTING KEVIN WHEN ZAC WAS NOT IN HIS CARE

Zac was initially placed in a six-month voluntary placement which did not require child protection involvement. The worker continued to visit Kevin and encouraged him to maintain a close relationship with his son. The worker organised a meeting with the foster care agency and the foster parents who agreed it was in Zac's best interests to have regular access with his father. The foster parents suggested Kevin see Zac at their home. Despite initial discomfort, Kevin made a few visits which helped Zac settle into his new family. At the end of the six months, Kevin decided it would be best for Zac to remain in care. Legislation required that child protection be notified in order to progress the placement to permanent care.

SUMMARY

Any placement of a child away from home is a serious matter requiring careful practice by those agencies involved. The moral censure in the community that greets parental substance misuse makes it particularly likely that invidious comparisons will be made between 'bad' neglecting parents and 'good' substitute caregivers. Such judgements do not serve well the needs of children, parents or even carers, all of whom need knowledge and assistance to maintain meaningful contact in the child's best interests. As many caregivers are drawn from the extended family, child placement can also awaken prior tensions, while providing an opportunity for some healing of disturbed family relationships, if the placement is handled well. We have suggested a range of strategies for workers across the service system to help children, parents and carers in both short- and long-term placements.

PART 4

BEING AT YOUR BEST

10

Self-care and professional development

Throughout this book we have referred frequently to the need for workers to examine their own values and attitudes and set clear expectations for themselves in what can be challenging work with parents and their children. In relation to each of the aspects of practice covered in the preceding chapters, in this final chapter we provide suggestions for worker self-care and professional development. While we speak in general terms, we acknowledge that the majority of workers delivering human services are women, many of whom are themselves primary caregivers, and that this has implications for the broader workforce, each organisation and individual staff members—for example, your own work–life balance, maternity leave, child care or unexpected carer's leave may impact on your availability for work, or your need for flexible work hours during school holidays, or other times when client families can be most in need.

Those who work in human services are likely to be of most benefit to their clients if they are themselves emotionally and physically well, if they have their own social support and recreation time, and are genuinely committed to the health and wellbeing strategies they promote. This requires good time management and discipline, but can be essential for a sustainable career. It may be helpful to seek out a mentor or role model in your workplace and ask about the strategies they use to switch off from work, or to debrief after a particularly difficult day.

Like the families you work with, as a worker you are shaped by your own personal and family life courses, and embedded in your particular social economy of family, friends and formal organisations. These will have an impact on how you approach and experience your work, and your need for a positive working environment and strategies for reducing stress and burnout. It is easy to see that workers who have travelled a personally rocky road to their work and who may be poorly supported at work and at home will have most need of these strategies, but there are also many challenges for workers who have led relatively advantaged lives and who therefore find themselves confronted with what can seem to be an alien culture. It is critical for all working in this area that you don't do this work alone, that you have access to good supervision and the ear of your colleagues to discuss your concerns and reactions on a day-to-day basis. This also helps to keep children and families safe.

With all its challenges, this work with children, their parents and wider families is immensely rewarding. Workers can be inspired by, and learn much from, parents who successfully manage to deal with their substance dependence and build new lives. It is a privilege to help a failing-to-thrive infant grow, and an anxious and worried school-child to join his peers in positive everyday developmental experiences. To assist parents and relatives to move on from old wounds and find the strength to help each other develops strengths in the worker, too. However, while alcohol and other drug treatment and family support do work to transform lives, they will not work for everyone, or all the time. It is important that workers remain optimistic and hopeful but also have incremental expectations of the changes that can be made in the short-term. It is also important to remember that setbacks are to be expected, and should be viewed as great learning opportunities, rather than indications of your failure to facilitate sustainable change. Remember that there is no magic dust that can instantly fix problems like substance dependence and the impacts of trauma. Organisations may need to be there for the long-term in order to witness a family achieving their goals. As a single worker, you may only play a small part in this journey, but each part is important.

It is common for workers at the interface between child and family support and alcohol and other drug treatment to experience feelings of fear, anger and hopelessness. Those workers primarily supporting parents and families can sometimes feel stigmatised along with their clients. Indigenous workers may concurrently experience racism and stigma associated with alcohol and other drug work (Roche et al., 2013). The same may apply to workers from other minority back- grounds. As previous chapters have indicated, many families in which there is problematic parental substance use have histories of trauma and experience high levels of interpersonal conflict. Consequently, parents and children struggle to gain emotional self-regulation. Some have learnt to act aggressively as a defence mechanism or in response to problems. Substance use can cause dramatic fluctuations in mood, behaviour and attitude. Behaviour can be erratic and unpredictable, which can make professional decision-making more urgent and there- fore more stressful.

The multiple needs and issues experienced by families can leave workers feeling overwhelmed. The slow pace of recovery and the likeli- hood of relapse can result in workers feeling powerless and ineffectual in their professional role. The association between alcohol and other drug abuse and violence can raise worker concerns for their own safety, in addition to concerns for the safety and wellbeing of infants, chil- dren, parents and other family members. The link between problematic substance use and criminal activity poses particular challenges for workers who often have to face well-founded fears. Additionally, like many in our society, workers might be touched in their own extended families by alcohol and other drug issues; they are not immune from emotional reactivity and may unwittingly over-identify with the parent or child. This makes for an emotionally charged work environment, whether conducted in clients' homes or in clinical or other settings. Stress, and its long-term consequence, burnout, can cause serious problems in the worker's ability to function effectively in the workplace.

Significant overlap between parental substance use, mental health, family violence and child outcomes means that, while no one worker could be expected to have knowledge and skills in all of the above, basic knowledge across each area is required for effective service provision and integration. This degree of complexity requires multidisciplinary and cross-sectoral training and development to increase the capacity of the workforce, promote shared understanding of roles and responsibilities, improve communication and foster collegiality and mutual professional trust. Professional development assists workers to develop the skills and knowledge they need to meet challenges that arise in practice and to implement self-care as a personal and professional responsibility to the self, the team and wider organisation, and ultimately children and families. Professional development helps to reduce stress, which is at times unavoidable, from becoming burnout. Workers with good supervision, a positive work–life balance and broad knowledge and skills are more likely to feel confident in their role and to achieve better outcomes for clients. They are also more likely to experience job satisfaction and to remain in the workplace.

While worker attributes play a part in work-related stress and burnout, organisational factors also play a key role. Stress and burnout are closely linked to job demands such as workload, role conflict, the physical working environment, the specific challenges of working in the human services sector, and the availability of resources. These include opportunities for career development, support from colleagues, good quality supervision, performance feedback, the degree of autonomy afforded, ability to participate in decision-making, positive reinforcements and rewards, flexible working conditions and opportunities for professional development. As stress and burnout result from the interaction between the individual and the organisation, professional development and self-care are joint responsibilities between the worker and the organisation.

INDIGENOUS WORKERS

Indigenous people face a unique set of challenges when working in the alcohol and other drug sector (Roche et al., 2010). Australian Aboriginal workers are often closely embedded within their community and consequently they are likely to experience and share many of the challenges faced by the families they work with. Baskin (2011) also speaks to this issue in Canada, arguing that appropriate practice must therefore begin with self-reflection and self-care. In addition to substance use, the challenges to be faced can include: increased rates of grief and loss; trauma; racial and other abuse; poorer physical and mental health; identity issues; high rates of child removal by protective services, both current and historic; incarceration; family breakdown; cultural dislocation; discrimination; and social disadvantage.

Indigenous workers may also be more likely to be performing a caring role within their extended family and community. The close connection to community can weaken boundaries between the personal and the professional self, particularly when workers are required to maintain cultural practices and reciprocity between community members. They may be called upon outside typical working hours and may be asked to become involved with members of their own extended family or kinship networks in a professional capacity. High rates of absenteeism and sick leave may stem from the greater difficulty in finding a work–life balance. It is also possible that workers who have been exposed to the same problems faced by their community have used, or continue to use, substances to help them cope.

While Indigenous people may face greater work stress than their counterparts, employee assistance schemes may not be suited to their needs unless they are culturally appropriate. A culturally safe workplace recognises the unique stressors faced by Indigenous people and the constraints within which their work is conducted. In Australia, the National Centre for Education and Training has drawn on Indigenous workers' experience to devise culturally sensitive ways of improving worker wellbeing (Roche et al., 2013). To balance work with family and community commitments, Indigenous workers may require flexible working hours and recognition of the need for cultural leave entitlements (Roche et al., 2013). Likewise, if you have been recruited to a position because you bring a unique knowledge and skill set due to your cultural background, it is important that you are open about any limitations you may have in other areas of training. Most employers are very happy to support ongoing professional development if there is a clear link between the training and the outcomes you are all trying to achieve for the people you are working with. You may find it helpful to seek out an appropriate mentor from another organisation.

SUPERVISION

Typically delivered one-to-one by a more experienced person, supervision can also be conducted in small group settings, or through a peer-to-peer model. Clinical supervision has a long history in child welfare practice, but is a comparatively recent addition to some parts of the alcohol and other drug sector. Clinical supervision is concerned with the skills and quality of a worker's practice, along with their knowledge, attitudes and beliefs, for the purpose of enhancing client outcomes. Clinical supervision is not only an important workforce development strategy, it is also useful in reducing stress and burnout and increasing job satisfaction and workforce retention. When provided by direct supervisors, clinical supervision is not always prioritised. Furthermore, direct line managers may not always be up-to-date with changing patterns of drug use, such as the proliferation of synthetic drugs, or changes to legislation in relation to mental health and drugs, which further limits support to workers often grappling with the complexity of issues at the interface of child safety and parental addiction. Along with regular opportunities for professional development, optimal clinical care for clients and high quality support for staff may require external supervision by an independent, qualified and experienced supervisor. For rural and remote areas, where there are greater gaps in services and qualified staff, electronic technology such as video-conferencing offers alternatives to face-to-face supervision (Roche, Todd & O'Connor, 2007).

BARRIERS TO WORKER SELF-CARE AND PROFESSIONAL DEVELOPMENT

- Withholding information from supervisors or other service providers through lack of trust in the supervisory relationship.
- Not understanding your own vulnerabilities or coping style and not implementing strategies for managing stress.
- Lack of organisational support for workforce development and training.
- Unrealistic workloads that do not reflect the complexity of the work undertaken.
- Lack of adequate supervision, including opportunities for peer supervision.

In the following sections we provide examples of particular challenges for workers from different aspects of your work with families and suggest some strategies for self-care and professional development.

ENGAGING PARENTS

Personal challenges

In Chapter 3 we noted how workers may respond with excessive pessimism or undue optimism to parents whose erratic behaviour, emotional liability and learnt distrustfulness make them difficult to engage. It is particularly challenging if parents present to the agency intoxicated or drug-affected, perhaps sleepy and uncommunicative, or agitated and finding it difficult to focus on the task at hand. Your reactions can be exacerbated by ignorance of what is involved in substance misuse and recovery, or by a personal or family history involving substance misuse which leaves you with a fixed position of what ought to be done. If you find yourself actively disliking a parent, over-identifying with them or becoming overprotective and wanting to do too much for them, it may be a sign that you are too driven by your own experiences or values, and this will inhibit real engagement and focus on their or their child's needs. Your own reactions to a client, however, can provide very useful therapeutic information to inform your work. For example, if you constantly feel intimidated by a particular parent, chances are that other people in their life also feel intimidated by them, and that this has created a life-long barrier for them in developing equal relationships. It is good to speak about these feelings during supervision or case reviews as they are a sign of your emotional intelligence, not a sign of weakness. Often communicating these reactions directly to clients can be transformative for them, too, and lead to new insights.

Self-care strategies

To care for yourself as a worker, you need to be willing to be self-reflective and consider how your own attitudes, values and experiences affect your work with children, parents and other family and network members. In particular, you need to be open to examining your own alcohol and other drug use, your reactions to alcohol and drug use by others, your responses to stress, and your parenting assumptions and practices. It is helpful to have realistic expectations about the degree and pace of client change, while accepting that change does indeed occur and that it can be facilitated. Self-care does not equate with self-centredness. To avoid over-personalising your experiences in the workplace, it helps to have a commitment to reflective practice in which clients' problems are considered in the context of the broader society— for example, the association between problematic substance use and poverty—and to view your own biography similarly in a broader light. You will need to be willing to seek assistance when becoming stressed.

Professional development

In the course of their work, a wide range of professionals regularly come into contact with substance-affected parents and their children. These include, but are not limited to, the medical profession, the legal profession, police, teachers, correction officers, counsellors, youth workers and child protection and family support workers. Depending on their role, worker knowledge, skill and experience will vary. Such differences also exist within the same field of practice. For example, the AOD sector is comprised of workers from a wide range of professional backgrounds. A significant minority do not have formal qualifica- tions and even those with relevant tertiary qualifications may not have specialist training in issues related to alcohol and other drugs (Roche & Pidd, 2010). Whatever your role and work setting, engaging parents with substance misuse issues requires you to have knowledge of the physiological effects of alcohol and other drugs, and of assessment and treatment modalities and strategies (e.g. the difference between detoxification and rehabilitation services, motivational interviewing and harm-reduction strategies), if only to help you understand what parents are trying to tell you, and the practical difficulties of their lives.

Make use of training offered within the service network, and bookmark useful internet reference sites. Taking part in cross-sec- toral workforce development initiatives can boost your capacity and enable you to share your knowledge and skills with workers from other disciplines and services. If you are employed in a child- and family-fo- cused agency, attending an alcohol and other drug conference could bolster your knowledge of alcohol and other drug-related issues. In the same way, attending a child welfare conference could be a useful form of professional development for those employed in the alcohol and other drug sector. Consider, too, whether you need further development of your engagement skills so that you are better able to explore with parents their priorities and point of view. Training in motivational interviewing increases worker confidence in engaging parents and results in less use of confrontational approaches, which leads to reduced stress and increased job satisfaction (Forrester et al., 2008). Workers knowledgeable in alcohol and other drug issues are more confident in dealing with related problems. Changes in drug patterns across time, and the profusion of synthetic drugs, suggest the need to periodically update professional development. Tools derived from intensive family preservation services, such as the values and strengths cards developed by St Luke's Innovative Resources, are a useful way of developing a common language and common goals with parents and children (see Useful websites and resources).

WORKING WITH CHILDREN

Personal challenges

The vulnerability of infants and children can be particularly confronting, especially if you have personally experienced what they are experiencing. In addition, as we noted in Chapter 4, workers often feel they lack the knowledge and skill to communicate appropriately with children, especially if their initial training and workplace roles have focused on communication with adults. It can be worrying to ask children to describe their lives if this places them in a position where they feel disloyal to parents or open to punishment. It is very common to be emotionally moved or overwhelmed by the needs and experiences of vulnerable children. This is especially the case if you lack knowledge of a developmental framework in order to organise your thoughts and observations.

Self-care strategies

Spend time with the child, observing and learning to communicate at the child's level, rather than precipitately pursuing your own agenda. Reflect upon your impressions of, and response to, the child, and the relationship between the strength of your response and the facts before you. Be alert to signs of secondary trauma, such as anxiety, strong feelings of identification with the child, dreams or nightmares. If disturbed, ask yourself: 'Of what does this remind me?' Take your dilemmas and choices to a supervisor (internal to the agency or external), and if you are experiencing re-awakened childhood distress, consider counselling. If you do not usually work with children and feel out of your depth, consult with more experienced colleagues in the agency or the service network, and consider some joint work with a child development professional.

Professional development

Understanding child development and the normal range of communication capabilities of children is indicated; seek appropriate training and ensure the agency has suitable reference sources at hand. Develop your ability to identify when children are at risk of abuse and neglect.

Expand your ability to use multiple approaches to communication with children individually and in groups, such as visual media, activities and narrative methods; where this is an issue across your worksite, advocate for specialist training and mentoring in this area. As Crompton (1980) suggested long ago, respect and flexibility are crucial in working with children, and it is important to let go of the fear of looking silly and simply engage with them as they need.

FORMING ASSESSMENTS

Personal challenges

The need for multidimensional assessment in this area exposes the worker to a deluge of information that can feel quite overwhelming.

Many workers report difficulty deciding how much or how little to focus on the parent's substance misuse, among the many presenting problems (see Chapter 5). Since substance misuse also carries moral overtones, and parents may be evasive and misleading in their accounts, one challenge commonly experienced is the difficulty of separating appropriate professional judgement from inappropriate judgement. Workers can find themselves unusually indecisive or blaming, to their discomfort and to the detriment of their work.

Self-care strategies

We have stressed throughout this book that respect and honesty can take you far in this work. Maintain open communication about what you need to know and why, and bring the family with you in the assessment process. Keep a clear mind on the scope and limits of your role, and negotiate information exchange accordingly. To manage the information deluge, develop a sequence of inquiry related to the goals set, keeping the immediate and long-term wellbeing of the children in view. Use the organisation's own assessment frameworks, supplemented where necessary. Use supervision to work through feelings of blame, confusion and inundation.

Professional development

Develop your working knowledge of the assessment frameworks used not only in your own agency, but in other agencies with which the family is involved. Use this knowledge to refine your understanding of your own particular contribution to holistic assessment, and the limits to what you do. Seek training or staff development on issues such as assessing the signs of drug use and relapse, and assessing children's safety and development. Some child and family services agencies find it helpful to have a staff member carry a portfolio interest in substance misuse assessment to assist their workers; similarly, an alcohol and other drug service can benefit from the presence of a worker trained in assessing children's wellbeing to act as a consultant to other staff members.

FOCUSING ON SAFETY

Personal challenges

Throughout the consultations that led to this book, workers made mention of their anxieties about the safety of children, parents (and especially women subject to partner violence) and themselves, given the failures of emotional and behavioural regulation that often accompany alcohol and other drug misuse, and the associated criminal activity in some instances. Workers may have their anxiety heightened when they try to act independently and do not seek sufficient assistance when anxious about children's safety and wellbeing, or when uncertain about how to approach parents or other family members. Sometimes they fail to share vital information with a supervisor (e.g. the presence of domestic violence). This may place both family members and themselves at further risk. Conversely, the supervisor may not trust worker discretion and might initiate unduly harsh responses to presenting concerns, thereby undermining a potentially good case plan and leaving workers feeling disempowered and more anxious.

It is difficult to achieve a balance: both ignoring and overreacting to threats from the family or its network can increase risk to yourself, and to women and children. Overreaction may increase hostilities between workers and parents and other family members; avoiding discussing serious issues with family members or avoiding taking necessary action due to potential for unpleasantness, or fears for one's own safety, not only extends uncertainty, but also potentially places children at greater risk of harm through reduced monitoring and support. This was clearly demonstrated in a case-file analysis of 186 children known to child protection in the UK. Overall, children were more likely to remain at home with parents who used heroin and if one parent was an immigrant. Strikingly, they were least likely to be visited and four times more likely to remain in households where there was family violence, which suggests the extent to which violence and intimidation can deter intervention among the most vulnerable infants and children (Forrester & Harwin, 2008). Inappropriate and/or inadequate interventions where domestic violence and substance misuse are present can also arise when workers inadvertently collude with those who perpetrate violence. This can arise for a number of reasons (White et al., 2013). For example, the worker might unwittingly display a level of acceptance of violence in order to establish or strengthen a working relationship with the parent. In addition to regular supervision, workers involved with families where violence is present should seek specialist input from domestic violence services.

Self-care strategies

We have suggested that respect and responsiveness to the parents' world views will be important tools in your capacity to manage risk (see Chapter 6). Some people respond to fear with aggression; seeing this as the parent's attempt to protect the child and the family can make it easier to work with the parent and reach the child (see Chapter 3). Avoid unnecessary confrontation; confrontation that occurs outside a relationship of established mutual respect is likely to be counterproductive (Miller & Rollnick, 1991). Build your negotiation skills, so that when you are asking clients to moderate or change their behaviour, you are also able to offer support in doing so, and some alternative ways of behaving. Even so, dangers to you or to family members, especially children, will arise, and they are the source of much worry. Home visiting is a crucial tool in this work yet it can be a source of risk. Develop agreements with parents about the conditions of home-based work, and carefully monitor your sense of safety in the home. If you do not feel safe, it is more than possible that the child, too, is not safe. Be critically reflective and seek to identify how personal and work-related stressors, particularly in response to risk situations and experiences of secondary trauma, impact on your role performance. You may need to actively pursue a more manageable workload and reliable and supportive supervision in the workplace, and insist upon making room for a better work–life balance to avoid stress developing into burnout.

Develop your capacity to identify risks and use a safety checklist and a crisis response framework approved by the workplace—for example, conduct joint visits to families when there are risks to worker safety or wellbeing, and make sure your movements are known to the agency. Practise your risk analysis and management skills; the more prepared you are, the more likely it will be that you will take appropriate and timely action when in a difficult situation. Do not place yourself or others knowingly in dangerous situations, but seek alternatives, such as legal interventions, if necessary. Contribute to a safe and respectful work environment in which colleagues and other professionals feel safe to express views and openly challenge decisions, particularly in relation to situations of risk or trauma; you will all benefit.

Professional development

While training in risk assessment and risk management will be useful, it needs to be supplemented by a supportive work environment to prevent and ameliorate the effects of secondary trauma. If you are a supervisor or manager, ensure that stress management and crisis management interventions are in place—for example, well-defined roles and reasonable workloads, time-management, conflict resolution and supportive counselling, along with safety guidelines and emergency management procedures relevant to your work-site, workforce and clientele. If you are a front-line worker, join with colleagues to make your needs known to management.

HELPING FAMILIES CHANGE

Personal challenges

Changing our emotions, our behaviour and our relationships is rarely easy, especially when biological, social and environmental forces join to hold us in established patterns. It comes as no surprise, then, that helping families to change their internal functioning can be daunting, as it asks the worker to adopt a stance that is simultaneously challenging and encouraging, realistic and optimistic. As we noted in Chapter 7, workers become discouraged when parents relapse into substance misuse and when children's wellbeing suffers. While it is right to feel responsible for the quality of your work, when this discouragement extends into a sense of despair and failure, you need to question whether you have claimed too much responsibility and left the family too little room to claim their own successes and failures. Given the sense of shame that may accompany parental substance misuse, if you demonstrate that you are personally over-invested in parents' success, you can make it difficult for them to share their struggles and relapses, and you will be taken by surprise when a crisis ensues. The challenge is to share the highs and lows with the family while maintaining a joint sense of purpose, rather than to simply ride the roller-coaster with them.

We have emphasised the need to balance helping parents change themselves, change their parenting and change the way the family as a whole works together. Not all workers can do all these things, but if you have such a broad mandate, you will need a flexible practice repertoire, and the ability to help the family hold these threads together. Such family work requires a distinctive blend of friendliness and professionalism, in which the professional listens to and learns from the family, and the professional's knowledge, life skills and contacts are made available to the family in a form they can use, free of mystique and jargon.

Self-care strategies

In this complex work, good organisation is important, and you will be stronger if you keep reflective case notes that help you detect trends and changes in the family as well as your own helpful and unhelpful behaviour. Partnership with the family will be an important source of strength. If you work with the family to identify suitable celebrations and rewards for major achievements, you can share in a sense of achievement. If you work with them to clarify the values that matter to them as a family, you can stimulate your own internal values conversation. If you can work with them to maximise the use of their strengths and what you have to offer, you will be less dragged down by their liabilities and your own limitations. Families need to experience joy to thrive; they must tune in to intrinsic developmental rewards. Some clients can articulate the need to develop new, socially sanctioned, stimulating activities that can fill something of the gap left by the loss of the effects of substances. It will be difficult for you to foster this internal motivation and help them find new external motivators if your own life feels joyless and overburdened; hence the importance of taking care of body and soul—good food, plenty of fresh air and exercise, fun, relaxation, time with family and friends, and new learning.

Professional development

Openness to learning and acquiring new skills and knowledge to expand your practice repertoire is vital. Programs such as Positive Parenting Program (Triple P) provide workers with the confidence to help parents learn child behaviour strategies (Sanders, 1999), while Parenting under Pressure (PUP) provides a model for addressing parenting in the context of substance-use (see Useful websites and resources). Training in strengths-based and narrative approaches, and in mutually supportive group work focused on families, can enrich the practice repertoire.

SUPPORTING FAMILIES THROUGH FORMAL AND INFORMAL NETWORKS

Personal challenges

For workers in services that have focused traditionally on a single adult client, the expectation to involve themselves in clients' social networks can be received with apprehension (see Chapter 8). Not only might this be intrusive and pose risks to privacy and confidentiality, it also calls for wider collaboration and conflict resolution skills than usual. To really see the network as more significant than the agency as a site for relapse prevention and relapse management interventions, and for child development opportunities, is to de-centre the worker and to entrust the pursuit of professional goals to informal helpers. Family group conferences are one way in which this approach has been formalised legally in some jurisdictions or for specific populations of children in others.

Similarly, the call for cross-sectoral and collaborative practice also de-centres the worker in favour of a relationship between the family and a wider care team. In service networks through which status and rewards are unevenly distributed, shared responsibility and open communication are required. This does not always sit easily with either low or high status workers. Workers must struggle with possible accusations that they have shared too little or too much information, and their roles are continually open to challenge and refinement (Vulliamy & Sullivan, 2000).

Self-care strategies

Somewhat paradoxically, the de-centred worker also needs to have a confident sense of self and grasp of his or her core role. It is around this that negotiation occurs. Your best protection against role uncertainty and communication failure is the respect and affirmation of your clients, their natural helpers and your colleagues in the service network. Often, the child provides the rallying point for this disparate set of actors. Winning your legitimacy is enhanced if you contribute to a shared pool of knowledge in which ideas are respected and constructive disagreement is encouraged to develop creative interventions and solutions with the child's best interests at the forefront of interaction with children, parents and extended family members.

Teamwork has its own set of skills and if you are asked to use these beyond the confines of your employing agency, it is helpful if you can develop them within the agency itself. With your colleagues, advocate as needed for an effective and sustainable workplace culture that supports individuals and teams to respond appropriately to the needs of children, families and the wider family through shared decision-making and teamwork based on mutual respect and trust.

Professional development

In Chapter 8 several suggestions were made regarding the development of inter-organisational relationships. With these in place, you will be better able to gain access to cross-disciplinary and inter-agency learning to expand your set of skills and knowledge. In addition, consider advanced training in report writing, a fundamental tool of collaborative case planning. Gaining the knowledge and skills to participate in, and if necessary to run, family group conferences for decision-making within the wider family network is also a good investment.

HELPING FAMILIES WHEN CHILDREN ARE IN CARE

Personal challenges

For all the grief and confusion that may accompany the process of removing a child from home and placing them in care, for some children this is a developmental and even life-saving necessity. Yet even this realisation does not always blunt the sense of personal failure, and of disappointment in the parents, workers feel if they have been working with parents to keep their children in their care. Placement is a time when parents may feel so angry, betrayed and despairing that it is difficult for workers to even keep open the lines of communication with them, especially if they have played some part in the child's placement. The temptation to cease contact and back away is strong.

Self-care strategies

Realistic debriefing in supervision is worthwhile. Without self-castigation, consider what you did and how, and what else might have been useful. Ascertain official projections for how long the placement might last, and implications for the future of the parent–child relationship, so that you will be in a position to similarly debrief the parents and help them make decisions about the present and future, if they come to wish this.

Professional development

Learn more about parental mourning for children in care (this has sometimes been called filial deprivation) and how this interacts with the substance abuse and recovery trajectory. If this is a frequent issue in your workplace, develop a personal or group study program focused on best practice with birth families and extended families during threatened or actual child removal.

Re-examine your agency's functions and associated educational material to explore the potential to strengthen the response of the wider service system to children who have been placed, their families and those who support them.

HOW WILL I KNOW IF I'M ON TRACK?

- You will know what the gaps in your training and experience are and be able to identify ways in which to acquire the knowledge and skills required to confidently fulfil your role.
- You will feel increased confidence in broaching the subject of alcohol and other drug use and associated issues of concern with parents, including its impact on children.
- You will feel confident collaborating or forming partnerships with

workers from different professional backgrounds—for example, general practitioners, nurses, social workers or psychologists regarding parental substance use.

- You will recognise threats to your own safety and wellbeing, and take steps to deal with them.
- You will have a work–life balance and know the limits of professional responsibility for clients.

SELF-CARE AND PROFESSIONAL DEVELOPMENT: WORKING WITH STELLA, JIM AND THEIR GIRLS

Stella was emotionally reactive and easily agitated. Jim tended to be hyperactive and rarely sat still. The worker had to resist being drawn into this elevated emotional climate. At the beginning of each visit, the worker listened to whatever was troubling them. Discussion was then brought back to the goals the worker and the family had agreed upon. In this way, the worker avoided feeling overwhelmed by the family's problems. Knowing the limits of her professional knowledge, she ensured the continuing involvement of the child health nurse to monitor the children's development. She also attended group supervision with colleagues who knew the family. The team provided constructive feedback on the worker's assessment of risk and safety factors for the children and her professional decision-making.

SELF-CARE AND PROFESSIONAL DEVELOPMENT: WORKING WITH KEVIN AND ZAC

The escalation in Kevin's drug use placed Zac at greater risk of harm. The worker brought her concerns to the attention of her team leader. In supervision, the decision was made to co-work the case and to conduct more frequent and longer home visits. Depending on the presenting concerns and the action that needed to be taken, the worker either visited alone or was accompanied by her team leader. Regular conversations were held not only with Kevin, but also with Melanie, who continued to reside in the home and to provide some care of Zac. While it was acknowledged that the case plan was resource intensive, rushing Kevin to relinquish care could have caused him to withdraw, leaving both parent and child with less support. Co-working the case reduced the worker's anxiety and her workload.

SUMMARY

In this chapter we have revisited the stages of practice covered in preceding chapters, from the perspective of the worker's needs for self-care and professional development. Generally, our suggestions fall into three main groupings: *building self-knowledge*, *developing safe practices* and *using the organisation well*. Just as we ask clients to do, *building your self-knowledge* and personal resources enhances your self-regulation of your emotions and behaviour. It is useful to develop reflective habits, tuning in to your own patterned and exceptional emotional and behavioural responses to clients and situations. Examine personal lenses and potential biases in supervision and try to ensure that personal or agency factors are not inhibiting effective communication and collaboration with clients, their significant others or with other professions or services.

Although we have argued that a respectful and collaborative relationship with service users is a key defence against worker harm, this does not negate the need to develop your *risk awareness and commitment to safe practices*. This includes knowing and adhering to organisational occupational health and safety policies and procedures, monitoring your own reactions to presenting concerns and seeking emotional and practical support from supervisors and colleagues, and using debriefing to manage workplace stress and improve work performance.

Using the organisation well to gain support and expand your knowledge base and practice repertoire includes engaging in good supervision based on mutual trust between supervisor and supervisee; as we have mentioned above, when this is not possible, seek alternative arrangements such as external supervision and peer support. Other possibilities include sharing knowledge and skills with colleagues on a formal and informal basis, such as peer reviewing cases in team meetings, or establishing a regular journal club where staff members share and critique articles of relevance and interest. In addition, mentoring relationships are professionally fulfilling for mentor and mentee, whether within or beyond the organisation. To improve services to families where parents misuse substances, the culture of peer support and collaborative learning must begin within each organisation but extend across inter-organisational boundaries. Where possible, multidisciplinary training across diverse sectors involved with parents and children fosters the development of shared understanding of issues, strategies and interventions.

In focusing on worker self-care and professional development in this final chapter, we envisage a workforce with people able to straddle the traditional divides between distinctive specialisms and fields of practice, in the interest of children and families. These will be workers who understand child development and are able to identify when children are at risk of abuse and neglect, and who also know about the physiological effects of alcohol and other drugs, and about appropriate assessment and treatment modalities and strategies—for example, the difference between detoxification and rehabilitation services, cycles of change, motivational interviewing and harm-reduction strategies. They will work within an effective and sustainable workplace culture that supports individuals and teams to respond appropriately to the needs of children, families and the wider family through shared decision-making and teamwork based on mutual respect and trust. This supportive work environment will ameliorate the effects of secondary trauma and it will help workers to avoid stress developing into worker burnout through a manageable workload balanced against other life domains, in turn aiding staff retention. Just as family life is complicated for parents who misuse substances and their children, so improving services for them is complicated. It is, nonetheless, both possible and necessary if we are to improve the lives of these children and help their parents on their recovery journey so that they can participate more fully in our communities.

PART 5

ADDITIONAL INFORMATION

KEY MESSAGES FOR PRACTICE

ORIENTATION

Parental substance misuse: the challenges (Chapter 1)

- Poorly regulated emotions and behaviour
- Distraction from children and parenting
- Direct harm to children's health and development
- Diversion of family resources to substances
- Distortion of social networks

Service system themes (Chapter 2)

Adult AOD services focus on:

- Parental self-regulation
- Reducing use and harm
- Supporting recovery
- Preventing and managing relapse

Child and family services focus on:

- Parent–child bonds
- Resourcing children's development
- Child safety
- Building family resilience

Task: Reconciling these themes

BEGINNINGS

Connecting with parents (Chapter 3)

- Reach out with respect to combat fear and shame and enable action
- Negotiate honestly but appreciate parents' reasons for non-disclosure and dishonesty
- Balance challenge with hope
- Blend personal with material services

Connecting with children (Chapter 4)

- Ensure children are seen and heard
- Promote a child-supportive environment
- Widen the communication repertoire with children
- Give developmentally appropriate information
- Involve children in decision-making as developmentally appropriate
- Demonstrate responsiveness and helpfulness directly to the child, in the home and in groups

Identifying what you need to know (Chapter 5)

- Assessment is continuous, dynamic and collaborative
- Assessment must be multidimensional, ecologically and developmentally informed
- Attend to both risks and resources
- Assess the contribution of the worker and services systems to problems and solutions

HELPING FAMILIES CHANGE AND GROW

Keeping children and families safe (Chapter 6)

- Be alert to actual and imminent harm (child abuse and neglect, family and community violence)
- Check the child's wellbeing against normal developmental milestones
- With parents and children, build a clear safety plan and monitor its implementation
- Invoke legal processes when the child is unsafe and the parents are not addressing this
- Support parents and children through legal intervention processes

Strengthening the family from the inside (Chapter 7)

Build child and family resilience by:

- Helping parents in their recovery journey: narratives of hope, aspiration and change
- Strengthening adult relationships and functioning
- Helping parents 'read' and respond to their children
- Helping the family develop reliable routines and enjoyable shared activities

Informal and formal family support (Chapter 8)

- Help the family review and develop its social network
- Resolve problematic links and build supportive, pro-family life linkages
- Find new sources of information and acceptable and enduring mentors. Ask: 'Who will help when I am gone?'
- Strengthen the flow of social and material resources, especially to children

- Strengthen children's educational and social participation
- Act as interpreter between the family and the service system
- Combat service system impediments to change
- Build professional communication and collaboration

When children are in alternative care (Chapter 9)

- Explore the experience and meaning of placement—both its griefs and its gains
- Facilitate safe parent–child contact: hold the pain of contact, encourage mutual respect
- Help the parent and child re-interpret the nature of family relationships—re-story the parenting narrative
- Provide information to facilitate mutual understanding and respect between carers and parents

THE WORKER IN CONTEXT (CHAPTER 10)

- Review your lived experience: Is it helping or harming your work?
- Reflect on your professional presentation with families—are you open and friendly, but honest and clear; do you support parents and children to 'speak the unspeakable' without responding with shock and censure; do you avoid unrealistic promises; are you consistent in following through on commitments?
- Seek information to fill knowledge gaps and training to fill skills gaps
- Build support laterally with colleagues and within safe supervision
- Build cells of learning and practice development within your organisation to enhance your own and colleagues' responsiveness to children and families

GLOSSARY OF TERMS

Agoraphobia
An anxiety disorder characterised by a fear of going out in public places. Agoraphobia often co-occurs with panic attacks.

Alcoholics Anonymous (AA)
A worldwide self-help organisation comprised of men and women who have a drinking problem and want to cease drinking. The program employed to help people achieve this goal of abstinence is known as the 'Twelve Steps'.

Antisocial behaviour
Aggressive, intimidating or destructive activities that are likely to cause alarm or distress to another person(s).

Anxiety
Anxiety is a normal emotional state people experience when they feel threatened, in danger or stressed. When people become anxious they can feel irritable, upset and tense. Although anxiety is experienced by everyone from time to time, for some people anxiety is persistent and severe, and can interfere with their daily functioning. People with anxiety problems may be constantly fearful and worried, or they may be so scared of certain situations that they can't face them.

Attachment
In relation to children, attachment refers to the bond between a primary caregiver and their child. To develop healthily a child needs to have a secure attachment to their primary caregiver, whereby they feel safe in that person's presence. Unresponsive, erratic or threatening care can

lead to attachment problems that have an ongoing negative effect on the child's development.

Blood-borne virus
A virus that can be transmitted from one infected person to another via blood to blood contact, such as through the sharing of injecting equipment.

CALD
Culturally and linguistically diverse; refers to minority groups of people (often from immigrant families) whose language and cultural heritage differs from the dominant culture.

Child abuse
Refers to the physical, emotional or sexual maltreatment or serious neglect of children.

Child protection services
Services, typically operated by governments, which intervene to protect children where parents or other carers are unable or unwilling to do so. If you think that a child might be at serious risk of neglect or abuse, these services should investigate and act upon your concerns.

Cognitive Behavioural Therapy (CBT)
A type of counselling that is used to treat a range of psychological problems and mental health issues. CBT predominantly challenges unhelpful thinking in response to a variety of situations, and is based on the theory that thoughts influence feelings, and feelings in turn influence behaviours. CBT is generally short-term, structured and goal-focused.

Collaboration
The process of working together to achieve agreed and shared goals, not merely cooperating around intersecting goals. Collaboration requires leadership, and the sharing of knowledge and learning to build consensus.

Confidentiality

Refers to the legal obligation of a health or mental health service, or a community support service, to keep a client's or patient's personal information confidential. Information can only be released if a client gives their permission, or in exceptional circumstances when instructed by a court of law, or to prevent harm to the client or others.

Depression

Depression is a mental disorder with symptoms including: depressed mood; loss of interest or pleasure; feelings of guilt or low self-worth; disturbed sleep or appetite; low energy; and poor concentration. Depression is a common problem all over the world.

Detoxification (detox or withdrawal)

The process of allowing the body to remove the physiological effects of the drug while managing the symptoms of withdrawal. Drug detox is performed in many different ways, depending on where you receive treatment, and may involve the administration of medication. It is generally completed before undertaking drug treatment, which should also include counselling and therapy.

Developmental delay

When a young child is slower to reach their developmental milestones than other children. Developmental delays may occur in different areas, including movement, communication and behaviour.

Developmental milestones

Tasks that children learn, or physical developments that commonly appear in certain age ranges. For instance, most children reach the developmental milestone of learning to walk between the ages of 9 and 15 months. Milestones generally develop in a sequential fashion and provide important information about a child's development.

Developmental stage

A period in the child's life that is characterised by a particular set of abilities, motives, behaviours or emotions that occur together.

Dialectical Behaviour Therapy (DBT)

A type of *Cognitive Behaviour Therapy* that is used to treat a range of unhelpful behaviours and mental health issues, including self-harm, borderline personality disorder and addiction. It teaches skills to help an individual enhance their interpersonal relationships, tolerate distress and better regulate their emotions.

Domestic violence

See *Family violence*.

Dual diagnosis

Dual diagnosis is when a person has a mental illness and a substance use problem. People with alcohol and other drug problems have higher rates of mental illness, including anxiety and depression, than the general community. The substance used can be a licit substance, such as alcohol or prescribed medication, or any illicit drug. Typically, the two conditions interact and make prognosis for each worse. Treatment is also more difficult.

Early intervention

The early detection and subsequent treatment of harmful drug use. The treatment can occur before the user is fully aware of the harms associated with their substance use.

Family and Systemic Therapy

Family therapy is a specialist area of counselling, usually undertaken by psychiatrists, psychologists, social workers and other counsellors with advanced training. While there are varied approaches to family therapy, they share the view that the family is a system in which the wellbeing of the family as a whole and its individual members are inter-related, so that it is useful for the whole family to work together to improve relationship dynamics, communication patterns and problem solving.

Family violence

Violence (either actual or threatened) that occurs within a family. It can include physical, verbal, emotional, psychological, sexual, financial or social abuse.

Foetal Alcohol Spectrum Disorders (FASD) and Foetal Alcohol Syndrome (FAS)

FASD describes a spectrum of disabilities and problems that are caused by prenatal alcohol exposure. Alcohol can cause damage to the unborn child at any time during pregnancy and the level of harm is dependent on the amount and frequency of alcohol use, moderated by factors such as intergenerational alcohol use, parent age and health of the mother (nutrition, tobacco use), and environmental factors like stress (exposure to violence, poverty). Alcohol use during pregnancy is widely recognised as the most common preventable cause of birth defects and brain damage in children.

Genogram

A family tree or map of family relationships across at least three generations, recording family members and relationships, major events, occupations, migrations, alliances and cut-offs, and further details such as communications patterns as appropriate to the phase and content of work undertaken with the client.

Handover

The transfer of some or all aspects of care for a patient from one mental health professional to another person or professional group.

Harm minimisation

A form of drug abuse prevention, which aims to minimise the adverse social and individual effects of drug use through supply, demand and harm-reduction strategies.

Harm-reduction strategies

Strategies that aim to reduce the harms associated with the use of substances, as opposed to focusing on preventing drug use itself and/or punishing those who use drugs. Examples include needle and syringe exchange programs to prevent the spread of blood-borne viruses (such as hepatitis C), and roadside alcohol (breath) testing.

Hepatitis C

A virus that causes liver inflammation and liver disease, it is spread through blood-to-blood contact. Infected persons may not feel ill but chronic sufferers may experience severe lethargy and other symptoms. There is no vaccination currently available for hepatitis C, but treatments are available and medical attention is recommended, especially for injecting drug users.

Hierarchy of needs

Refers to the psychologist Abraham Maslow's theory of development. It understands that everyone has five basic needs that vary according to their degree of importance. Maslow proposed that people must have their basic physical needs (such as water and food) met before they can successfully focus on and achieve the next set of needs in the hierarchy.

Lapse

See *Relapse.*

Maintenance therapy

Also known as Opioid Replacement Therapy, maintenance therapy is treating drug dependence by prescribing a different drug (such as methadone) that is pharmacologically similar to the drug of dependence, but without the high.

Mandated intervention

An intervention required by a legal authority.

Mandatory reporting

Refers to the legal obligation to report suspected cases of child abuse and neglect. Mandatory reporting requirements can vary across jurisdictions.

Maternal and Child Health Services

A service that provides support and information for families with children aged 0 to 6 years. In Victoria, Australia, there are free maternal and child health centres in every local government area in the state.

Motivational interviewing (MI)

A client-centred and directive counselling approach that aims to elicit behaviour change by helping clients explore and resolve ambivalence about problematic behaviour.

Narcotics Anonymous (NA)

A community-based organisation, where members meet regularly to help each other lead a drug-free life. NA is modelled on *Alcoholics Anonymous*.

Narrative approaches

Developed by Michael White at the Dulwich Centre (see Useful websites and resources) and David Epston, narrative approaches to counselling and community work view problems as external to the people who experience them. The narrative approach centres people as experts on their own lives, and practitioners work collaboratively with them to explore the stories that shape their lives, with a view to then retelling those narratives in ways that will enable them to bring their inherent strengths to bear upon the problems that beset them.

Neglect

When a primary caregiver, who is in a position to do so, fails to provide a child with the care that is essential to the child's physical and emotional development. Included in the category of neglect is: (a) emotional neglect, where a caregiver deliberately or ignorantly does not provide the child with warmth, encouragement or support; and (b) physical neglect, where the caregiver withholds, or fails to provide, basic physical necessities, including clothing, housing, medical care, etc.

Neonatal Abstinence Syndrome (NAS)

Following birth, when a baby is no longer exposed to the medications or drugs used by their mother during pregnancy, they may experience signs of withdrawal. Signs include irritability and high-pitched crying, increased breathing rate, fever, tremors, sneezing, vomiting/diarrhoea and problems with feeding/sucking, sleeping and weight gain. It is difficult to predict which babies will experience NAS, and treatment often includes medication and an extended stay in a special care nursery.

Open-ended questions

Typically beginning with words such as 'what' and 'how', open-ended questions are designed to encourage full and meaningful answers. They are the opposite of close-ended questions, which usually result in one word or yes/no answers.

Out-of-home care

Utilised when care is provided to children who cannot live with their own families. Children may need to live in out-of-home care for different reasons and for different periods of time. There are a range of out-of-home care options, depending on the needs of the child, including foster care, kinship care and residential care.

Outreach

Outreach is a broad term and the definition varies from service to service. In general outreach refers to providing services to clients in their own environment, which can be on the street, in their home, in a hospital, etc.

Parentification

Parentification is a form of role reversal whereby a child is inappropriately given the role of meeting the emotional and/or physical needs of the parent, and as a consequence does not have their own needs met.

Permanent care orders

These children's court orders give custody and guardianship of the child until they reach legal adulthood to a suitable person other than the parent, without changing the child's legal identity. They are used when the court deems that a child must be removed from their family and placed permanently with another family. Permanent care differs from foster parenting and adoption. Foster care is temporary care of the child in another family, while adoption means that the new parent becomes the child's legal parent.

Pharmacotherapy

The treatment of substance dependence through the administration of medication. In the case of opioids this refers to the prescription of other drugs (e.g. methadone, buprenorphine) as maintenance therapy.

Play therapy

A form of psychotherapy where a child is encouraged to express, or act out, their experiences, feelings and problems in play rather than by talking. Play therapy takes place under the guidance or observation of a therapist.

Polydrug use

The use of more than one drug at the same or different times. Many people will have a preferred drug or a drug of choice but will use other substances. Many will use drugs in combination to either enhance their effects (e.g. alcohol plus another depressant such as GHB) or to counteract the effect of another drug (e.g. alcohol plus a stimulant like cocaine or caffeine, or cannabis to help with the after-effects of LSD or amphetamines).

Pro-social development

Refers to the development of an individual so they have a tendency to think about the welfare of other people, to feel empathy for them and to act in a way that benefits others.

Protective factors

Characteristics of the person or their environment that enhance resilience and protect individuals from developing problems.

Psycho-education

When information about psychological problems and skills training is provided to a client and/or associated party such as family members.

Psychosis

Psychosis describes a condition whereby a person loses contact with reality. A psychotic state is characterised by the presence of delusions, hallucinations and/or thought disorder. Psychotic symptoms can be part of an ongoing disorder (e.g. schizophrenia, schizoaffective disorder) or can occur once in an individual's lifetime.

Recovery

Recovery generally refers to the *process* of achieving one's own personal goals for health and wellbeing in relation to alcohol or other drug dependence, but it also sometimes refers to an end *state* of freedom from substance dependence.

Relapse and lapse

A relapse occurs when an individual slips back into old behaviour patterns. Sometimes this is distinguished from a lapse, which is a single event of drug use or old behaviours. Intervening early can prevent a lapse from becoming a relapse. See also *Stages of Change model.*

Relapse prevention

A set of cognitive and behavioural strategies that can help people cope with stressful or high-risk situations that might trigger a relapse. A mental health worker can help an individual devise coping strategies to suit them.

Respite care

Similar to short-term foster care, respite care gives full-time foster carers or birth families a regular break from the care of their child.

Risk factors

Characteristics of the person or their environment that increase the likelihood that the person develops a disorder or experiences adverse outcomes.

Safety plan

A plan an individual can make for times when they feel unsafe or at risk of being hurt. The content of the plan will depend on the person's individual needs. A person can make a safety plan either on their own or with the help of someone else, including a health care worker.

Secondary trauma

Helping or wanting to help someone who has experienced a traumatic event or events can also lead to stress and signs of trauma in the helper.

Self-medication

The use of alcohol and/or drugs to reduce the discomfort caused by physical or psychological problems.

Solution-Focused Brief Therapy (SFBT)

Based on the work of Steve de Shazer and Insoo Kim Berg, SFBT is a collaborative approach that seeks to break the dominance of problems in the client's life by inviting him or her to concentrate on what is working well, and to do more of it. The work contrasts with therapies that have a strong retrospective focus, with some use of few or even single sessions of solution-finding counselling. Aspects of this approach have shaped strengths-based practices.

Stages of Change model

Recovery from substance use generally involves a series of steps or changes that a person goes through at their own pace before they make permanent lasting change. Most people go through the stages several times (relapse) in a process called the 'cycle of change' before lasting change is made. The stages involved are:

- **Pre-contemplation**, in which the person is unconcerned about their drug use. At this stage, the benefits of use outweigh negative consequences; people are therefore unlikely to want to change.
- **Contemplation** involves having mixed feelings about substance use; people at this stage are aware of some of the negative consequences of use and are open to receiving information or education.
- **Preparation** is when people have an intention to give up and are making plans to cease use.
- **Action** involves making significant efforts to stop using.
- **Maintenance** involves abstaining from use and preventing relapse.
- **Relapse** is when the person resumes using alcohol or other drugs and goes back to an earlier stage of the model; this stage is considered an opportune time to consider which strategies did or did not work and to try to stop using again.

Stigma

Associating negative qualities with having a mental illness or a substance use problem. People may avoid seeking help or discussing problems with friends due to feeling stigmatised or being judged.

Strengths-based approach/practice

This approach draws on the traditions of solution-focused and narrative approaches, seeking to reduce stigmatisation and an excessive attention to problems and to harness the competencies and helpful problem-solving behaviour of individuals and families in the service of their wellbeing and aspirations.

Substance abuse

Refers to the harmful or hazardous use of psychoactive substances, including alcohol, illicit drugs and inhalants, or the misuse of prescribed medication.

Substance dependence

A set of symptoms that develop after repeated substance use. These typically include: a strong desire to take the drug; difficulties in controlling its use; continuing to use it despite harmful consequences; tolerance; a higher priority given to drug use than to other activities and obligations; and signs of physical withdrawal.

Sudden Infant Death Syndrome (SIDS)

Also known as cot death, SIDS describes the unexpected death of a baby where there is no apparent cause. In many countries, SIDS is the most common cause of death of babies who are aged between one month and a year.

Trauma

In psychological terms, trauma refers to an experience or experiences that are emotionally painful, distressing or shocking and that can often have lasting effects on the individual.

Treatment plan
A document that outlines the planned course of therapy. It may be formalised or consist of informal case notes, depending on the level of documentation needed by the individual. For some examples of more formal treatment plans, see: Victorian Government Health Information, Chief Psychiatrist's homepage at www.health.vic.gov.au/chiefpsychiatrist.

Withdrawal symptoms
Physical or psychological symptoms that result from stopping or reducing the use of a drug that had been used consistently and at high levels.

Withdrawal services
Services provided to people who are likely to experience *withdrawal symptoms* (see above). There are different types of withdrawal services, including:
- residential withdrawal, which involves a short stay in a community residential drug withdrawal service or hospital;
- home-based withdrawal, which is supervised withdrawal occurring in the client's home. The service is provided by a registered nurse and a medical practitioner when the withdrawal is of mild/moderate severity and support is available from a family member or friend; and
- outpatient withdrawal which is available for people who will experience mild/moderate withdrawal and whose withdrawal can be appropriately managed without admission to a residential service.

REFERENCES

Abar, B., LaGasse, L.L., Wouldes, T., Derauf, C., Newman, E., Shah, R., Smith, L.M., Arria, M.A., Huestis, M.A., DellaGrotta, S., Dansereau, L.M., Wilcox, T., Neal, C.R. & Lester, B.M. (2013). Cross-national comparison of prenatal methamphetamine exposure on infant and early child physical growth: A natural experiment. *Prevention Science.* 15:767–76.

ANCD (2007). *Compulsory Treatment in Australia.* Australian National Council on Drugs. Research Paper 14.

Arney, F., Chong, A. & McGuinness, K. (2013). The power of family: Supporting family decision making approaches with Aboriginal families to promote the safety and wellbeing of children. In F. Arney & D. Scott (eds). *Working with Vulnerable Families: A partnership approach.* 2nd edn. Melbourne: Cambridge University Press.

Atkinson, J. (2002). *Trauma Trails, Recreating Song Lines: The transgenerational effects of trauma in Indigenous Australia.* North Melbourne: Spinifex Press.

Australian Institute of Health and Welfare (2014). *National Drug Strategy Household Survey detailed report 2013.* Drug statistics series no. 28. Cat. no. PHE 183. Canberra: AIHW.

Barlow, J., Sembi, S., Gardner, F., Macdonald, G., Petrou, S., Parsons, H., Harnett, P. & Dawe, S. (2013). An evaluation of the parents under pressure programme: A study protocol for an RCT into its clinical and cost effectiveness. *Trials.* 14:210.

Bartu, A., Sharp, J., Ludlow, J. & Doherty, D.A. (2006). Postnatal home-visiting for illicit drug-using mothers and their infants: A randomised controlled trial. *Australian and New Zealand Journal of Obstetrics and Gynaecology.* 46(5):419–26.

Baskin, C. (2011). *Strong Helpers' Teachings: The value of Indigenous knowledges in the helping professions.* Toronto, ON: Canadian Scholars' Press.

Bell, J. & Harvey-Dodds, L. (2008). Pregnancy and injecting drug use. *British Medical Journal.* 336:1303–5.

Bell, M. (2002). Promoting children's rights through the use of relationships. *Child and Family Social Work.* 7:1–11.

Berg, I. & Kelly, S. (2000). *Building Solutions in Child Protective Services.* New York: W.W. Norton & Company.

Blythe, B., Heffernan, K. & Walters, B. (2010). Best practices for developing child protection workers' skills: Domestic violence, substance abuse, and mental health training. *Revista de Asistenta Sociala.* 2:51–64.

Bronfenbrenner, U. (1979). *The Ecology of Human Development: Experiments by nature and design.* Cambridge: Harvard University Press.

Callaghan, T., Crimmins, J. & Schweitzer, R.D. (2011). Children of substance-using mothers: Child health engagement and child protection outcomes. *Journal of Paediatrics and Child Health.* 47:223–7.

Campbell, L. (2002). Interagency practice in Intensive Family Preservation Services. *Children and Youth Services Review.* 24(9/10):701–18.

—— (2009). Defining the 'case' to be 'managed' in services to children at risk of harm and their families. In E. Moore (ed.). *Case management for Community Practice.* South Melbourne: Oxford University Press, 367–87.

Campbell, L. & Mitchell, G. (2007). Victorian family support services in retrospect: Three decades of investment, challenge and achievement. *Australian Social Work.* (60)3:278–94.

Chudley, A.E., Kilgour, A.R., Cranston, M. & Edwards, M. (2007). Challenges of diagnosis in Fetal Alcohol Syndrome and Fetal Alcohol Spectrum Disorder in the adult. *American Journal of Medical Genetics Part C (Seminars in Medical Genetics).* 145C:261–72.

Contole, J., O'Neill, C., Mitchell, G. & Absler, D. (2008). *Counting the Kids: Final Evaluation Report.* Melbourne: Odyssey Institute of Studies, Odyssey House Victoria. (Access via www.odyssey.org,au, then follow links to info and resources, brochures and publications.)

Council of Australian Governments (2009). *Protecting Children Is Everybody's Business: National Framework for Protecting Australia's Children 2009–2020.* Canberra: Commonwealth of Australia.

Covington, S. (2007). Working with substance abusing mothers: A trauma-informed, gender-responsive approach. *The Source.* Berkeley, CA: National Abandoned Infants Assistance Resource Center. 16(1).

—— (2012). Curricula to support trauma-informed practice with women. In N. Poole & L. Greaves. *Becoming Trauma Informed.* Toronto, Ontario, Canada: Centre for Addiction and Mental Health (CAMH).

Crompton, M. (1980). *Respecting Children: Social work with young people.* London: Edward Arnold.

Cunningham, S. & Finlay, K. (2013). Parental substance use and foster care: Evidence from two methamphetamine supply shocks. *Economic Inquiry.* 51(1):764–82.

Dawe, S., Frye, S., Best, D., Moss, D., Atkinson, J., Evans, C., Lynch, M. & Harnett, P. (2007). *Drug Use in the Family: Impacts and implications for children.* Canberra: Australian National Council on Drugs.

Dawe, S. & Harnett, P. (2007). Reducing potential for child abuse among methadone maintained parents: Results from a randomized controlled trial. *Journal of Substance Abuse Treatment.* 32:381–90.

—— (2013). Working with parents with substance misuse problems: A Parents Under Pressure perspective. In F. Arney & D. Scott (eds). *Working with Vulnerable Families: A partnership approach.* 2nd edn. Melbourne: Cambridge University Press.

Dawe, S., Harnett, P.H., Rendalls, V. & Staiger, P. (2003). Improving family functioning and child outcome in methadone maintained families: The Parents Under Pressure program. *Drug and Alcohol Review.* 22:299–307.

De Bortoli, L., Coles, J. & Dolan, M. (2013). Parental substance misuse and compliance as factors determining child removal: A sample from the Victorian Children's Court in Australia. *Children and Youth Services Review.* 35:1319–26.

De Civita, M., Dobkin, P.L. & Robertson, E. (2000). A study of barriers to the engagement of significant others in adult addiction treatment. *Journal of Substance Abuse Treatment.* 19(2):135–44.

Deren, S. (1986). Children of substance abusers: A review of the literature. *Journal of Substance Abuse Treatment.* 3(2):77–94.

Dunlop, K. (2014). A Qualitative Study of Odyssey House Victoria's 'Horse Play' Program. Unpublished thesis. The University of Melbourne.

Elder, G. (1978). Family history and the life course: The family and the life course in historical perspective. In T. Hareven (ed.). *Transitions.* New York: Academic Press. 17–64.

Elgen, I., Bruaroy, S. & Laegreid, L.M. (2007). Complexity of foetal alcohol or drug neuroimpairments. *Acta Paediatrica.* 96(12):1730–3.

Elliott, B., Mulroney, L. & O'Neil, D. (2000). *Promoting Family Change: The optimism factor.* Crows Nest, NSW: Allen & Unwin.

Feingold, A., Kerr, D.C.R. & Capaldi, D.M. (2008). Associations of substance use problems with intimate partner violence for at-risk men in long-term relationships. *Journal of Family Psychology.* 22(3):429–38.

Forrester, D. (2000). Parental substance misuse and child protection in a British sample. *Child Abuse Review.* 9(4):235–46.

Forrester, D. & Harwin, J. (2008). Parental substance misuse and child welfare: Outcomes for children two years after referral. *British Journal of Social Work.* 38:1518–35.

—— (2011). *Parents Who Misuse Drugs and Alcohol: Effective interventions in social work and child protection.* Chichester: Wiley-Blackwell.

Forrester, D., Holland, S., Williams, A. & Copello, A. (2012). An Evaluation of the Option 2 Intensive Family Preservation Service. Cardiff University/Tilda Goldberg Centre for Social Work and Social Care, University of Bedfordshire.

Forrester, D., Kershaw, S., Moss, H. & Hughes, L. (2008). Communication skills in child protection: How do social workers talk to parents? *Child and Family Social Work.* 13:41–51.

Frederico, M., Jackson, A. & Dwyer, J. (2014). Child protection and cross-sector practice: An analysis of child death reviews to inform practice when multiple parental risk factors are present. *Child Abuse Review.* 23:104–15.

Garbarino, J. (1992). *Children and Families in the Social Environment.* New York: Aldine de Gruyter.

Gilligan, R. (1999). Enhancing the resilience of children and young people in public care by encouraging their talents and interests. *Child and Family Social Work.* 4(3):187–96.

Goodman, R. (1997). The strengths and difficulties questionnaire: A research note. *Journal of Child Psychology and Psychiatry.* 38(5):581–6.

Gruenert, S., Ratnam, S. & Tsantefski, M. (2004). *The Nobody's Clients' Project: Identifying and addressing the needs of children with substance dependent parents.* Melbourne: Odyssey Institute of Studies, Odyssey House Victoria.

—— (2006). Identifying children's needs when parents access drug treatment: The utility of a brief screening measure. *Journal of Social Work Practice in the Addictions.* 6(1/2):139–53.

Gruenert, S. & Tsantefski, M. (2012). Responding to the needs of children and parents in families experiencing alcohol and other drug problems. *Prevention Research Quarterly*. North Melbourne: Australian Drug Foundation. 17.

Harbin, F. (2002). Therapeutic work with children of substance misusing parents. In F. Harbin & M. Murphy (eds). *Substance Misuse and Child Care*. Dorset, UK: Russell House Publishing.

Harnett, P.H. (2007). A procedure for assessing parents' capacity for change in child protection cases. *Children and Youth Services Review*. 29:1179–88.

Harnett, P. & Day, C. (2008). Developing pathways to assist parents to exit the child protection system in Australia. *Clinical Psychologist*. 12(3):79–85.

Harwin, J., Alrouh, B., Ryan, M. & Tunnard, J. (2013). Strengthening prospects for safe and lasting family reunification: Can a Family Drug and Alcohol Court make a contribution? *Journal of Social Welfare and Family Law*. 35(4):459–74.

Hedges, K.E. (2012). A family affair: Contextual accounts from addicted youth growing up in substance using families. *Journal of Youth Studies*. 15(3):257–72.

Higgs, P., Owada, K., Hellard, M., Power, R. & Maher, L. (2008). Gender, culture and harm: An exploratory study of female heroin users of Vietnamese ethnicity. *Culture, Health and Sexuality*. 10(7):681–95.

Hogan, D.M. (1998). Annotation. The psychological development and welfare of children of opiate and cocaine users: Review and research needs. *Journal of Child Psychology and Psychiatry*. 39(5):609–20.

Hollingsworth, L.D., Swick, D. & Choi, Y.J. (2011). The role of positive and negative social interactions in child custody outcomes: Voices of US women with serious mental illness. *Qualitative Social Work*. 12(2):153–69.

Holman, M.M. (1998). Motivational interviewing: An intervention tool for child welfare case workers working with substance-abusing parents. *Child Welfare: Journal of Policy, Practice, and Program*. 77(3):275–89.

Hudak, M.L. & Tan, R.C. (2012). The Committee on Drugs & The Committee on Fetus and Newborn. Neonatal drug withdrawal. *Pediatrics*. 129:e540–60.

Humphreys, C. (2007). Domestic violence and child protection: Exploring the role of perpetrator risk assessments. *Child and Family Social Work.* 16(4):360–9.

Humphreys, C., Regan, L., River, D. & Thiara, R.K. (2005). Domestic violence and substance use: Tackling complexity. *British Journal of Social Work.* 35:1303–20.

Jeffreys, H., Hirte, C., Rogers, N. & Wilson, R. (2009). *Parental Substance Misuse and Children's Entry into Alternative Care in South Australia.* Adelaide: Department for Families and Communities, Government of South Australia.

Jones, H.E., Dengler, E., Garrison, A., O'Grady, K.E., Seashore, C., Horton, E., Andringa, K., Jansson, L.M. & Thorp, J. (2014). Neonatal outcomes and their relationship to maternal buprenorphine dose during pregnancy. *Drug and Alcohol Dependence.* 134:414–17.

Kalland, M., Kinkkonen, J., Gissler, M., Merilainen, J. & Siimes, M.A. (2006). Maternal smoking behavior, background and neonatal health in Finnish children subsequently placed in foster care. *Child Abuse & Neglect.* 30:1037–47.

Kelly, J.J., Davis, P.G. & Henschke, P.N. (2000). The drug epidemic: Effects on newborn infants and health resources consumption at a tertiary perinatal centre. *Journal of Paediatrics and Child Health.* 36(3):262–4.

Keyser-Marcus, L., Alvanzo, A., Rieckmann, T., Thacker, L., Sepulveda, A., Forcehimes, A., Islam, L., Leisey, M., Stitzer, M. & Svikis, D. (2014). Trauma, gender and mental health symptoms in individuals with substance use disorders. *Journal of Interpersonal Violence.* 30(1):3–24.

Kinney, J., Haapala, D. & Booth, C. (1991). *Keeping Families Together: The Homebuilders model.* New York: Aldine de Gruyter.

Klee, H. (1998). Drug-using parents: Analysing the stereotypes. *International Journal of Drug Policy.* 9(6):437–48.

—— (2002). Overcoming the barriers. In H. Klee, M. Jackson & S. Lewis (eds). *Drug Misuse and Motherhood.* London: Routledge.

Kumpfer, K.L. & Fowler, M.A. (2007). Parenting skills and family support programs for drug-abusing mothers. *Seminars in Fetal & Neonatal Medicine.* 12:134–42.

Lambert, M.J. (1992). Psychotherapy outcome research: Implications for integrative and eclectic therapists. In C. Norcross & M. Goldfried (eds). *Handbook of Psychotherapy Integration.* United States: Basic Books.

Lawrence, H.R., Kelley, M.L., Murphy, E.M., D'Lima, G.M., Milletich, R.J., Hollis, B., Cooke, C.G. & Stockstad, M. (2015). Child care in families with SUD mothers or fathers. *Drug and Alcohol Dependence.* 146:e170–1.

Lloyd, M.H. & Akin, B.A. (2014). The disparate impact of alcohol, methamphetamine and other drugs on reunification. *Children & Youth Services Review.* 44(2014):72–81.

Luthar, S.S., Cushing, G., Merikangas, K.R. & Rounsaville, B.J. (1998). Multiple jeopardy: Risk and protective factors among addicted mothers' offspring. *Development and Psychopathology.* 10:117–36.

Man-kwong, H. (2004). Overcoming craving: The use of narrative practices in breaking drug habits. *International Journal of Narrative Therapy and Community Work.* No 1. Republished at http://www.dulwichcentre.com.au/overcoming-craving.html (accessed 23 December 2014).

Manning, V., Best, D.W., Faulkner, N. & Titherington, E. (2009). New estimates of the number of children living with substance misusing parents: Results from UK national household surveys. *BMC Public Health.* 9:377.

Miller, W.R. (1989). Matching individuals with interventions. In R.K. Hester & W.R. Miller (eds). *Handbook of Alcoholism Treatment Approaches.* New York: Pergamon Press.

Miller, W.R. & Rollnick, S. (1991). *Motivational Interviewing: Preparing people to change addictive behavior.* New York: Guilford Press.

Miller, W.R. & Rollnick, S. (2002). *Motivational Interviewing: Helping people change.* 2nd edn. New York: The Guilford Press.

Minnes, S., Singer, L.T., Arendt, R. & Satayathum, S. (2005). Effects of prenatal cocaine/polydrug use on maternal–infant feeding interactions during the first year of life. *Journal of Developmental and Behavioral Pediatrics.* 26(3):194–200.

Mitchell, G. & Campbell, L. (2011). The social economy of excluded families. *Child and Family Social Work.* 16:422–33.

Morris, K. & Connolly, M. (2012). Family decision making in child welfare: Challenges in developing a knowledge base for practice. *Child Abuse Review.* 21(1):41–52.

Murray, M. & Tsantefski, M. (2008). Therapeutic groups for children of substance-dependent parents. *Children Australia.* 33(4):22–3.

Nafstad, P., Fugelseth, D., Qvigstad, E., Zahlen, K., Magnus, P. & Lindemann, R. (1998). Nicotine concentration in the hair of nonsmoking mothers and size of offspring. *American Journal of Public Health*. 88(1):120–4.

Osterling, K.L. & Austin, M.J. (2008). Substance abuse interventions for parents involved in the child welfare system: Evidence and implications. *Journal of Evidence-Based Social Work*. 5(1–2).157–89.

Pajulo, M., Savonlahti, E., Sourander, A., Piha, J. & Helenius, H. (2001). Prenatal maternal representations: Mothers at psychological risk. *Infant Mental Health Journal*. 22(5):529–44.

Pascoe, J.M., Kokotailo, P.K. & Broekhuizen, F.F. (1995). Correlates of multigravida women's binge drinking during pregnancy: A longitudinal study. *Archives of Pediatric and Adolescent Medicine*. 149(12):1325–9.

Prochaska, J.O. & DiClemente, C.C. (1986). Toward a comprehensive model of change. In W. Miller & N. Heather (eds). *Addictive Behaviors: Processes of change*. New York: Plenum Press. 3–28.

Prochaska, J.O., DiClemente, C.C. & Norcross, J.C. (1992). In search of the structure of behavior change. In J.D. Fisher, J.M. Chensky & A. Nadler (eds). *Initiating Self-Changes: Social psychological and clinical perspectives*. New York: Springer-Verlag.

Richter, K.M. & Bammer, G. (2000). A hierarchy of strategies heroin using mothers employ to reduce harm to their children. *Journal of Substance Abuse Treatment*. 19:403–13.

Riley, E.P. & McGee, C.L. (2005). Fetal Alcohol Spectrum Disorders: An overview with emphasis on changes in brain and behavior. *Experimental Biology and Medicine*. 230(6):357–65.

Ritter, A., King, T. & Hamilton, M. (2013). *Drug Use in Australian Society*. South Melbourne: Oxford University Press.

Robertson, E.B., David, S.L. & Rao, S.A. (2003). *Preventing Drug Use Among Children and Adolescents: A research-based guide for parents, educators and community leaders*. 2nd edn. Bethesda, MD: National Institute on Drug Abuse, US Department of Health and Human Services.

Roche, A.M. & Pidd, K. (2010). *Alcohol & Other Drugs Workforce Development Issues and Imperatives: Setting the scene*. National Centre for Education and Training on Addiction (NCETA). Adelaide: Flinders University.

Roche, A.M., Todd, C.L. & O'Connor, J. (2007). Clinical supervision in the alcohol and other drugs field: An imperative or an option? *Drug and Alcohol Review*. 26:241–9.

Roche, A.M., Tovell, A., Weetra, D., Freeman, T., Bates, N., Trifonoff, A. & Steenson, T. (2010). *Stories of Resilience: Indigenous alcohol and other drugs workers' wellbeing, stress and burnout.* National Centre for Education and Training on Addiction (NCETA). Adelaide: Flinders University.

Roche, A.M., Trifonoff, A., Nicholas, R., Steenson, T., Bates, N. & Thompson, M. (2013). *Feeling Deadly: Working Deadly. A resource kit for Aboriginal and Torres Strait Islander alcohol and other drug workers and their managers and supervisors.* National Centre for Education and Training on Addiction (NCETA). Adelaide: Flinders University.

Rose, D. (2010). Living with Drugs in the Family: The needs and experiences of siblings. Unpublished thesis. Melbourne: The University of Melbourne.

Rosenberg, L. (2011). Addressing trauma in mental health and substance use treatment. *The Journal of Behavioral Health Services & Research.* 38(4):428–31.

Ryan, J.P., Choi, S., Sung Hong, J., Hernandez, P. & Larrison, C.R. (2008). Recovery coaches and substance exposed births: An experiment in child welfare. *Child Abuse & Neglect.* 32(11):1072–9.

Sanders, M.R. (1999). Triple P-Positive Parenting Program: Towards an empirically validated multilevel parenting and family support strategy for the prevention of behavior and emotional problems in children. *Clinical Child and Family Psychology Review.* 2(2):71–90.

Schuler, M.E., Nair, P., Black, M.M. & Kettinger, L. (2000). Mother–infant interaction: Effects of a home based intervention and ongoing maternal drug use. *Journal Clinical Child Psychology.* 29(3):424–31.

Schuler, M.E., Nair, P. & Kettinger, L. (2003). Drug exposed infants and developmental outcomes. *Archives of Pediatrics and Adolescent Medicine.* 157:133–8.

Scott, D. (2013). Working with and between organisations. In F. Arney & D. Scott. *Working with Vulnerable Families: A partnership approach.* 2nd edn. Port Melbourne: Cambridge University Press.

Scott, D., Arney, F. & Vimpani, G. (2013). Think child, think family, think community. In F. Arney & D. Scott. *Working with Vulnerable Families: A partnership approach.* 2nd edn. Port Melbourne: Cambridge University Press.

Scully, M., Geoghegan, N., Corcoran, P., Tiernan, M. & Keenan, E. (2004). Specialized drug liaison midwife services for pregnant opioid dependent women in Dublin, Ireland. *Journal of Substance Abuse Treatment.* 26:329–35.

Snyder, R., Shapiro, S. & Treleaven, D. (2012). Attachment theory and mindfulness. *Journal of Child and Family Studies.* 21:709–17.

Stevenson, J. (1999). The circle of healing. *Native Social Work Journal.* 2(1):8–21.

Suchman, N.E., Decoste, C., McMahon, T.J., Rounsaville, B. & Mayes, L. (2011). The mothers and toddlers program, an attachment-based parenting intervention for substance-using women: Results at 6-week follow-up in a randomized clinical pilot. *Infant Mental Health Journal.* 32(4):427–49.

Sun, A.P. (2007). Relapse among substance-abusing women: Components and processes. *Substance Use & Misuse.* 42:1–21.

Tsantefski, M. (2010). Holding the Mother Holding the Baby. Unpublished PhD thesis. Melbourne: The University of Melbourne.

Tsantefski, M., Humphreys, C. & Jackson, A.C. (2014). Infant risk and safety in the context of maternal substance use. *Children and Youth Services Review.* 47:10–17.

Turnell, A. & Edwards, S. (1999). *Signs of Safety: A safety and solution oriented approach to child protection casework.* New York: W.W. Norton & Company.

Unger, J.B. (2012). The most critical unresolved issues associated with race, ethnicity, culture, and substance use. *Substance Use & Misuse.* 47(4):390–5.

United Nations Office on Drugs and Crime (2014). *World Drug Report 2014.* Vienna: United Nations Division for Policy Analysis and Public Affairs.

Vulliamy, A.P. & Sullivan, R. (2000). Reporting child abuse: Pediatricians' experiences with the child protection system. *Child Abuse & Neglect.* 24(11):1461–70.

Walsh, C., MacMillan, H.L. & Jamieson, E. (2003). The relationship between parental substance abuse and child maltreatment: Findings from the Ontario Health Supplement. *Child Abuse & Neglect.* 27(12):1409–25.

Walsh, F. (2006). *Strengthening Family Resilience.* 2nd edn. New York: Guilford Press.

Werner, E. & Smith, R. (1992). *Overcoming the Odds: High risk children from birth to adulthood.* New York: Cornell University.

White, M., Roche, A.M., Long, C., Nicholas, R., Gruenert, S. & Battams, S. (2013). *Can I ask...? An alcohol and other drug clinician's guide to addressing family and domestic violence.* National Centre for Education and Training on Addiction (NCETA). Adelaide: Flinders University.

Wu, M., LaGasse, L.L., Wouldes, T.A., Arria, A.M., Wilcox, T., Derauf, C., Newman, E., Shah, R., Smith, L.M., Neal, C.R., Huestis, M.A., DellaGrotta, S. & Lester, B.M. (2013). Predictors of inadequate prenatal care in methamphetamine using mothers in New Zealand and the United States. *Maternal Child Health Journal.* 17:566–75.

USEFUL WEBSITES AND RESOURCES

The following links provide a range of information and resources relevant to working with families affected by parental alcohol and other drug use. They are only intended to be examples, rather than a comprehensive list.

INFORMATION ON ALCOHOL AND OTHER DRUG USE AND TREATMENT

General and broad information
- www.adf.org.au
- www.alcoholconcern.org.uk
- www.drugabuse.gov
- www.drugscope.org.uk
- www.project6.org.uk
- www.samhsa.gov

Workforce development
- www.ccsa.ca
- www.fdap.org.uk
- www.matuaraki.org.nz
- www.nceta.flinders.edu.au

Resources for partners and families
- www.adfam.org.uk
- www.fds.org.au

Peer support
- www.aa.org
- www.aa.org.au
- www.crystalmeth.org

- www.dualrecoveryanonymous.org
- www.na.org.au
- www.smartrecovery.org

Motivational interviewing

- www.motivationalinterviewing.org

Foetal Alcohol Spectrum Disorders

- www.fasdtrust.co.uk
- www.nofas.org
- www.nofasd.org.au

Hepatitis and Blood Borne Viruses

- www.hepatitisaustralia.com.au

AOD Practice Policies and Guidelines

- alcoholresearchuk.org
- www.health.nsw.gov.au/policies/gl
- www.turningpoint.org.au

Stages of change model

- www.health.gov.au

INFORMATION ON CHILD DEVELOPMENT AND PARENTING

Family life course

- www.elder.web.unc.edu

Maternal and Child Health Services

- www.betterhealth.vic.gov.au
- www.mcai.org.uk

Raising Children and Parenting

- www.parenting.com
- www.raisingchildren.net.au
- www.triplep.net

Research on Children & Youth
- www.aracy.org.au
- www.rip.org.au
- www.earlychildhoodaustralia.org.au

Sudden Infant Death
- www.cdc.gov/sids
- www.lullabytrust.org.uk
- www.sidsandkids.org

Mentoring
- www.bigbrothersbigsisters.org.au

INFORMATION ON INTERVENTIONS FOR SUBSTANCE-USING PARENTS AND THEIR CHILDREN
- www.adfam.org.uk
- www.childwelfare.gov/pubs
- www.health.vic.gov.au/aod/pubs/ (Parenting Support Toolkit)
- www.nspcc.org.uk (FEDUP)
- www.odyssey.org.au
- www.pupprogram.net.au
- www.regen.org.au/playgroup

INFORMATION ON CHILD ABUSE
- www3.aifs.gov.au/cfca
- www3.aifs.gov.au/cfca/publications (Reporting abuse and neglect)
- www.childhelp.org
- www.nspcc.org.uk

INFORMATION ON FAMILY VIOLENCE
- www.anrows.org.au
- www.dvrcv.org.au
- www.odyssey.org.au (Breaking the Silence, Can I Ask?)
- www.safeathome.org.au (My Safety Plan)

- www.safehorizon.org
- www.womensaid.org.uk

INFORMATION ON MENTAL HEALTH AND DUAL DIAGNOSIS

- www.beyondblue.org.au
- www.dualdiagnosis.co.uk
- www.dualdiagnosis.org
- www.mifa.org.au/index.php/fact-sheets
- www.sane.org
- www.traumasociety.com.au

TOOLS FOR COLLABORATION

- www.partnertool.net
- www.vichealth.vic.gov.au/publications/the-partnerships-analysis-tool

INFORMATION ON PARTICULAR POPULATIONS

- www.aifs.gov.au/cfca
- www.damec.org.au
- www.drugabuse.gov/pubs/minorities (Drug Use Among Racial/Ethnic Minorities)
- www.fnha.ca
- www.kina.org.nz
- www.samhsa.gov/specific-populations/racial-ethnic-minority
- www.ukdpc.org.uk

INFORMATION ON NARRATIVE AND STRENGTHS-BASED INTERVENTIONS

- www.dulwichcentre.com.au/what-is-narrative-therapy
- www.innovativeresources.org
- www.signsofsafety.net/

INDEX